MARCO SPIES

BRANDED INTERACTIONS

*Creating the
Digital Experience*

BRANDED INTERACTION DESIGN

There are now many handbooks that introduce readers to interactive and user experience design in a structured and detailed way – from the development of personas to the creation of wireframes. Branding as an independent subject, however, is only mentioned in passing. Alongside these, there are plenty of manuals on corporate design and corporate identity that provide strategic and creative assistance for designers, but these often ignore interactive media. At the request of colleagues and students, I searched in vain for a book that brought together brand strategy and design principles for interactive media – an approach that I have followed in practice and in my teaching in recent years. Thus was born the idea of writing a book on branded interactions to fill that gap.

Branded interaction design goes far beyond graphic design. On the internet, a brand must fulfil multiple requirements. Websites are sales, service and marketing channels all in one, and the needs of web users may be different from those of traditional target groups. There are also complex technical environments, whose limits and possibilities must be considered during the design process. Browser-based apps, such as corporate websites, microsites and online shops, are only one part of interactive brand identity. The importance of mobile apps for smartphones and tablets has grown enormously and will continue to do so. In addition to screen-based media, interactive touchpoints are increasingly found in public spaces, in the form of installations or interactive billboards. The goal of Branded Interaction Design (from here on abbreviated as BIxD) is to replicate the same brand experience at every brand touchpoint (TOUCHPOINTS, P. 116).

The spectrum of a brand's identity is now broader than ever: logo, typography, page layouts, images, animation, navigation, interaction, sounds, words, 3D. Digital media brings the classic brand disciplines together and expands them to include the potential for interaction and flexibility. An example of this is the use of interactive and animated logos. The requirements and design potential of interactive media demand a complex, multidisciplinary process that focuses on the needs and behaviour of the user. Only then will the results work for the brand and only then will the medium be used to full advantage.

WHO NEEDS THIS BOOK?

Time and again I hear the same complaints from managers at digital agencies: 'We're great at implementation and our work is wonderful. We win awards. And our products pass usability tests with flying colours. But getting to that point is often very tedious and, in the countless discussions and feedback sessions with our clients, lots of our original ideas are lost.' Everyone is familiar with discussions of this kind; they are sometimes unavoidable and, in the best cases, can be useful, especially if clients are arguing from their own field of interest. However, when personal taste comes into play, long discussions should be avoided. But those who consistently base UX and visual design on strategic requirements and can make this convincing to clients should be able to demonstrate a clear and objective chain of reasoning, making many discussions unnecessary.

This book is intended to provide help and inspiration for all those involved with or interested in the design of interactive brands, whether beginners or professionals. It can be used by freelancers, lone designers who work for smaller local companies, and by concept developers and designers at big agencies working on international brands.

It's useful for:

- screen and interface designers
- interaction designers
- content developers and information architects
- Flash and motion designers
- information designers and generative designers
- corporate designers
- product designers

In addition, the book offers helpful information on project planning and methods for all those who work on BIxD projects, on both the agency and the client side:

- brand consultants and strategic planners
- project and product managers
- brand and marketing manager
- web and software developers

THIS BOOK'S STRUCTURE

The BIxD process is presented in five phases:

1 DISCOVER
2 DESIGN
3 DEFINE
4 DELIVER
5 DISTRIBUTE

The methods involved and their role in the overall process are described and illustrated with lots of practical examples. You can choose to work through the book from beginning to end, but this is not essential. Each subsection will provide practical guidance for specific everyday problems and serve as a useful reference. All chapters contain methodological examples and interviews with experts from leading brands and interactive agencies.

SET-UP

Before we begin working on the concept and design, the project must first be properly set up. The Set-Up chapter (P. 20) discusses what a good brief should include, what the ideal team make-up is, what to consider when planning a schedule or budget and what you need to know about the technical framework of a project.

PROCESS

The Process chapter (P. 40) explains the difference between the 'waterfall model' and agile project development, defines the individual process steps and lays out the roles of the participants.

DISCOVER

In the Discover chapter (P. 51) we introduce research methods that help the design team to gain a better understanding of businesses, brands and users. These include various auditing procedures, as well as working with personas and scenarios. A requirements matrix helps to compare and evaluate the findings and insights.

DEFINE

The Define chapter (P. 113) describes how goals can be turned into metrics, how to employ a user journey to identify the key brand touchpoints and what strategic models for positioning a brand designers should know and use before they begin developing ideas.

4
—
5

DESIGN

The development of ideas, concept and design is the focus of the Design chapter (P. 173). Here we learn how to generate and evaluate ideas, how to structure content and how to define the look and feel and the design vocabulary for BIxD projects. Information about prototyping and testing the design is also included.

DELIVER

The Deliver chapter (P. 253) describes how to produce materials and templates and how to document these in the form of style guides. In addition, it shows how user experience (UX) guidelines can be employed to create dynamic brand signatures, such as moving interactive elements. The successful completion of a BIxD project also includes a post-launch quality assessment.

DISTRIBUTE

At the end of the BIxD process, the design is implemented and, if applicable, rolled out in different markets. The mediation of the design idea and the training of employees and service providers play an important role here, as the Distribute chapter (P. 301) demonstrates.

GOOD PRACTICE

The Good Practice sections between chapters are designed to show what successful branded interactions look like. Illustrated examples from the fields of service design, branding on websites and mobile apps, brand communication in public spaces, brand development and brand management illustrate a full range of digital brand experiences.

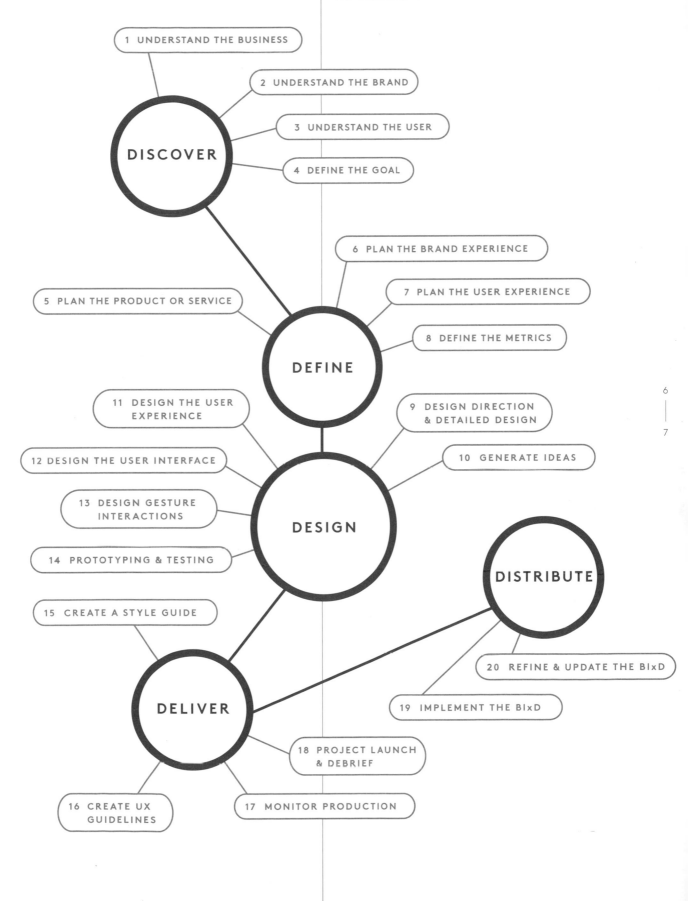

CONTENTS

DISCOVER

51

THE ANALYSIS PHASE

GOOD PRACTICE I

97

Service Design

DEFINE

113

THE STRATEGY PHASE

GOOD PRACTICE II

157

Brand Design

DESIGN

CONCEPT AND VISUALS

DELIVER

DOCUMENTS AND PRODUCTION

253

GOOD PRACTICE IV

285

Brand Communication
in Public Spaces

DISTRIBUTE

BIxD ROLLOUT AND UPDATES

301

GOOD PRACTICE V

333

Brand Management

INTRODUCTION

Since the turn of the century, globalized markets and digital communication have not only changed corporate values and consumer lifestyles, but have also altered the realm of brand design. Rules and guidelines for digital branding (TOUCHPOINTS, P. 116) are not just 'nice to have' but are now an essential part of modern brand management.

Integrated brand communication must therefore take into account the wide range of digital touchpoints available. The target groups of global brands are more heterogeneous than they were twenty years ago, and the pace at which we must keep up is steadily increasing. We spend less time with traditional forms of media, and an increasing amount of time with digital ones. Devices such as smartphones and tablets have contributed to this growth, making us familiar with using touchscreens and gestures, as well as a keyboard and mouse. The speed of innovation continues to grow faster. The work of brand designers in this environment can be summed up in three hypotheses, which form the basis for this book.

HYPOTHESIS 1

Modern brand management functions according to the rules of the digital world.

The growing number of digital devices and formats creates a variety of touchpoints between brands and clients or interested parties. These can be used by companies for sales and marketing, and also for services or for product innovation. However, they also pose completely new challenges for many companies. The time-honoured mechanisms for brand management no longer work. Brands must learn to let go, to accept the direct influence of consumers through interactive and social media and to integrate this into their work.

Take the example of luxury brands, which were able to remain uninvolved in digital media for a long time. Scarcity was fashionable and made a brand more attractive. During the first decade of the new millennium it was widely believed that e-commerce did not work for luxury brands. Their websites were used only for product presentation. Video was incorporated at an early stage to show fashion, since seeing clothing on a body in motion is a significant advantage over the static quality of print media. But from around 2009 onwards, luxury and fashion brands began to realize that digital channels could do more. Ralph Lauren led the trend for online selling and most fashion brands now operate online stores (INTERVIEW, P. 232), as well as offering mobile apps that allow users to

view, personalize and try out products – such as clothes – virtually.

The lifestyles of consumers have also become more complex. Classic consumer typologies usually fall short (BEHAVIORAL ARCHETYPES™, P. 135). The paradigms have shifted; viewing users as people with individual needs and motives for action instead of merely as part of a socio-demographic segment forces brands to realign their strategies, which can be summarized in five points:

- *Coherence over consistency:* A visually consistent look is still important. However, the question of meaningful and playful interaction with touchpoints and services needs to come first.
- *Sustainability instead of a short-term message:* Added value and services can make the brand more relevant to consumers and are more memorable than this season's advertising message.
- *Interaction and dialogue instead of top-down communication:* Brands should meet their clients at eye level. Interactivity and social media allow customers to be included in decision-making processes, and so sustain customer loyalty.
- *Continuous evolution instead of progress in spurts:* Interactive branding can be developed and optimized easily and quickly (this is called lean UX).
- *The interface is the brand, not the logo:* Static brand visuals are only one element of brand design. But an open brand does not mean that anything goes.

The importance of a stable core brand and a shared understanding of this core by everyone working for the brand is vital.

HYPOTHESIS 2

Because these major changes are not yet reflected within many companies, external support is needed.

In the current situation, for many companies it does not make sense to permanently hire creative specialists whose business advantages – interdisciplinary, cross-media and cross-sector thinking – can very quickly be lost. Yet more and more companies recognize that they need these creative skills to face the challenges of the future. Therefore, interactive designers and agencies are increasingly becoming vital strategic partners and are being included in brand planning at an early stage. In the past, interactive agencies did not play this role because they were often only included at the end of the 'strategic food chain' for the task of execution alone. In the past, the procedure was often: first the process, then the project, then the

product, then the designer. But designers are now increasingly being included in the early phases, to identify problems, define processes, write briefs and develop products. Rather than simply providing a channel for communication, they are now becoming sounding boards for businesses. One consequence of this change is that companies now regard websites and mobile apps as customer products and services, in the same way that traditional goods and services are.

HYPOTHESIS 3

Work processes and roles within interactive projects are changing – for both clients and agencies.

Linear workflows such as the classic waterfall model (P. 43) have proven to be too rigid for use on digital projects, which must be able to respond quickly to the demands of the ever-accelerating growth of technology and the risks of the unstable global economy, in which projects are often put on hold at short notice, changed and restarted.

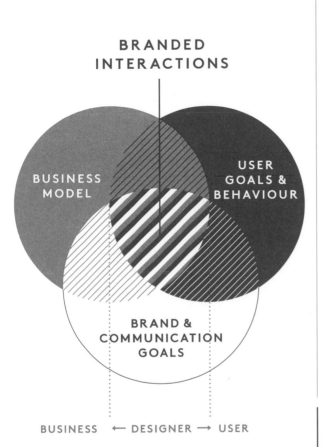

BRANDED
INTERACTIONS

BUSINESS
MODEL

USER
GOALS &
BEHAVIOUR

BRAND &
COMMUNICATION
GOALS

BUSINESS ← DESIGNER → USER

WHAT ARE BRANDED INTERACTIONS?

Branded interactions are digital brand experiences that take place at the intersection of business objectives, brand objectives and user goals. Branded interaction design can therefore be an important mediator between companies and customers.

Nonetheless, innovation is key to surviving in a crisis environment. Both innovation and results are achieved faster and more easily with the use of agile development.

In agile development, team members easily switch between roles. Rigid job descriptions beome obsolete. Managers, designers, concept developers, planners and developers view each other as equal partners in the design process and work together – without wrangling and delineating responsibilities. This means that job descriptions change. For both clients and agencies, the hallmarks of successful project teams are now interdisciplinary working and being able to engage both with technical systems and with people. The resulting division of labour is tricky for large agencies, which find themselves obliged to restructure and rely on small interdisciplinary teams.

THE CHANGING ROLE
OF AGENCIES

Changes in the role of agencies are part of a trend known as 'design thinking', first defined a decade ago and more recently accelerated by the increasing digitization of everyday life.

When design thinking made the cover of *Business Week* in 2004, it was identified with the design agency IDEO. IDEO'S founder David Kelley, along with Terry Winograd and Larry Leifer, gave the name 'design thinking' to a process for generating innovative ideas in all areas of a company. Now design thinking is an established model used to break up existing patterns of thought in the planning and design of products and services. Empathy, integrative thinking, an interdisciplinary approach and experimentation are considered essential for developing innovative, customized solutions. Design thinking consists of six steps that are presented here as part of the BIxD process, albeit in a slightly altered form.

THE SIX STEPS OF THE DESIGN THINKING PROCESS

1 **UNDERSTAND** – Ask the right questions; define needs and challenges

2 **OBSERVE** – Research and analyse existing situations

3 **POINT OF VIEW** – Synthesize collected information

4 **IDEATE** – Generate, visualize and evaluate different solutions

5 **PROTOTYPE** – Create prototypes to test and improve selected ideas

6 **TEST** – Test the prototype in practice

IN THE DECADE OF DESIGN

What caused the shift that expanded the concept of 'design' into new areas? In the boom years of the 1960s and 1970s, Western corporations competed over quality, with the engineer as the ultimate professional role model. In the 1980s and 1990s, companies were engaged in price wars in saturated markets, and business economics became the leading discipline. It may be too early to say for certain, but it looks as if design may be the distinguishing factor of the 2000s and 2010s. This assessment matches the theories of Joseph Pine and James Gilmore, who claim that, since the late 1990s, the experience has become the driving force of economic development, with the 'experience economy' replacing the service economy of the 1980s and 90s.

Design has become vital for all companies whose profitability depends on continuous innovation. 'Design thinking', the incorporation of creative and visual strategies into product management and corporate management, has now reached board level. Design not only helps to advertise products and make them more attractive; it also makes it possible to open up new markets, add value, optimize processes and reduce costs. Ideally, it also creates markets where no market formerly existed.

The rise of design has been driven by the digital revolution. Products such as Apple's iTunes no longer obey academic distinctions between information, product and environment design. Digital design means more than designing a user-friendly online shop or booking portal. It combines information design, interaction design, product, environmental and service design, as well as many other design disciplines. It has become a core discipline for businesses, bringing together brand management, product development, service operations and marketing initiatives to create a unified customer experience. Digital interfaces become vital long-term touchpoints for a brand.

THE EXISTING AGENCY LANDSCAPE

Changes in the design landscape have been driven by newer specialized agencies who have realized that design and design management are keys to corporate success. The prime example is Apple, the company that is like no other for design as a business model and that employed this philosophy to create one of the strongest corporate brands of all time. Nonetheless, the so-called 'new media' were once ridiculed, and the bursting of the dotcom bubble in 2000 seemed to favour those who regarded the internet as a flash in the pan, at worst socially harmful and at best not a serious environment for brand management. That has long since changed.

INTERACTIVE DESIGN IS THE CORE DISCIPLINE OF BRAND MANAGEMENT

All traditional design, branding and ad agencies have tried to expand into interactive media in recent years, but often with only limited success. In the field of visual branding, the potential of digital media – interaction, multimedia, generative software – is still largely untapped. Agile CD/CI approaches that consistently incorporate new media are the exception.

Traditional agencies tend to encounter two problems. Firstly, integrating interactive media usually means significant restructuring, especially since demand management and agile development can't be integrated without changing the company organization. Secondly, interactive products and apps are more closely connected to a company's core business than traditional advertising and branding agencies are used to working. Many marketing departments now recognize this trend, and view digital marketing as a unifying discipline. Marketing plans that do not include interactive media are no longer viable. The same is true for sales. Brand managers now value the long lifespans of well-designed interactive experiences.

USER EXPERIENCE DESIGN: HUMAN-CENTRED DESIGN

The main difference between interactive design and the design of print media is that behind the outer layer of design, we are not just dealing with paper but with a machine – a machine that may sometimes require more patience from its users than they actually possess. The trick of interactive design is not only to design the look of the interface, but also the way it responds, ideally in a way that adapts to people. This requires the designer to have both a high degree of empathy for the user and a full understanding of how the medium works.

'This is the role that agencies must now fill. Clients need us to bring them business ideas. We need to expand beyond our traditional role of being great communicators. We need to be great thinkers and problem solvers as well. They need us to understand how their consumers and markets are changing, and then bring them strategies that fundamentally improve their competitive position. Finally, they need us to turn those ideas and strategies into reality – by building transformational experiences.'

CLARK KOKICH, CEO of Razorfish, *Digital Outlook Report 09*

THE MEDIUM: SYSTEMS THAT CHANGE OVER TIME

Branded interactions must stem from the brand itself. Like all interactive applications, they are dynamic systems that are constantly changing through interaction with the user, either through simple decision-making, such as selecting a menu option, through automated personalization or via user-generated web content. Contemporary brand management makes use of the open nature of interactive media and allows customers to actively participate.

DESIGN: THE INTERFACE IS THE BRAND

If the provider of an interactive application is a business, the medium is a touchpoint for their brand. Just as we associate a brand with the sales assistant when we shop in a store, our experience of an app or a website is reflected onto the brand itself.

BRANDED INTERACTION DESIGN AND CORPORATE IDENTITY

Flexible corporate identities that cover the design of every aspect of the brand experience are still the exception. Classic corporate design is based on a graphic system with a framework of more or less rigid rules; it may include variants for different static uses, but the design elements themselves cannot usually be changed. Rightly so, say critics of the latest digital media-driven approach, because a brand needs stability and durability. That may be true, but in an environment where everything is in flux, change is the greatest constant. What's more, digital branding is not only the preserve of marketing specialists and agencies, but may occur beyond the traditional territory of brand management. Product evaluations, forum discussions, field reports, product parodies and picture galleries are all user-generated, and it would be wrong to try to stop them. Those who listen to their existing and prospective customers will find it easier to produce branded interactions that are both relevant and effective.

'An interface is humane if it is responsive to human needs and considerate of human frailties. If you want to create a humane interface, you must have an understanding of the relevant information on how both humans and machines operate. In addition, you must cultivate in yourself a sensitivity to the difficulties that people experience. That is not necessarily a simple undertaking. We become accustomed to the ways that products work to the extent that we come to accept their methods as given, even when their interfaces are unnecessarily complex, confusing, wasteful, and provocative of human error.'

JEF RASKIN, *The Humane Interface*

SET-UP

PLANNING A PROJECT

If you properly implement the BIxD process at an early stage, you can avoid scheduling and budget problems later.

At the beginning of a new project, you need to define the project's expected scope and the desired goal. The more concrete this definition is and the better it reflects your client's ideas, the more accurate and successful the project plan will be. Often, however, a client does not have specific expectations. Perhaps only the company's strategic objectives are provided and the client is looking to an agency for help in defining the project. In this case, experience from similar projects can help to advise clients during the brief phase. But even those who are heading a BIxD project for the first time can – with a little help – get a good grasp of the task at hand. This chapter shows you how.

THE BRIEF

'Projects generally begin for one of two reasons: something is broken or something doesn't exist.'

DAN SAFFER, *Designing for Interaction*

Clients come to an agency with different questions and expectations. The real motivation for the project is not always clear – even to the clients. They may only know that there is a problem, and something must be done about it. Therefore, the first step is to find out what the project is actually about. You need to get a basic idea of what the project's goal is, and you need to answer various questions. How big is the client thinking? How would we approach this project ourselves? How long it will take? Who should be on the team? Do we need outside specialists? Who will be responsible for the technical implementation?

At the beginning of a project there are many questions that cannot be answered until the project is up and running. But a thorough brief will help you to get an initial overview and, most importantly, will help you to calculate the costs. However, the brief should not be understood as a contract. Briefs are live documents that should be continually updated and supplemented. An agile project approach (WORKFLOW MODELS, P. 42) will make this possible.

☰ WHAT'S IN THE BRIEF?

1 THE PROJECT AND THE GOAL

- **TASK**: What task has the client assigned the agency or designer? What is its scope? What's the medium?

- **GOALS**: What is the project objective? How will we know it's a success? The goal should be specific, measurable, attainable, relevant, time-bound, and formulated in a positive way.

- **TARGET GROUP**: Who do we want to reach? Are there predefined target groups and segments? Have personas already been created?

2 PROJECT CONTEXT

- **PROJECT BACKGROUND**: What purpose does the project serve? What is its background and motivation? How does this project relate to other projects?

- **INFORMATION** about the company, the product, the brand (especially when working with a first-time client) and the company's previous digital projects.

- **IDENTIFYING THE COMPETITORS**: Market studies and product or company comparisons should be made or reviewed.

- **SCHEDULE AND BUDGET**: Deadlines should be specific: for example, 'On 14 April, the new products will be introduced at a press launch...' A rough costing helps us determine how big we should be thinking.

- **OTHER PARTIES INVOLVED**: Who are the project stakeholders? Who makes the decisions? Which service providers are involved?

- From a client perspective, what **SUCCESSFUL SOLUTIONS** have been found by competitors or in other projects with similar objectives?

3 PROJECT REQUIREMENTS

- **CONSTRAINTS**: These may be technical, such as the use of a specific technology, or brand-related; for this reason, you should always request existing CD/CI manuals or style guides.

- **PRIORITIES**: What must be included in the initial product? What can be added in later versions?

- **REQUIREMENTS** that go beyond the field of design (e.g. marketing), so that these can be taken into account and additional costs avoided later.

- **CONTENT**: What content and materials are available at the start of the project that could be used?

4 THE DELIVERABLES

- **SERVICES**: What results does the client expect? In what form?

- Are **POINTS OF CONTACT** (**POC**s) for other teams or service providers required?

BRIEF PARAMETERS

Regardless of the size of the project, the brief for a BIxD project contains certain key parameters: the project objective; the project's background and the client's motivation for implementing the project; the agency's tasks and expectations; the functional and non-functional requirements and restrictions. It also specifies the deliverables – the products or services to be delivered – as well as giving details of the client company, the brand and the target group, based on user insights and market research.

There are many reasons for companies to commission a BIxD project, and the context and foundation for the project are not always immediately apparent. It may be helpful to compile the brief in collaboration with the client, especially if you're familiar with the company or have worked with them before.

'Successful solutions are often made by people rebelling against bad briefs.'

PAUL ARDEN, *It's Not How Good You Are*

REBRIEFING

Even if the client has already compiled a brief, it may still be advisable for you or your agency to summarize the project in your own words and expand on it with your own ideas and suggestions. This 'rebrief' ensures that the client and the designer have the same basic understanding from the start.

THE TEAM

'*A happy team makes a tough task look simple.*'

The SCRUM principle

The more complex and uncertain a project is, the more important the team composition is. The team members should complement each other professionally and speak a common language despite their different disciplines. A team's size and composition should be determined by the brief and an initial project definition. The experience of the team members is often the deciding factor.

TEAM SIZE AND COMPOSITION

As a general rule, the greater the experience of the individual members, the smaller a team can be; this makes communication easier between the team members and with the client. The smallest design team consists of a concept developer with strong consulting and organizational skills and a technically savvy visual designer. The team size can then be scaled upwards as required. But beware: the larger the team, the harder internal and external communication becomes and the faster the cost increases.

BIxD projects can vary greatly: developing digital products and services requires close cooperation between the design team and the development team and with the client's product management team. These teams can be hard to coordinate. All team members need to keep everyone in the loop, both to ensure that everything is kept under control with regards to the client, and also in order to avoid the friction that communicating through the wrong channels can cause.

A TACTICAL APPROACH TO TEAM COMPOSITION

A few years ago, we worked with the agency Neue Digitale (now Razorfish) and developed the interactive corporate design for a leading mobile communications company in only three months. The design team consisted of a creative director, two information architects, an art director and a UI designer. There was also a strategic planner, who represented the stakeholders on the agency side, and a project manager whose sole responsibility was time and budget management. At 6pm every day, the project's status was discussed and the next day's tasks defined. We met with the design team in a different room. A team plan hung on the wall that described everyone's responsibilities. Any points of contact – for the client, developers or other agencies – were added to the team roster.

When working under pressure, visualizing the project as a sporting challenge can help get team members to commit to the job. We drew up a team plan that looked like a football pitch, showing not only our own 'players', but also the client's team on the other side. The idea was not to show the client as an opponent, but to illustrate the concept of 'man-to-man marking' and make the responsibilities of each member clear. The creative director deals with the brand manager, and the strategic planner is the agency's internal sounding board for service and sales, while the visual designer and the UX designer bounce off each other. Since then, I've often worked on complex

projects with teams compiled in a similar way and have found that having team members who work well together is more vital than any individual member, no matter how experienced.

☰ ROLES IN THE BIxD CORE TEAM

▸ **DESIGN TEAM LEAD** (usually the creative director or design director): Guides the team, curates content, controls quality and ensures that the design fits the previously defined strategy.

▸ **UX DESIGNER** (usually one or more information architects or concept developers): Develops content structure, class hierarchies and interaction elements and creates page layout and navigation in close collaboration with the visual designers.

▸ **VISUAL DESIGNER** (usually one or more art directors and UI designers): Creates the look and feel, the visual language, the page structure and navigation, working in close collaboration with the UX designer.

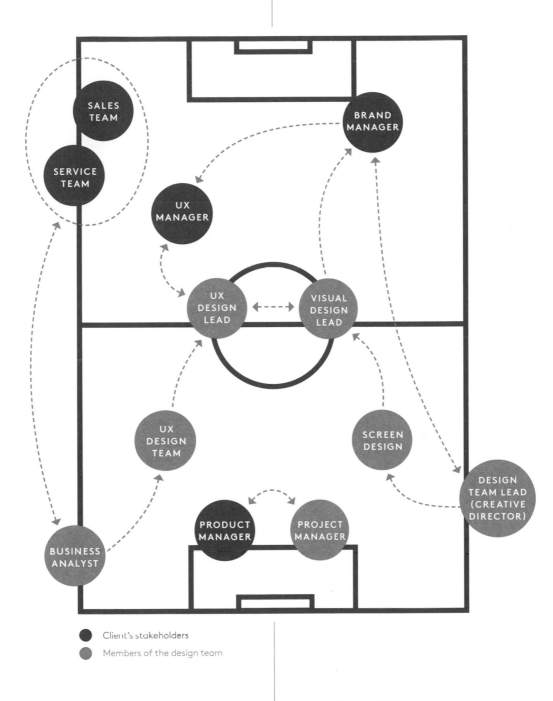

Client's stakeholders
Members of the design team

TACTICAL TEAM PLANNING

The analogy to tactical planning on a football pitch helps to visualize the roles of the team members on the client and design teams' side.

ADDITIONAL PLAYERS

Specialists who can be consulted when required or who form a temporary part of the team:
• strategic planners • researchers • business and system analysts • usability testers • motion and sound designers, photographers, 3D specialists, architects • software developers • project and account managers • content managers • concept developers • copywriters

DISCOVER

DEFINE

DESIGN

STRATEGIC CONSULTATION

USER EXPERIENCE DESIGN

(AUDIO)VISUAL DESIGN

DELIVER **DISTRIBUTE**

TECHNICAL DEVELOPMENT

STRATEGIC CONSULTATION
- BRAND STRATEGY
- MARKET RESEARCH
- E-BUSINESS CONSULTANT
- DIGITAL PLANNING (COMMUNICATION STRATEGY)

USER EXPERIENCE DESIGN
- SERVICE DESIGN
- INFORMATION ARCHITECTURE DESIGN
- USABILITY ENGINEERING
- GAME DESIGN
- INTERACTION DESIGN

(AUDIO)VISUAL DESIGN
- INFORMATION DESIGN
- CORPORATE DESIGN
- INTERFACE/UI DESIGN
- SOUND DESIGN
- MOTION DESIGN
- EXHIBITION DESIGN

TECHNICAL DEVELOPMENT
- TECHNICAL ARCHITECTURE
- APP DEVELOPMENT
- PHYSICAL COMPUTING
- FLASH/HTML DEVELOPMENT

WHO'S PART OF THE PROCESS?

The BIxD process includes experts from different fields: strategic consulting, UX and visual design and technology. If possible, all disciplines should be involved in the Discover phase **(P. 46)**.

PROJECT PLANNING

At the beginning of the project, the project requirements have not yet been fully established, so it is not yet known how long the design and development will take. An experienced designer, however, should be in a position to compile a rough project plan and a cost estimate together with the project manager. The project manager often cannot do this alone, however, because he or she cannot assess what needs to happen and when, and how long different stages will take to complete. UX designers find it easier to make a reasonable assessment.

A BIxD project can take anywhere from three weeks to three years. A linear project plan only makes sense when the task is contained and manageable and the outcome is known from the start. When a product is being developed, or with a technically innovative project, the sequence of steps is not as clearly defined. Instead, the project is divided into cycles or iterations, in which the outcome of the next stage is always defined first. In projects of this kind, it is better to appoint a permanent team for a set period of time and then use an agile or scrum-based framework (PROCESS, P. 40). The original plan should be kept in mind over the entire project period and adjusted if necessary. Every project should allow enough leeway in both time and budget. For projects where the deadline is fixed, it must at least be possible to change the project's scope.

☰ THE SEVEN STEPS OF PROJECT PLANNING

1 ESTABLISH THE PROJECT'S STATUS: At which point are you joining the project? Is there already an analysis or a basic strategy? Is an in-house employee or an external consultant already involved? If a strategy exists and research has been carried out, you need to understand the results and question them if need be.

2 USE AGILE PLANNING FOR DEVELOPMENT PROJECTS: Developing a digital product or service always involves unknown variables that require special attention. Designers should be involved in projects like this from the beginning because their perspective can be valuable. However, this means that designers must be willing to deal with technical and strategic issues.

3 DECIDE ON A TEAM SIZE AND CONSULT THE STAKEHOLDERS: A larger team does not necessarily mean a faster project, but requires more coordination. Multiple stakeholders mean multiple consultation sessions (STAKEHOLDER ANALYSIS, P. 54).

4 NOT EVERYTHING CAN AND SHOULD BE PLANNED IN DETAIL: It is not always helpful to break down the project into small task sets, even if the project manager thinks these will be easier to control. Often the direction of a project will change mid-route and unexpected elements will have to be incorporated. It is crucial to have a fixed goal, but the process should not be forced to proceed in a particular way just because it was agreed at the start of the project. Development projects are better suited to an agile approach.

5 PLAN A REALISTIC SCHEDULE: Tell the client what works and what won't. Often the client's project manager is under time pressures because too much time was wasted at an early stage or because the plan is unrealistic due to a lack of experience. The design agency may be blamed for this later on, so be sure to explain your reasoning to your contacts so they can pass these on to their superiors, and factor in a time buffer.

6 MAKE COST ESTIMATES TRANSPARENT: If clients can clearly see what they are getting for their money, what competitors are offering no longer seems as important. Creative processes are difficult to compare. One advantage of BIxD is that the stages of the process and the intermediate results are well planned and communicated in advance.

7 CREATE A COMMUNICATION PLAN: A communication plan includes the roles and responsibilities of both the client and agency. It is created together with the client and the design team at the start of the project and dictates who talks to whom and who is responsible for what. In case of problems, escalation levels should be defined.

TECHNOLOGY

Ideally, at the start of a BIxD project, no choice of a specific platform should have been made. The client's project lead belongs to the marketing department. And those who are directly responsible to the executive board should be assertive enough to compete during the project planning with marketing and IT. Branding and corporate design decisions must be made at the top level. The requirements are defined from a business, brand and user perspective. Design and development teams take a conceptual approach together and then agree on a technical solution. This greatly simplifies the design process and ultimately leads – assuming there is an interactive team with enough technical experience – to a better product.

Unfortunately, in practice, things often don't work that way. The choice of platform has already been made when IT tells the design department that the system needs a branded interface, but it has to be produced as cheaply as possible since the IT design budget has been spent on the system evaluation and in-house requirements workshops. However, because no designer was included in these workshops, technical specs and content have been decided with no thought to what the target audience wants or what would benefit the brand. In this situation, it's no surprise when the focus groups, made up of people from production, marketing and sales, look at the project with scepticism and doubt whether the long-planned relaunch will bring the improvements that were promised.

If an external consultant with a design background is brought in early on, he or she can consider the requirements and contribute ideas that are innovative enough to reposition the product or brand. A consultant will look at the expectations of the target group and decide, together with the marketing and sales teams, how services and content can be best presented. Because the consultant has an objective view of the company, he or she can also oversee the process and moderate corporate policy issues.

COOPERATING WITH THE DEVELOPMENT TEAM

Regardless of how things stand when the project begins, interaction with the development or tech team is extremely important throughout a project. Communication should be established between the development and art departments as early as possible, even if both are based under a single agency roof. Call a meeting for the project partners to get to know one another, so that areas of crossover within the project can be discussed and the following key issues clarified:

- Who speaks when, how often and in how much detail with whom?
- What technical constraints exist at the start of the project?
- In which phase should the first feasibility checks be made?
- What documents does the design team supply?
- Is the documentation of the rules clear enough?
- Where can design and implementation occur in parallel in time-critical projects?

Project development benefits hugely if a programmer from the development team can sit down with the designers early on or if weekly meetings are scheduled. Misunderstandings can be clarified at an early stage, and clients generally like to see their service providers cooperating. It is also good for designers to learn about the developer's mindset. Once the platform has been selected, the system (e.g. a content management system) should be explained to the designer, who should then try it out (TRY IT YOURSELF, P. 231).

DEVELOPERS HAVE A SYSTEM OVERVIEW – DESIGNERS HAVE THE USER PERSPECTIVE

Despite working closing together, keeping a healthy distance from your development partners should stop you from becoming getting too attached to a specific technology. Collaboration with developers is fertile, but it is their job to view things with the system in mind. Designers should be advocates for the user and for the company. It is our job to disregard technological specifics and suggest solutions that may be a technical challenge to implement; this is the only way that innovation can happen.

Even if the final implementation of the project lies with the client's own IT department or an external service provider, it makes sense for the front-end development (e.g. HTML templates, CSS style sheets or Flash prototypes) to be led by the design team. The way a design is technically implemented is crucial to the feel of an app and therefore part of the brand experience.

DESIGN AND TECHNOLOGY

TOM ACLAND
NEUE DIGITALE/RAZORFISH

Neue Digitale/Razorfish develops complex web projects for major brands. How does this collaboration between design and technology work?

We used to assume that there was a kind of pattern that could be used to design a project from brief to delivery: a kind of meta-process. Over the last two years, this has changed. For example, within twelve weeks of the release of a new platform – the iPad – we were working on a major strategy project that would have a huge impact on how the sales departments of a global corporation did business. This shows how fast and flexible design teams – as well as development teams – need to be to match the pace of technology.

In terms of the collaboration between design and technology, this means that we rely on flexible work processes that can change depending on the task. But to stop the whole thing from descending into chaos, we need rituals that stay the same from project to project. This includes a daily exchange. Not in the sense of a meeting that is artificially set up, but a daily ritual that includes project members from all disciplines so we can discuss what is going on. Not to find solutions, but to talk to each other.

How do you create these rituals and what are they like?

In the beginning we adapted a lot of methods from software development. First, we used these approaches for technical implementation. There are patterns taken from agile software development that were created fifteen or more years ago – although originally with other objectives. Back then, the focus was on risk-managing huge projects in which there was no transparency, as well as situations in which the requirements were not clear and agility was needed. We initially developed these patterns as blueprints, to find out if the processes would also work for things other than implementation, and indeed they could and can, because they are very human and very easy to use. Things like using tactile and accessible tools, like Post-Its on the wall, where the project team can see them. These creative tools are easily transferable.

You initially explained this change or this process-based paradigm shift with the speed with which changes occur in technology...

The idea of flow today is completely different from what it was five years ago. Back then, a funnel model was used; we could make predictions about media efficiency and what the pull-through on the sales results would be.

Now we need to generate insights very quickly, perhaps weekly, effectively running the whole model in fast-forward mode.

Here's an example. Last week Seat, a client of ours, received a letter from a ten-year-old, who had drawn a car design for Seat with a very cute caption: 'You can use these ideas and actually build the car.' The creative team made a stop-motion film that showed the letter being opened, the car design being built and then driving away. That was something that was created within a few hours and then could be played back into the brand flow.

Other examples can be seen in the use of topical issues that appear in the media. This is how we stay relevant. But we can only do this if we can act quickly and in the interests of the brand.

How does all this affect the cooperation with a client? In a purely project-driven client relationship, something like this would probably not be possible.

It depends on the task. But one thing is certain. When we meet with clients, we often discuss processes and no longer try, as in the past, to define specific areas of responsibility, e.g. this is our domain, that is the agency's domain, or this is the domain of another company department. Instead the whole thing needs to be viewed from the perspective of the consumer or target group in order to be able to determine what roles, processes and exchange tools are required – regardless of who is responsible for what – so that it's possible to react quickly, even when the project is complex.

It takes a while before these things are resolved with a client. Then it is more a question of what everyone has to offer. It is no longer a top-down approach, where someone says: 'You're responsible for this, you're responsible for something else.' But if everyone sees an opportunity to contribute, then the process and flow can evolve. If you have a good idea, then it should be possible for the idea to be adapted and implemented by the group.

If this can happen, then it doesn't matter where the idea originated. The prerequisite for this, of course, is that everyone has a clear picture of the goal and keeps others in the loop, so clashes are avoided.

This means, however, that when you're working with a client, you're not perceived as a service provider but as a consultant. But providing and implementing a completed strategy is more typical of a service model, while a consultant works with clients as if they were part of the same team.

I think the question is: what would I do if I were the decision maker? Unity of purpose helps to alleviate conflicts. That's a utopian goal, and I don't believe it's always possible to achieve it, but it is the model that we should strive for to get better results.

But how does an agency get into this position? How do you convince the client that you are working on a retainer level?

Nowadays, the complexity and fast pace of things put everyone under pressure, even the client. When we experience this daily as clients or as agency team members, then it is clear that we don't have time to hold on to the old processes. A different model is needed; contemporary stress levels mean that we should start viewing these constructs as a thing of the past. I believe these fixed process models have more to do with ROI optimization (return on investment), which may indeed be part of a mature market. However, at the moment I feel that we are not in a mature phase, but rather in an inventive phase, and if we are to survive, we need to space to explore and make mistakes.

I would go further and say that it's not just a matter of speed but a fundamental change in the way we work. The old processes, in which everything was defined – timeline-based models – were often supported by software. We are now moving away from digital organization methods. People now work with Post-Its and more playful methods. In principle, this reflects our approach to technology. We spend less time sitting in front of a computer and are constantly switching between media.

That's an interesting counterpoint to the theme of maturity, because mature technologies allow and encourage a level of humanity. In the past we were rather slavishly tied to our machines, but we are now reaching a point where the computing power available to us is there to make things easier.

I also believe that this is a new kind of freedom. Brands need to rethink themselves and open up their structure, particularly as regards how they communicate and present themselves. The interactivity of brands should encourage open social interaction.

That's right. And I think this is more necessary in the execution (from a campaign or marketing point of view) than in the strategy. I think that diversity and the 'long tail' principle demand a kind of openness, an ability to react. You can't always plan everything in advance but you must always be ready to respond. It's even more important in this environment that a brand not only has a clear positioning, but also that it has a face and is clearly differentiated from other dynamics. After all, clients and consumers are seeking a pole that they can use to orientate themselves. The principles of the brand must remain clear, otherwise you get totally lost in the details.

How can an interactive agency manage the balancing act between the appearance of stability in an unstable medium, and, on the other hand, using this lack of stability to remain open so that consumers can anchor themselves?

That is a very interesting question. That is our challenge; that's the challenge for the market. To answer the question, I'd say that if an agency with digital DNA can't do it, who can? Everyone struggles with the same challenge.

The habit of constantly changing direction, constantly finding new things and incorporating them is much closer to our technologist genes than those of others in the marketplace.

Nevertheless, our objectives are not completely different. The only question is: who does it first and who gets it right? Our competitors and the market will answer this. But it's clear we've got to move further up in the value creation chain. In the past, we were always reliant on instructions from others. The challenge for us in this competitive situation is to make this dependence obsolete – and to be in a position to shape these things or even to take them over completely ourselves.

Particularly in an environment that is changing so quickly, it makes no sense to wait for a technology that will remain standard for the next ten years.

Yes, that's right. The interesting thing here is that standards are often easy to comply with. The non-observance of standards is often not a design issue, but a conscious business decision. A gap between standards and deliberate disassociation from standards does not actually occur very often. But the point here is: You start with the design issue and then deal with the standards. You don't begin with the question 'How can we make this thing reasonably user-friendly?'

You said: You start with a problem, then develop the design and then deal with the technological issues. Nevertheless, the designer is increasingly required to possess more technical savvy because new technologies make more things possible and the range of potential options gets a lot larger. Especially if you don't take standard solutions into account, there's an incredible range of possible technologies that can be used to solve a particular problem. How much technical knowledge does a designer need to work effectively with the development team? Is there somewhere the designer often goes wrong? What causes the

biggest misunderstandings between designers and developers?

I am innately a techie, so it feels a little traitorous to say that designers usually go wrong when they place their own demands in the background by blindly accepting it when a techie tells them something is too difficult. I've often found that what seems to be the optimal solution from a purely technical point of view can turn out to be completely wrong from the perspective of the user or designer. In this kind of situation, the designer's view ought to win out, but this often doesn't happen because designers are too daunted by the technology. I even think the techies are pleased when someone says: 'I understand this is difficult to do, but the product will be so much better if we work out a way of doing it.'

However, designers can be pompous in their arguments and lost in their own world. The best designs are driven less by technical ideas than by observation or by recognizing an actual problem on a human level. You have to treat the technical understanding of potential users as if it were your own. If you follow human-centred design principles and observe the people you're designing for, you free yourself from the pressure of asking how much training you need, because all you really have to do is observe.

Tom Acland is the managing director of Razorfish Germany in Frankfurt am Main.

PROCESS

GIVING STRUCTURE TO A PROJECT

A clearly defined design process helps us to move in the right direction and ensures that the goal defined at the beginning is the one we reach at the end.

A good workflow helps the team without constraining its creative freedom. The BIxD process presented in this book has been tested many times in practice. It combines UX design and design thinking with a strategic CI/CD approach. It can be used to develop anything from international corporate presentations and e-business web portals to smaller interactive branding projects for an exhibition stand or public space. The basic structure of the BIxD process also matches contemporary agency processes, so that the key methods and deliverables are relatively easy to integrate.

WORKFLOW MODELS

In 2000, when I worked for what was then one of Germany's leading web design agencies, a workflow map filled three A3 pages. Most of the space was taken up by describing the points of contact between different disciplines. There were many things to consider, especially regarding the task handover between strategy and design and between design and technology. Large-scale portal concepts were written up in Microsoft Word. Application concepts included descriptive text, wireframes and use cases. These documents often ran to hundreds of pages and were therefore unwieldy. During the design process, if a single module was changed, the entire document had to be searched and updated in every place that the module appeared. The application concepts were handed over to programmers and visual designers and the necessary information had to be made available to both groups. When questions came up mid-project, half the concept team had already moved on to the next project.

To reduce inefficiency, alternate workflows were tested. Significant improvements were made by incorporating technology into the process. We were trained in Unified Modeling Language (UML), which allowed us to set up the information architecture and interaction sequences for websites using predefined templates. We also learned to describe the elements of interfaces as objects with certain characteristics and behaviours. The programmers were familiar with this type of description so this reduced uncertainty when the concept was handed over. There was only one problem with this: this approach was the

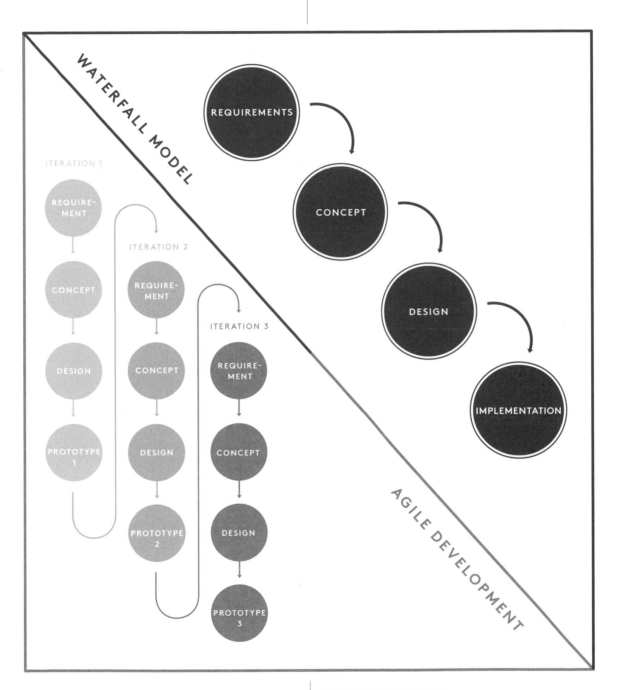

WATERFALL MODEL

AGILE DEVELOPMENT

ITERATION 1

ITERATION 2

ITERATION 3

REQUIRE-MENT

CONCEPT

DESIGN

PROTOTYPE 1

REQUIRE-MENT

CONCEPT

DESIGN

PROTOTYPE 2

REQUIRE-MENT

CONCEPT

DESIGN

PROTOTYPE 3

REQUIREMENTS

CONCEPT

DESIGN

IMPLEMENTATION

WORKFLOW MODELS

Two development models for interactive projects. With the waterfall model, each phase is completed before starting the next phase. In agile development, sub-steps are implemented in iterations called sprints. Early prototyping helps reduce risks.

complete antithesis of the way that most creatives think and work. When we were developing a cross-media interactive style guide for adidas, we chose another path. After the task flows (DEFINE, P. 113) were defined, the information architecture was developed in close collaboration with the designers. Working in short iterations or cycles, concept developers and designers got used to work processes that were then developed further.

What did I learn from this? There is no such thing as an agency process approach that always works. A linear, precedent-based process – the so-called waterfall model – makes sense if you're familiar with the tasks and can plan, and if the project's course is predictable. But this approach inevitably fails if the result is not predictable from the outset, if deviations in the plan based on new information and ideas are not only allowed but encouraged, or if a team is not used to collaborative working. In these cases, an agile development approach can help. In this type of product development process – based on the Japanese work philosophy of *kaizen* – the whole team works closely together in short predefined cycles known as sprints. An agile approach is not only useful for projects that involve collaborations between design and technology; it also works within individual design disciplines or between strategy and design.

Regardless of the approach you choose, you need a framework that defines the release stages and high-level phases and that allows the project to be planned while giving the team the freedom they need. The framework described in this book – the BIxD process – is precisely this kind of framework.

✔ THE IDEAL WORKFLOW IS

- ▸ modular and flexible in its methods and stages
- ▸ scalable in breadth and depth
- ▸ extendable if special topics need to be included
- ▸ easy to communicate and
- ▸ comprehensible to employees and clients binding and results-orientated

THE BRANDED INTERACTION DESIGN PROCESS

Whether you're using the waterfall model or agile development: the BIxD process provides a stable framework for the project that describes who does what and when. In its basic form, it divides the creative process into five steps, from analysis and summarization of ideas towards an approach that begins to live and change as soon as it is put into practice. This basic concept is familiar to all designers and is found in many agency processes to varying degrees.

In practice, a project is rarely as straightforward as the model suggests. There will always be influences from outside the project, some tasks running in parallel and many interdependent on each other. However, a clearly defined work process is absolutely necessary for a successful BIxD project. The workflow is not an end in itself but a safeguard. It promotes careful planning and project control, and provides quality assurance and structured cooperation with the client. In short, it ensures that a design team tackles projects in a way that is both strategic and creative, while performing at a high level of quality and profitability.

At first glance, the BIxD process seems linear. But within each phase and beyond it, there may be parallel work streams and iterations. In principle, the design phase can be completely organized in sprints (WORKFLOW MODELS, P. 43). In the Distribute phase, an agile approach becomes even more valuable, since it allows new requirements to be incorporated regularly and evaluated during rollout and operation (P. 319).

THE PROJECT PHASES

Regardless of the scope of the BIxD project, it should always include the following five phases. Specific methods and techniques must be decided case by case. The product at the end of each phase (the deliverables) also may vary. Particularly with larger projects, each phase should end with a result that allows both the client and the agency, in cases of doubt, to withdraw from the project at that point – perhaps because the company's strategy or the market has changed – without everything having been for nothing. Benchmarks for acceptance and approval should be established at various points: before the end of the Define phase, at the design direction presentation or DDP (P. 176) and at the end of the project. Everything else can be flexible. Depending on the client, you can plan for more or fewer checkpoints, in the form of reviews with the client to adjust the project's direction if need be.

PHASE 1: DISCOVER

The brief is the starting point of the project and is followed by the Discover phase, which includes stakeholder and user interviews, analysis of target groups and competitors, brand and usability audits and other methods, which are presented in the next chapter. The Discover phase focuses on learning about the target group, summarizing the client and the stakeholders' perspective of the project and understanding the assignment ('See everything'). At the end of the Discover phase, a requirements matrix is created and the requirements are weighed against each other. We find trade-offs that must be resolved in the next phase in collaboration with the client.

PHASE 2: DEFINE

During the Define phase, the requirements are developed and specified in a metrics catalogue. Decisions also begin to be made. We sort through the requirements and initial ideas to create structure and focus. To do this, we need an explicit goal, which is defined for the design team in a creative brief ('See as one').

PHASE 3: DESIGN

After the approval of the metrics catalogue and strategy presentation in the Define phase, the interface can be created. The Design phase is roughly divided into two parts. The end of the first part is marked by an important benchmark: the design direction presentation (DDP), in which the information architecture, the app's look and feel and the visual vocabulary of its key features

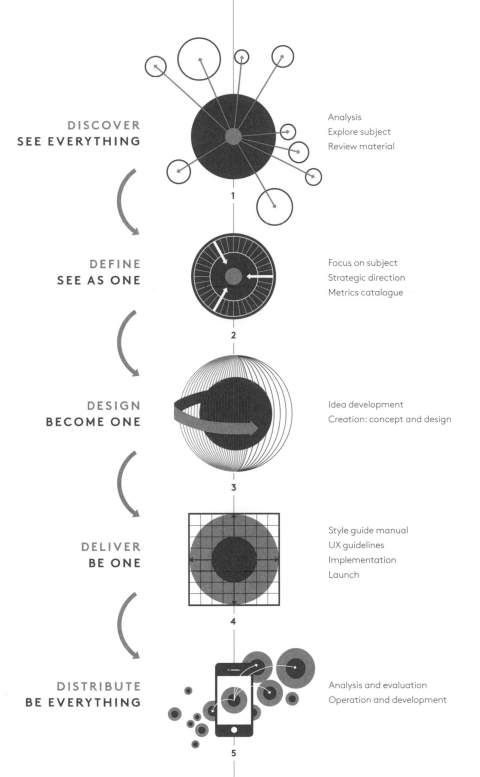

DISCOVER
SEE EVERYTHING

Analysis
Explore subject
Review material

1

DEFINE
SEE AS ONE

Focus on subject
Strategic direction
Metrics catalogue

2

DESIGN
BECOME ONE

Idea development
Creation: concept and design

3

DELIVER
BE ONE

Style guide manual
UX guidelines
Implementation
Launch

4

DISTRIBUTE
BE EVERYTHING

Analysis and evaluation
Operation and development

5

46
—
47

SEE EVERYTHING, SEE AS ONE

The outline of the design process, from a philosophical viewpoint.

are presented. The DDP is subject to the client's approval. In the second part of the Design phase, all other design modules (or templates, in the case of websites) are designed and described in functional diagrams (or wireframes for websites). This results in the detailed design documentation (DDD), which is a collection of all design-related documents, including wireframes, process flows and layouts, and explains how the technical implementation will happen.

PHASE 4: DELIVER

After the detailed design documentation has been approved comes the Deliver phase. A style guide is created to document the visual design rules. User experience guidelines are used to regulate the interactive principles. All content and design materials are created simultaneously. The design team supports the technical implementation of the project with quality assurance metrics and asset production. After the launch, the project should be carefully documented as a case study that is circulated both internally and externally.

PHASE 5: DISTRIBUTE

The Distribute phase focuses on the implementation of the style guide within the company and the implementation of the rules in the realization and rollout. An updatable online style guide – or better still a web-based brand management system – helps during the so-called design management process and allows for flexible updates. The Distribute phase also includes the continuous development of digital products and services. Here, a lean UX or agile development process can help to ensure smooth cooperation between the client, development team and design team.

1

DIS SCOVER

THE ANALYSIS PHASE

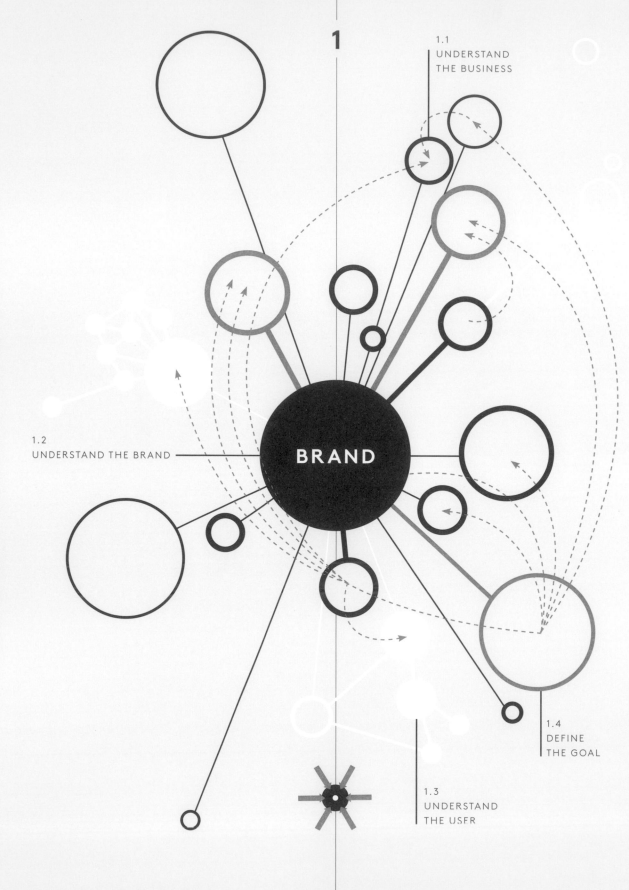

1.1
UNDERSTAND
THE BUSINESS

SET-UP / PROCESS —— **DISCOVER** / DEFINE / DESIGN / DELIVER / DISTRIBUTE

1.2
UNDERSTAND THE BRAND

BRAND

1.4
DEFINE
THE GOAL

1.3
UNDERSTAND
THE USER

The Discover phase is a journey of discovery with the aim of getting to know your client, their brand and their customers and gaining a full understanding of the project.

If you want to get to know another culture, you should go to the place it sprung from. This also applies to companies. Only those who understand their client's brand and business will be able to create a successful digital presence. The Discover phase means actively finding your starting point and exploring the potential of the project. There are three key sources of information: the business model, the brand and message strategy, and the goals and expectations of the users. Requirements from these three areas will be compiled into a target matrix (P. 88), reconciled and later evaluated. It is important for designers to be involved in this step in order to develop a design that's on strategy. The research and assessment methods used in this phase are described in the pages that follow.

1.1

UNDERSTAND THE BUSINESS

To develop digital services for a client, the design team needs input from the stakeholders. Many questions can be answered by holding a kick-off workshop, but it can also be useful to conduct individual interviews with stakeholders. Existing material on the company, the brand and the target audience should be collected and sifted. Finally, it is helpful to take a closer look at the competition and make an analysis of best practice examples that will allow you a better understanding of the client's business.

STAKEHOLDER ANALYSIS

Stakeholders are anyone who engages, creates, operates and uses branded interactions, as well as those who have the knowledge required to build, operate or use the system. At the beginning of a project – and before you invite anyone else to a kick-off workshop – the stakeholders should be identified and analysed. This analysis can be a brief list of all project participants or a complex graph in which the stakeholders are evaluated for their impact on the project. The stakeholder analysis is an internal document for the design team, but it can also serve as the basis for a communication plan agreed with the client.

THE STAKEHOLDERS ARE:

- the project manager/the client's project team
- representatives from different company departments
- the project sponsors (those funding the project)
- your own team
- testers and focus groups
- the end user or the app's future users
- external service providers needed for implementation

✔ **WHAT YOU SHOULD KNOW ABOUT THE STAKEHOLDERS**

▸ What is their role in the project?

▸ What do they know that others do not?

▸ What is their position in the company?

▸ What are their needs, priorities, hopes, expectations, fears?

▸ What are their interests/(brand) affinities?

▸ What is their view of the company's goals?

In addition, there are other stakeholders who may initially be overlooked, but who can nevertheless influence the success of the project. For example, imagine an interactive window installation that runs at night in a flagship store in a large city. The local traffic authority must test road safety; someone must take care of the technical maintenance; the store's cleaning staff must be informed, etc.

OTHER STAKEHOLDERS INCLUDE:

- (local) authorities
- legal experts
- security experts
- maintenance companies
- trading partners of the company
- middlemen and delivery people

In addition, there may be other people and departments on the client's side who may suddenly become influential during the project. Depending on the project, these may include the company's sales, service, marketing, engineering or editorial departments, or company offices in other locations.

The stakeholders can be marked on a map to illustrate their relationships and their relevance to the project. The greater their influence, the closer to the project centre the stakeholder should be positioned.

THE KICK-OFF WORKSHOP

All stakeholders who have a significant impact on the project should be invited to the kick-off workshop. Attendees will receive an agenda in advance and should come prepared.

Once when working with an international client, I took part in a kick-off workshop where the company's brand manager, sales manager, service manager and project manager were all sitting down at the same table for the first time. Each gave a short presentation on their own department's goals for the project. The individual presentations contained so much material for discussion that the workshop had to end before we, as an agency, were able to present our point of view. We just listened and asked questions. But we had not made the trip in vain. We had succeeded in bringing the different departments together and the project stakeholders realized that they needed a shared vision for the project first. This provided a great basis for the work that followed.

FOCUS GROUPS

Focus group workshops are sometimes held during the Discover phase. A focus group composed of the client's customers can help you gain a better understanding of the target group. To find the right composition for the focus group, the target group should first be defined and then discussed with the client. If the client works primarily in the B2B field, he or she should be able to provide a contact list of business clients. The goal is to create a focus group that is diverse and relevant.

First of all, focus group members should be questioned about their personal experiences as users. This can be done with questionnaires or interviews. Specific aspects of the user experience should then be tackled in open discussion. The design team must identify in which phase of the customer experience cycle the customer is located and what their customer journey to this point has been like (THE CUSTOMER LIFE CYCLE, P. 120). Have they had any particularly positive or negative experiences? Focus groups are particularly fruitful when they are incorporated into long-term product development, but you must be sure to switch the participants regularly to ensure their feedback is relevant and up-to-date. For example, since 2004, Deutsche Bahn has had a customer advisory board made up of 32 members, who fulfil an advisory role for the German train operator's passenger services division.

In-house focus groups (for example, when planning an employee portal) should be treated with caution. Stakeholders who talk a lot without really having anything to say but who have been included by the project manager for political reasons can distort the research results.

Focus groups sometimes run alongside an entire project to ensure market acceptance. But beware. Although it makes sense to include focus groups during the Discover phase, in the Design phase you should carefully consider the extent to which stakeholder and focus group participation is desirable and beneficial.

STAKEHOLDER INTERVIEWS

Individual stakeholder interviews are particularly useful when, for example, there is concern that employees may not describe a situation realistically if their boss is present in the workshop. On-site interviews also provide a picture of how and where the employees work. It is important to prepare for these interviews and to let the staff know the purpose of the meeting from the start. At the same time, keep the interview informal and make it clear that you have not been briefed by the company management, but are there for your own reasons. Discussions about specific topics or ideas should be avoided and the underlying motivations and problems explored instead.

✓ POSSIBLE QUESTIONS FOR INDIVIDUAL INTERVIEWS

- ▸ What is your role in the company?
- ▸ What do you think the key business goals are?
- ▸ Describe the products/services your company offers.
- ▸ Who is your target audience?
- ▸ What makes your company better than others?
- ▸ What industry trends do you think will be important in the near future?
- ▸ What is your role within the project?
- ▸ What could make the project fail?
- ▸ What is the motivation behind the project from your perspective?
- ▸ At what point would you consider the project a success?

QUESTIONNAIRES

It is the agency or design team's job to moderate the kick-off workshop and ask the right questions. In preparation, you need to compile a questionnaire that can be taken to the workshop and completed during the stakeholder interviews. The questions should cover:

- the company and the brand
- the project process, roles and benchmarks
- target groups and customer insights
- digital strategy and marketing
- corporate identity and style guide issues
- technical factors

Each question should be given a unique ID number, to make later discussions about specific points easier. In addition to the interviewee's responses, you should also record how important a requirement is for each stakeholder. This can be done using points ratings from 1 to 10 or by using priorities:

1 imperative, absolutely vital
2 important, should be implemented
3 optional, could be implemented
4 noted, could be considered in future

The questionnaire, of course, can be sent to the client in advance. In this case, it is useful to add a column saying whether the question is to be answered in writing or discussed during the workshop. The questionnaire can be expanded over the course of the project and can be used as a preliminary version of a PRD.

SURVEYS

If the interviewees are too far away to talk on site, interviews can be organized via Skype or FaceTime. If it is not possible to conduct interviews directly, perhaps because the company management is against it, written surveys can be done using web-based survey tools. These are also a good option if you want to survey a large number of people to get more representative results.

ID	STAKEHOLDER	PRIORITY			RESPONSE
		Vital	Important	Optional	
1	Pavan Patel, Corporate Communications Director			X	IN WRITING

Can you describe one of the departments involved in the project, and the workflows they use to communicate with other departments and in-house clients?

....

....

....

ID	STAKEHOLDER	PRIORITY			RESPONSE
		Vital	Important	Optional	
2	Martha Mayer, Brand Manager	X			WORKSHOP

What kind of additional creative input is available that would be relevant to the development of this project?

INPUT		AVAILABLE	RELEVANCE
Design strategy for the brand itself (strategy paper, CI guidelines for offline communication,)	→	YES	HIGH
Design strategy for product development / design (instructions for product development)	→	YES	HIGH
Design requirements for packaging materials	→	NO	LOW
Design standards for offline communication	→	YES	LOW
Design standards for POI	→	YES	LOW
Any visual materials for the product launch	→	NO	HIGH
Prototypes or product samples	→	YES	HIGH
Other design-related materials	→	YES	LOW

QUESTIONNAIRE

Sample questions for a stakeholder questionnaire at the start of a project.

	1	**1.1**	**1.2**
PAGE ID	1	1.1	1.2
PAGE TITLE	HOME	FAQ	CONT
CONTENT / FUNCTIONALITY	→ Intranet homepage with teasers, News, Events, FAQ and About Us	→ Frequently asked questions about the company and its services.	→ De Po
INTEGRATED CONTENT	→ Multiple subpages with news stories	→ How To Find Us (PDF), corporate structure (PDF)	→ Mc
TARGET GROUP	→ All	→ All	→ All
RESPONSIBLE FOR CONTENT	→ Peter Peterson	→ Anna Anderson	→ Ar
UPDATES	→ Not clear when the Spotlight and About Us sections have been updated. No recent updates to the Events section. Regular updates to subpages.	→ Content is up-to-date but page does not include a 'last updated' date.	→ Nc
NOTES	→ Page looks sparse and dull. Notice for recently updated pages is very small and unattractive. Most of the content is rarely updated.	→ Page could be expanded by adding press information that is currently located on a separate page	→ Pa th
URL	→ www.example.com	→ www.example.com/faq	→ wv
TYPE OF CONTENT	→ News page. Subpages include articles and lists of links	→ FAQ	→ Cc
RESTRICTED ACCESS?	→ No	→ No	→ Nc

CONTENT AUDIT

Excerpt from a content audit for a corporate intranet site. The content is evaluated page by page. Here we see samples of the notes on the homepage and a FAQ subpage. Content audits can be very extensive.

CONTENT AND SERVICE AUDITS

A project never starts from absolute zero. There will always be pre-existing content and functions that can or should be incorporated. For example, for the relaunch of a company website or online shop, content can be adapted from existing editorial content or product catalogues. A relaunch is a chance to ditch old content, to develop new formats and to adjust the structure or ways of accessing the content.

Especially with complex content, such as online magazines, knowledge portals or presentations of specific products and services, it can be tricky for outsiders to navigate their way through structures that were first established years ago. In cases such as these, you should include the content providers (e.g. for intranet projects, the company's own departments) in the content audit.

CARD SORTING

Card sorting helps us understand the mental models of the target group, seeing how content and concepts fit together in their minds. The method is useful for structuring and prioritizing complex information and content: e.g. finding meaningful menu names to use in product or information catalogues.

To begin, concepts, descriptions and images relating to content, features and functions are collected and written on index cards. If there are already category suggestions, you can write them on larger cards, to which the content can be assigned. The cards are spread out on the table and the test subjects are asked to group the cards and sort them into categories. They may also suggest their own categories. The maximum number of categories can be predetermined. A card sort should be done using seven to ten test subjects. The cards may also be numbered so that they can be easily counted and analysed.

60
|
61

ⓘ A wealth of information and examples on card sorting is available on the website for the book *Card Sorting: Designing Usable Categories* by Donna Spencer.
→ bit.ly/1EJqP1t

SET-UP / PROCESS —— **DISCOVER** / DEFINE / DESIGN / DELIVER / DISTRIBUTE

✿ EXAMPLE OF A COMPETITOR AUDIT

★★★☆☆	Idea/originality
★★★★☆	Visual design
★★★★★	Brand fit
★★★☆☆	Value (information/content)
★★★☆☆	Ease of use/navigation
★★☆☆☆	Media appropriateness
★★☆☆☆	Technical excellence
★★★☆☆	**TOTAL SCORE**

A sample scale that could be used to audit a competitor's product or service.

COMPETITOR AUDIT AND BENCHMARK ANALYSIS

A close examination of your competitors is invaluable for any type of design project. After all, it's important to know how others have solved similar problems if you're planning to do it better. But a competitor analysis for a BIxD project can be particularly extensive. For web projects, you should analyse competitors' websites, noting their features and evaluating the branding and user experience. It's a way of learning what works and what doesn't, how special features are rendered graphically and conceptually, and how they can be most effectively branded.

If there's a focus group, it is useful to get the members to test the competitor's products. The same is true for services that are not necessarily offered by competitors, but are considered best practice in similar market segments. When you compare the products and services of your competitors according to predetermined criteria, you are creating a benchmark analysis.

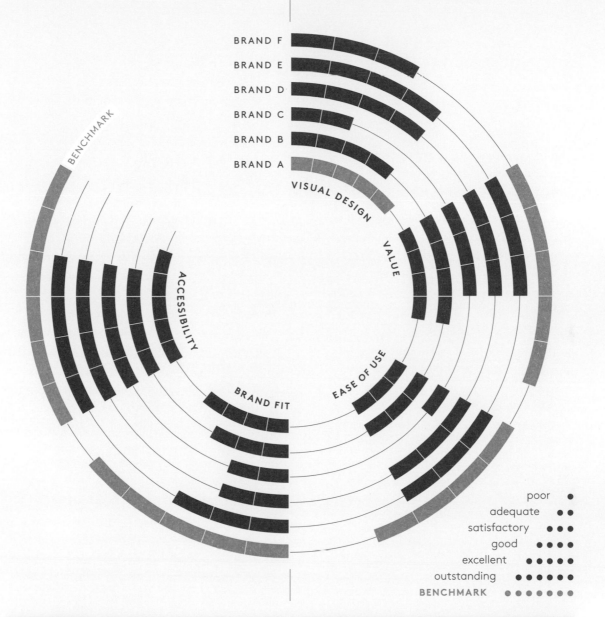

Legend:

poor	●
adequate	●●
satisfactory	●●●
good	●●●●
excellent	●●●●●
outstanding	●●●●●●
BENCHMARK	●●●●●●●

	BRAND A	BRAND B	BRAND C	BRAND D	BRAND E	BRAND F
VISUAL DESIGN	●●●●●	●●●●	●●	●●●●	●●●●	●●●
VALUE	●●●●	●●●●	●●●	●●●	●●●	●●●●●
EASE OF USE	●●●	●●●	●	●●●	●●●	●●●●
BRAND FIT	●●●●	●●●	●●	●●	●●●	●●●●
ACCESSIBILITY	●●●●●●	●●●●	●●●●	●●●●	●●●	●●●●●●●
TOTAL SCORE	●●●●	●●●●	●●	●●●	●●●	●●●●●

BENCHMARK ANALYSIS

A benchmark analysis is used to compare competitors
and rate them in a range of categories.

PRODUCT ANALYSIS

Understanding a company's business model means dealing with its products. Taking a factory tour or making test purchases to become more familiar with the product portfolio should be part of the Discovery phase. Of course, product analyses differ from industry to industry. Some products are intangible: those of electricity suppliers, for example, or insurance companies. Other products are tangible and can be easily investigated using a five-senses analysis. This may sound strange at first, but anyone who has applied a five-senses analysis to two different yoghurts will not only taste the difference, but see, hear, smell and feel it when opening the lid.

The aim of product analysis is to acquire as much information as possible on a product's strengths and weaknesses and understand what makes the product unique. A product's USP (unique selling proposition) and design are often based on its unique attributes.

✔ THE FIVE SENSES ANALYSIS

▸ What does the product look like?
▸ What does the product taste like?
▸ What does the product sound like?
▸ What does the product feel like?
▸ What does the product smell like?

RISK/REWARD™: USER CONDUCT IN PRODUCT CATEGORIES

In product analysis, we soon discover how different products can be, not only in their tangibility, but also in our different expectations as consumers and our willingness to explore the product. However, human reactions towards some product categories, and therefore towards brands in these categories, are often irrational.

Car buyers usually engage intensely with the product: they take test drives, they read brochures, watch ads and seek out information about the car model and brand. This makes sense because, in the best case scenario, they will own the vehicle for a long time. However, the same is true for a product such as a life insurance policy, but in this case, most people prefer to delegate the buying decision to a consultant and rarely understand the basic product features. It's vital to take consumer behaviour in the specific product category into account when considering how to promote a product via digital channels.

The Leo Burnett agency uses a specially developed tool called Risk/Reward™. Product categories are divided into a matrix with two axes. Risk describes how expensive or time-consuming it is for the consumer to choose a brand within a product category. In contrast, Reward refers to the pay-off that a user can expect, e.g. in the form of social approval or personal satisfaction. For example, the purchase of a light bulb is characterized by low risk but also low reward. Expectations are therefore kept accordingly low: a message promising a better life would be pointless. Smartphones, however, are high risk/high reward products, so the brand promise can be correspondingly bolder.

RISK/REWARD™ FOR DIGITAL CHANNELS

Different product categories are characterized by different user behaviour (burden, passion, entertainment, routine). In order to provide added value for the users, the behavioural dynamics of the category should be taken into account in the design.
© Leo Burnett Worldwide

'Interrogate the product until it confesses its strengths.'
ALFREDO MARCANTONIO

SECONDARY RESEARCH

In addition to the Discover methods described here, there are, of course, many ways to stay informed about a given topic. Publications, white papers, trade magazines, newspaper articles and blog posts about social, economic, political and technological trends relevant to the topic are required reading at this stage of the project. Relevant social media communities can be a useful source of information. And of course, market research and consumer analysis will provide relevant data about the target group, competitors and market.

64

65

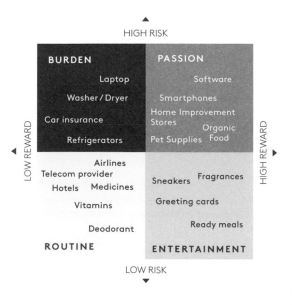

BURDEN — Laptop/Midsize or compact car/ Telecom providers/Banking/ Internet providers/Digital camera/ Large home appliances/Mattress/ Computer printer/Hair colouring kits

PASSION — Airline tickets/Hotels or resorts/Video game system/Toys/Pet supplies (excl. food)/Designer jeans

ROUTINE — Skincare/Paint/Hair products/ Over-the-counter medicines/ Detergent/Toothpaste/Shaving cream/Batteries/Toilet paper

ENTERTAINMENT — Fragrances/Fashion apparel/ Accessories/ Vitamins/Pet food/ Beer/Chocolate/Juice/Carbonated drinks/Cookies/Chips/Mints

1.2

SET-UP / PROCESS ——— **DISCOVER** / DEFINE / DESIGN / DELIVER / DISTRIBUTE

UNDERSTAND THE BRAND

The user experience is the brand experience. The experience that people have when using a digital app will have a sustained effect on their evaluation of the brand, just as personal advice in a store or over the phone would. In order to make a digital app brand-appropriate, we must first analyse and understand the current and target positioning of the brand. Brand positioning is a complex discipline, but some basic methodology can be applied.

BRAND PERSONALITY

For the new positioning of a brand product or company brand it is helpful – and quite entertaining – to get customers to describe the brand's personality. Sometimes this triggers internal discussions but the outcome is always productive. A lack of self-awareness or confusion about the future direction can become apparent. If the actual and target personalities differ greatly from one another, both personalities can be described. In this way, the vector from the current to the target state is clear. If they are very different, this is an indication that any brand relaunch will need to push the message more strongly. The task of the participants in a brand personality workshop is to imagine your company/product/brand as a person and try to answer the following questions:

- How old is this person?
- Is the person a man or a woman?
- To which ethnic group does this person belong?
- Where does the person live (city/countryside, house/apartment, in which city or country)?
- Is the person single/married; does he or she have children?
- What is the person's occupation, field and position?
- What are the person's hobbies and is the person socially committed?
- Describe the person's character: introverted, extroverted, loyal…?
- What is the person's political affiliation?
- What kind of car does the person drive?

The questions can be expanded or narrowed down. Of course, the brand personality does not replace market research. But it can help the design team to gain a better understanding of the brand. Occupation and social status reflect the brand's performance and positioning; personality sheds light on the brand's emotional value, as well as the perception of the brand in terms of corporate responsibility. Apple turned the brand personality of its personal computer into a persona in an ad campaign: 'Hello, I'm a Mac,' says the protagonist of the commercials, who, in contrast to his formally dressed colleague, a PC, appeared much more relaxed and friendly. The campaign ran from 2006 to 2009 on TV and online and was broadcast in different versions in the US, UK and Japan.

→ bit.ly/apmK

With start-ups, we use the brand personality as a tool to develop a unified image of the new brand. For larger brands, it soon becomes apparent if there is a consistent perception of the brand or if the brand personality is unclear, perhaps due to repositioning or to losing its edge for other reasons.

A note of caution, however. Problems can arise if questions are asked about the brand personality in the same workshop in which personas are created, as things can easily become confused. The brand personality is not about the target group or the brand's lead users, i.e. users that any company would like to have and therefore wants to address. Instead, the purpose is to develop an understanding of how the brand itself behaves towards its current and potential customers (BRAND BEHAVIOUR, P. 129).

66

67

ℹ The brand personality is an easy way to get familiar with the brand. In order to analyse the current brand positioning in the market, we use strategic positioning models, which are discussed in the Define chapter (P. 113).

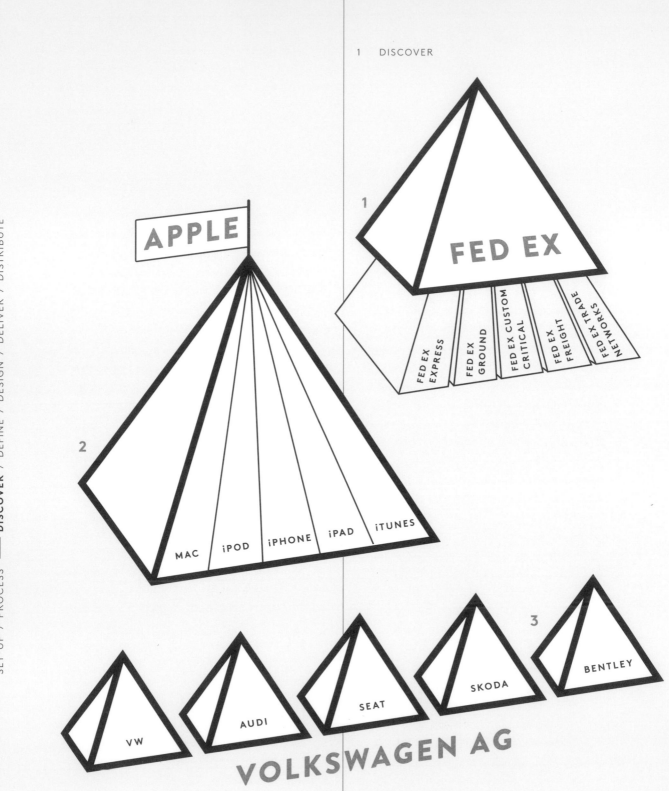

BRAND ARCHITECTURE MODELS

1. FedEx is an example of a master brand strategy.
2. Apple uses a sub-brand architecture.
3. Volkswagen AG employs a freestanding brand strategy.

BRAND ARCHITECTURE

The term 'brand architecture' refers to the structure of the relationships between a company's individual sub-brands. We can distinguish between three basic types of brand architecture:

1 MASTER BRAND ARCHITECTURE

With a master brand architecture, also called a monolithic brand strategy, a company's products and divisions are presented as a single identity. Product brands are subordinate to this identity both in name and look. An example of this is the software producer SAP. However, there may be brand extensions that use a generic descriptor added to the name of the umbrella brand, as in the example of FedEx.

2 SUB-BRAND ARCHITECTURE

A sub-brand architecture, also called an endorsed brand strategy, is when several independent companies or product brands are positioned beneath an overarching master brand. Thus, a brand preserves a separate identity but also benefits from the master brand. The connection can be made visually and in the brand name – e.g. by adding a description such as 'powered by…' or 'A member of the … group' – but the name may not necessarily include a direct link. Lufthansa runs some of its companies, such as Lufthansa Cargo and Lufthansa Italia, as endorsed brands, while its frequent flyer programme Miles & More bears the name of the parent company below its own logo.

Apple's product line – ranging from iPod to iTunes – can also be regarded as a sub-brand architecture. In addition to the uniform naming and visual identity of Apple products, the shared user experience is the dominant brand-specific feature.

3 FREESTANDING BRAND ARCHITECTURE

In a freestanding brand architecture, also called an individual brand strategy, a parent company has a portfolio of multiple co-existing brands that are independent in name and visual identity. The name of the parent firm is often unknown to customers and is only of interest to the business community. The freestanding brand strategy is predominately found in the consumer goods sector, where individual product brands owned by the same company are apparently in competition with each other. A freestanding brand strategy allows each brand to react very quickly to market changes, without affecting the other brands. A typical example is Procter & Gamble, which owns around fifty brands including Braun, Wella, Gillette and Dolce & Gabbana. Another is Volkswagen AG, which operates its various car brands (VW, Audi, Seat, Skoda, Bentley, and others) independently.

In large international companies that operate across multiple business sectors, the brand architecture can be very complex. Particularly in the case of corporate mergers or acquisitions, a strategy must be developed at an early stage to cover how the newly purchased or created brands will be dealt with. Brand architecture is relevant to the development of a comprehensive BIxD style guide and in creating a web landscape that reflects the hierarchy of brands or their specific target repositioning.

For companies that use a master brand or sub-brand strategy, brand architecture provides a suitable entry framework for a global web presence, guiding a user through the site to a sub-brand.

For example: over the past decade, the industrial conglomerate Linde has bought up many of its competitors and become the world leader in industrial gases. Today the firm includes subsidiaries in more than a hundred countries. In design terms, a visual balancing act was required, because while the Linde corporate colour is blue, the branding of many of its purchased former competitors is red (BOC and associates). Both colours are still represented in the company portfolio. There is also the Linde Group, a corporate brand that aims to appeal to investors, journalists and prospective employees on the web. The complex brand structure is reflected on the Linde homepage (P. 336).

EVALUATE CD/CI

While a UX designer focuses predominately on the business model and user requirements, as visual designers we have to be familiar with corporate design and branding guidelines. In addition to style guides for the various design disciplines, we should look at brochures and other publicity materials and evaluate how far the practice deviates from the rules. If there are obvious difficulties with following any of the guidelines, this is a sign that these issues should be raised in the BIxD project and should be resolved differently. By incorporating a social media analysis, we learn how users and clients treat the logo, brand name and other brand elements. This user-generated content forms a point of contact with the brand (TOUCHPOINTS, P. 116) that the company itself cannot directly control, but which can provide information about the perception and vulnerability of the brand.

1.3

UNDERSTAND THE USER

The user is an unknown variable. Who is actually sitting on the other side of the screen? Target groups are complex. But by using various quantitative and qualitative research methods, we can learn more about them, ask them questions and describe them demographically to calculate the 'average consumer'. The advertising agency Jung von Matt in Stuttgart is home to an installation representing 'Germany's most average living room', furnished with everything that is typically German.

Using quantitative research methods, it is possible to determine what percentage of a target group are men or women, how much they earn, how many play football or ski, and how many surf the internet in their spare time. This is useful for planning campaigns and calculating costs per thousand, the currency in which print ads are charged. Nonetheless, these are still averages – abstract statistics that say very little about how an individual brand experience should be designed.

USER INSIGHTS

For this reason, we need more insights and information about the behaviour of our users. This section explains how we analyse target groups and divide them into user groups, how personas (PERSONAS, P. 79) are developed and how to put ourselves into a persona's position. Our aim is to plan and design in a user-centred, not an organization-centred way. Only when we know our users can we create interactive services that are relevant to them.

PERSONA A

PERSONA B

PERSONA C

TARGET GROUPS
OR
CUSTOMER
SEGMENTS

PERSONA D

PERSONA E

PERSONA F

PERSONA G

PERSONA H

TARGET GROUPS AND PERSONAS

Personas are individually and vividly described representatives
of the target group or a customer segment.

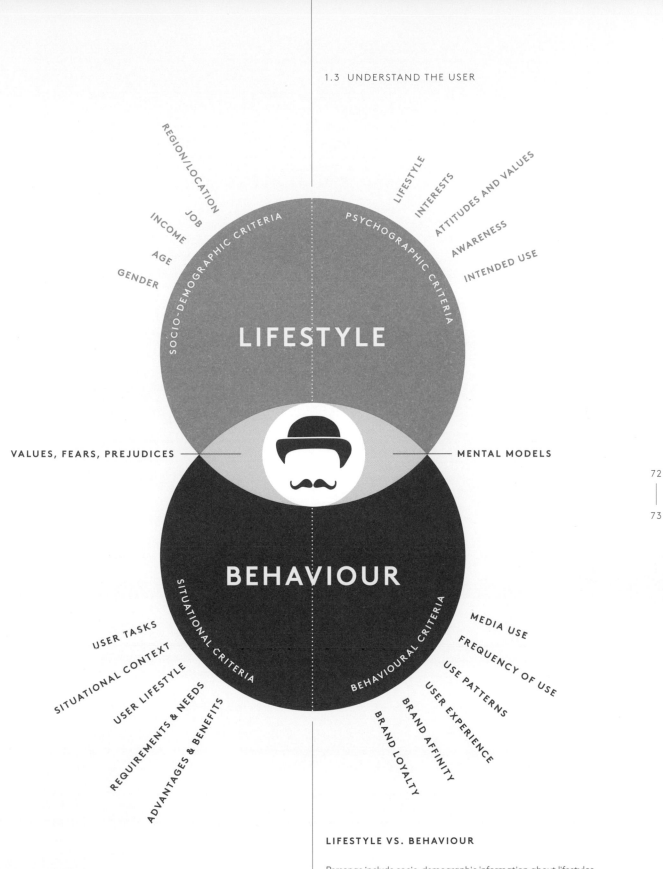

REGION/LOCATION
JOB
INCOME
AGE
GENDER

SOCIO-DEMOGRAPHIC CRITERIA

PSYCHOGRAPHIC CRITERIA

LIFESTYLE
INTERESTS
ATTITUDES AND VALUES
AWARENESS
INTENDED USE

LIFESTYLE

VALUES, FEARS, PREJUDICES ———

——— MENTAL MODELS

BEHAVIOUR

SITUATIONAL CRITERIA

USER TASKS
SITUATIONAL CONTEXT
USER LIFESTYLE
REQUIREMENTS & NEEDS
ADVANTAGES & BENEFITS

BEHAVIOURAL CRITERIA

MEDIA USE
FREQUENCY OF USE
USE PATTERNS
USER EXPERIENCE
BRAND AFFINITY
BRAND LOYALTY

LIFESTYLE VS. BEHAVIOUR

Personas include socio-demographic information about lifestyles
as well as behaviour. Behaviour is usually more difficult to
determine, but is more useful for segmentation purposes.

MENTAL MODELS

A mental model represents a person's thoughts and associations about a particular subject. Mental models include experiences, existing factual knowledge and intuitive ideas and perceptions. They affect a person's behaviour and the way he or she approaches certain topics and issues and develops solutions. Mental models often operate as a kind of 'script' for everyday situations, a term coined by the American cognitive scientist Roger Schank.

'A script is a set of expectations about what will happen next in a well-understood situation. In a sense, many situations in life have the people who participate in them seemingly reading their roles in a kind of play. The waitress reads from the waitress part in the restaurant script, and the customer reads the lines of the customer. Life experience means quite often knowing how to act and how others will act in given stereotypical situations. That knowledge is called a script.'

ROGER SCHANK, *Tell Me A Story*

During the Discover phase, you should try to collect a persona's scripts and to understand and anticipate these in order to create a better contextual response. If we know, for example, that a person may misunderstand a certain wording because of his or her mental model (e.g. because the person's script includes something other than the 'typical' meaning), we can react to this and work out alternatives.

TARGET GROUP ANALYSIS AND SEGMENTATION MODELS

The aim of target group analysis is to ensure that both the message and the design of an app will serve the needs of its future users. Unless we know exactly whom we're targeting, we won't be able to reach the right level of brand value in the Define phase. How progressive is a brand? How expensive should it be or seem? Which interaction options can it credibly offer? Each of the segmentation models listed below is a different way of answering questions about a target group's affinity for technology, its demands and its level of engagement. But all of these models are limited in some way, and none of them is a panacea, even if it may sometimes be touted by agencies as if it is. The models help us to form a picture of the target group and to find clues for brand positioning. Which is the most effective is ultimately a matter of personal judgment. At think moto, we usually begin by working with the Sinus Milieus and then use Digital Lifestyles to learn more about online behaviour. The Digital Lifestyles can then be mapped over the Sinus Milieus.

1   LIFESTYLE MODELS

Every company has a definition of its target group
– sometimes very precise, sometimes less so. At the
very least, rough socio-demographic categories will
have been established. Systems such as the Sinus
Milieus (P. 76), developed by the Sinus Institute in
Germany, define target groups by assigning them
to social milieus or lifestyles. Often companies
create target group profiles for multiple segments
that are rather similar to the personas described
below. The segmentation may be based on a range
of different criteria.

→   www.sinus-institut.de/en

2   LIMBIC MAP

Another way to learn more about the conscious
or unconscious motivation of the target group is
to use a Limbic Map, a method developed by the
brand specialists at Gruppe Nymphenburg. The
insights underlying the Limbic Map are based
on neuromarketing principles. Using the map,
target groups can be classified according to their
psychological personality traits and divided into
seven consumer types (e.g. Adventurer. Performer,
Traditionalist). The Limbic Map is an aid to
understanding the buying decisions and emotional
spectrum of the target group and helps to identify
ways to address them and position the brand in
regard to its competitors. These findings are useful
not only for traditional visual branding, but also
for interaction design. Users whose values are
strongest in the area of fun and imagination make
different demands on a website design than users
who value efficiency, logic and functionality. The
Limbic Map allows the attitudes of the target group
to be visualized and classified, showing overall
tendencies and helping to distinguish between
different personas and their motivations.

3   DIGITAL LIFESTYLES

As part of Digital Life, the world's largest study
of internet users, the brand research company
TNS identified six digital lifestyle types (P. 77).
In addition to general socio-demographic data,
the study compared people's digital behaviour
(e.g. frequency of internet access, social media
use and other online activities), as well as their
attitudes towards the internet (e.g. with regard to
data protection or online friendships). Behaviour
(i.e. consumption) and attitude (involvement) are
not directly linked; it is the interaction between
the two that creates digital user engagement.

TNS distinguished six user segments: Influencers,
Communicators, Knowledge Seekers, Networkers,
Aspirers and Functionals. Influencers, for example,
are characterized by a high level of commitment
and a wide range of digital activity. They are
primarily younger users who see the internet
as a vital part of life and a platform to express
themselves. When you compare the characteristics
of these digital lifestyle profiles, you can see
similarities and differences between the six
segments. Networkers have a similar consumption
level to that of Influencers, but they use the
internet primarily for direct communication

SET-UP / PROCESS —— **DISCOVER** / DEFINE / DESIGN / DELIVER / DISTRIBUTE

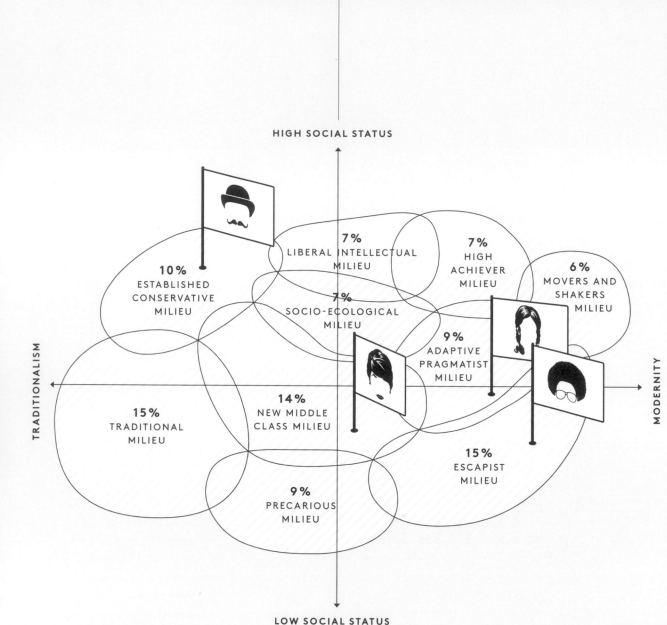

HIGH SOCIAL STATUS

10%
ESTABLISHED
CONSERVATIVE
MILIEU

7%
LIBERAL INTELLECTUAL
MILIEU

7%
SOCIO-ECOLOGICAL
MILIEU

7%
HIGH
ACHIEVER
MILIEU

6%
MOVERS AND
SHAKERS
MILIEU

9%
ADAPTIVE
PRAGMATIST
MILIEU

TRADITIONALISM

MODERNITY

15%
TRADITIONAL
MILIEU

14%
NEW MIDDLE
CLASS MILIEU

9%
PRECARIOUS
MILIEU

15%
ESCAPIST
MILIEU

LOW SOCIAL STATUS

SINUS MILIEUS: POSITIONING BY LIFESTYLE

Sinus Milieus group together demographic characteristics
such as income, profession and age with values and attitudes
towards work, family, leisure time and consumption.
See more at: www.sinus-institut.de/en
Reprinted with the kind permission of the Sinus Institute.

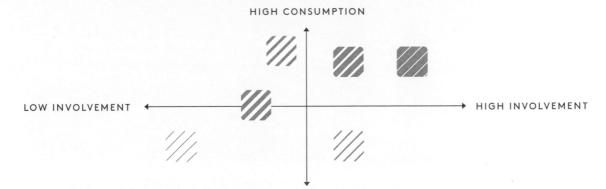

HIGH CONSUMPTION

LOW INVOLVEMENT ← → HIGH INVOLVEMENT

LOW CONSUMPTION

 INFLUENCERS
The internet is an integral part of my life. I'm young and use the mobile web often and everywhere. I am a blogger, an avid social network user with many friends from social networks. I'm also a big online buyer and use my phone for shopping. I want to make sure that as many people as possible hear my online voice.

 NETWORKERS
The internet is important for me to build up and maintain relationships. My life is pretty hectic, both at work and at home. I use social networks to stay in touch with people for whom I otherwise would not have time. I often use the internet at home and am open to interacting with brands and taking advantage of promotional offers. However, I'm not really someone who expresses their opinions online.

 COMMUNICATORS
I just love to talk and express myself, whether face to face, online, on my phone or on social networks, either by instant messaging or by email. I want to express myself in the online world in a way that is not possible in the offline world. I have a smartphone and use it to access the internet at home, at work or at university.

 ASPIRERS
I want to build a personal online presence. I am a newbie in the internet world, which I access via my phone or in internet cafes, but mostly from home. At the moment I'm not online all that much, but would like to be, especially using a mobile device.

 KNOWLEDGE SEEKERS
I use the internet to expand my knowledge, find information and stay informed about world events. I do not particularly care for social networking, but I like to be in contact with like-minded people who can help me, especially when making purchasing decisions. I'm very interested in current issues.

FUNCTIONALS
The internet is a functional tool; I don't use it to express my opinions online. I use it to write and receive emails, get news, follow sports or check the weather, and also to shop online. I'm not interested in the latest developments (e.g. social networks), and I am worried about data protection. I'm older and have been using the internet for a long time.

76

77

TNS DIGITAL LIFESTYLES

These six digital lifestyle segments are the result of a comprehensive study of online behaviour, which was first conducted worldwide by TNS in 2010. The results of the study can be viewed interactively at: 2010.tnsdigitallife.com

SET-UP / PROCESS —— DISCOVER / DEFINE / DESIGN / DELIVER / DISTRIBUTE

with friends and for a much smaller range of activities. They also differ in their usual means of accessing the web: Influencers tend to make greater use of mobile devices, while Networkers prefer to surf from home.

Using these Digital Lifestyle segments, the target group for a digital brand can be defined in relation to its online behaviour and attitudes to the internet. In this way, designers can match the interactive objectives of users and find them where they spend most time online.

→ www.tnsdigitallife.com

---

7 WAYS TO IMPROVE YOUR EMPATHY WITH UNFAMILIAR TARGET GROUPS

1 **CREATE PERSONAS**: These help you and your team to see things from the perspective of other users, or of your client (P. 79).

2 **USING MOOD BOARDS TO CREATE A PERSONA**: Visualize the persona in the context of his or her everyday life (P. 83).

3 **WHAT'S IN YOUR BAG**: Make a photo collage that includes things that the persona has in his or her bag (P. 83).

4 **A DAY IN THE LIFE**: Imagine a persona and describe a typical day in his or her life (P. 87).

5 **CONDUCT STREET INTERVIEWS**: Consult people on the street; ask them if you can record the interview on video. Soundbites help convince clients (P. 87).

6 **CONTEXT ANALYSIS**: If possible, visit your target group at home or at work (wherever they will use your app).

7 **CONDUCT A SHOPPER TEST**: Buy the product where the target group buys it, and look around you!

WHEN IS THE TARGET GROUP NOT THE TARGET GROUP?

Companies are often able to describe the buyers of their product or service fairly accurately. Existing target group profiles, however, should be reviewed with interactive media in mind. On the internet, you may find that you are dealing with a different target group than appears to be the case at first glance. For example, advertising for a premium airline may focus on executives as a target group, but the airline's website – especially its booking system – is not generally used by the executives themselves but by their PAs, who may never fly with the airline themselves. It is therefore crucial to know and understand these users. It is vital to imagine how real people use a website or a mobile app, not just people in the abstract. Personas can help with this.

PERSONAS

Personas are descriptions of typical representatives of a target group or a specific target group segment. Based on market research, they are not intangible statistical averages but fictional individuals who are described according to their desires, goals and expectations. Personas help us to imagine how a certain person would behave and react in a specific situation, e.g. when using an app.

PERSONAS ARE:
- hypothetical, i.e. they are not real people
- archetypal, i.e. not averages but individuals
- specific, i.e. they have personalized characteristics, experiences and behavioural patterns.

Designers need empathy to understand a persona. You could look at your own circle of acquaintances for real people who belong to the target group. When Nintendo undertook a comprehensive relaunch of both its website and brand in 2006, it was necessary to understand the complex target groups. Traditional 'heavy gamers' were joined by new 'casual gamers'. The game manufacturer had previously focused on a very young audience, but it now wanted to be a brand that was accessible to all lifestyles and that also appealed to adults who had no real gaming ambitions. In the future, its web presence needed to interest and inform the new target groups, as well as satisfy the high information and service needs of heavy gamers. I could find examples of the different user segments with my own social circle. Felix, my thirteen-year-old cousin who played with Pokemon cards and a Gameboy and later with a DS and Wii, represented the traditional Nintendo user. But Felix's mother also belonged to the target group, as a representative of the 'purchaser' segment. Because Felix was still too young to buy his own games, it was she who decided which games he was allowed to play and which ones he was not. Nintendo helped her by making product descriptions as clear as possible and offering a broad range of products for the youngest heavy gamers.

Although personas are fictional, they are based on the characteristics of real users. Therefore, it is necessary to collect information for the target group. These personas act as realistically as possible and are given specific goals, attitudes and behaviours:

- personal data (name, photograph...)
- socio-demographic data (age, gender, occupation, marital status...)
- psychographic data (desires, values, lifestyle, hobbies...)
- technographic data (devices owned, user behaviour...)
- geographical data (town, country, culture...)

✓ WHY WE WORK WITH PERSONAS

Working with personas brings many benefits, and it's always worthwhile if the client can be convinced to pay for the relatively low amount of extra work involved. The client can also be included in the process and the results can be used elsewhere in the company. Here are a few reasons for using personas:

▸ They enable effective communication about the target group within the design team and with the client. They put you in the user's position and help you to see things from this perspective throughout the design process.

▸ In the Discover phase and afterwards, they allow you to identify requirements from a user perspective, to prioritize these and assess the need for specific features. These requirements can be documented in use cases and user scenarios (P. 83), or as user stories if you are using the lean UX process (P. 319).

▸ They make the work quantifiable and can be used to evaluate new marketing or promotional projects.

▸ They help us to define test cases and user scenarios, and provide profiles for the recruitment of test subjects.

NAME, AGE AND OCCUPATION OF THE PERSONA
Target group segment or Sinus Milieu

1	**PERSONAL PROFILE** →	A persona profile should include information on age, occupation, family, residence, daily routines, etc.
2	**HOUSEHOLD INCOME** →	The available monthly household income.
3	**VALUES / OBJECTIVES** →	The persona's lifestyle values. The persona's likes and dislikes.
4	**GOALS** →	Personal desires and life goals.
5	**DEMANDS ON THE PRODUCT OR SERVICE** →	What are the persona's expectations of the product?
6	**POTENTIAL PAIN POINTS** →	What will annoy or frustrate the persona when using the product?
7	**RELEVANT BRAND TOUCHPOINTS** →	In which context would this persona encounter the brand?
8	**MEDIA USE** →	Frequency and type of digital media used.

PERSONAL MOTTO →

USER SCENARIO	REQUIREMENTS	BEHAVIOUR
→	→	→
→	→	→
→	→	→

PERSONA TEMPLATE

Personas are not part of your project documentation, but it is helpful to keep a detailed record of them.

WHAT'S IN YOUR BAG?

The contents of a bag are usually personal items and can
give an in-depth insight into the personality of the owner.

PERSONA MOOD BOARD

The persona mood board visualizes the preferences and lifestyle of a persona in the form of a collage of images. It contains images of branded clothing, favourite websites, lifestyle, workplace, the persona's car and hobbies, favourite colours, food, and so on.

WHAT'S IN YOUR BAG?

The contents of a bag say a lot about its owner. We can tell what's important to them, whether they smoke and if so, which brand, what kind of car they drive, whether they love kitsch, are superstitious or are a meticulous planner. Parents often keep pictures of their children in it. A bag contains a personal inventory: the things that are important to people. It is a reflection of a personal lifestyle. It shows patterns of behaviour and personal values and can provide information on the location, age, marital status, hobbies, brand affinities and personal tastes of a persona. It's also fun to compile the collages together. There are also photo blogs and websites, as well as a Flickr group, devoted to the question 'What's in your bag?'

→ bit.ly/QQNZFv

USE CASES AND USER SCENARIOS

What people say and what they do are often two different things. In order to create a relevant user experience, we need to understand behaviour in a particular context. Using personas and user scenarios allows us to imagine the values, preferences and personality traits that characterize user behaviour. In order to do this, we first need to define the most important user scenarios and use cases, matching them with the user motivation and the interface that will be used to reach the desired result. We then describe these scenarios, anticipating not only the behaviour of the user, but also that of the app or interface. User scenarios for different phases in the customer life cycle show us how to make users aware of the app, involve them and take their requests seriously, as well as how to avoid losing them.

User scenarios describe how a user will interact with an existing or planned system. They can be used as both a tool for analysis as well as for design. When we employ user scenarios for analysis, we speak of 'current-state scenarios'. If we are using them to create future interaction processes, for example, a newly developed website, we call them 'future-state scenarios'. Current-state scenarios are mainly used in the Discover phase. Future-state scenarios can be used in the Define and Design phases.

SET-UP / PROCESS ──── **DISCOVER** / DEFINE / DESIGN / DELIVER / DISTRIBUTE

MIGUEL — HEAVY GAMER — SCENARIO 01.1.1

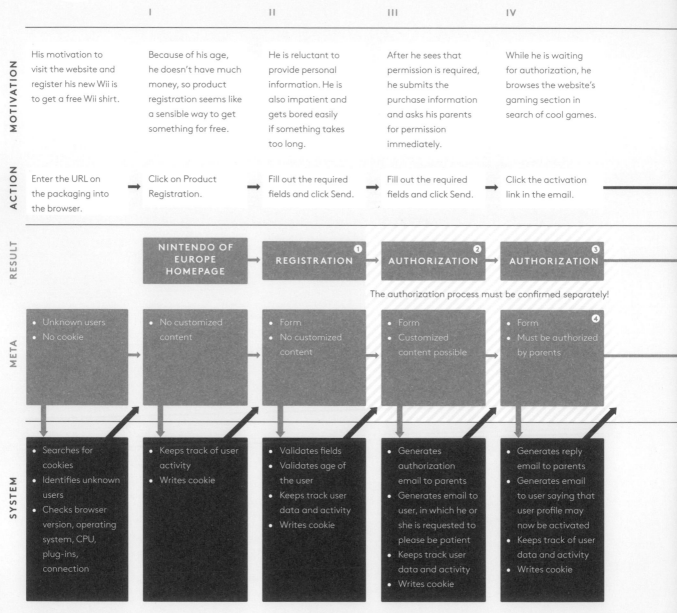

	I	II	III	IV
MOTIVATION	His motivation to visit the website and register his new Wii is to get a free Wii shirt.	Because of his age, he doesn't have much money, so product registration seems like a sensible way to get something for free.	He is reluctant to provide personal information. He is also impatient and gets bored easily if something takes too long.	After he sees that permission is required, he submits the purchase information and asks his parents for permission immediately.	While he is waiting for authorization, he browses the website's gaming section in search of cool games.
ACTION	Enter the URL on the packaging into the browser.	Click on Product Registration.	Fill out the required fields and click Send.	Fill out the required fields and click Send.	Click the activation link in the email.
RESULT		NINTENDO OF EUROPE HOMEPAGE	REGISTRATION ❶	AUTHORIZATION ❷	AUTHORIZATION ❸

The authorization process must be confirmed separately!

META	• Unknown users • No cookie	• No customized content	• Form • No customized content	• Form • Customized content possible	• Form ❹ • Must be authorized by parents
SYSTEM	• Searches for cookies • Identifies unknown users • Checks browser version, operating system, CPU, plug-ins, connection	• Keeps track of user activity • Writes cookie	• Validates fields • Validates age of the user • Keeps track user data and activity • Writes cookie	• Generates authorization email to parents • Generates email to user, in which he or she is requested to please be patient • Keeps track user data and activity • Writes cookie	• Generates reply email to parents • Generates email to user saying that user profile may now be activated • Keeps track of user data and activity • Writes cookie

USER SCENARIO

A user scenario for Miguel, a persona from Nintendo's target group segment 'Heavy Gamers'.

V

VI

VII

VIII

He receives an email informing him that his account is now authorized. In the email, he finds a link for his user profile.

Now he wants to receive the promotional gift as soon as possible.

He completes the registration process and is excited about receiving a Wii shirt.

He leaves the site because he has everything he wanted. He will visit again, but now he wants to play games.

Click on Activate Profile.

Click on Register Product.

Fill in the required fields and click Submit.

Fill in the required fields and click Submit.

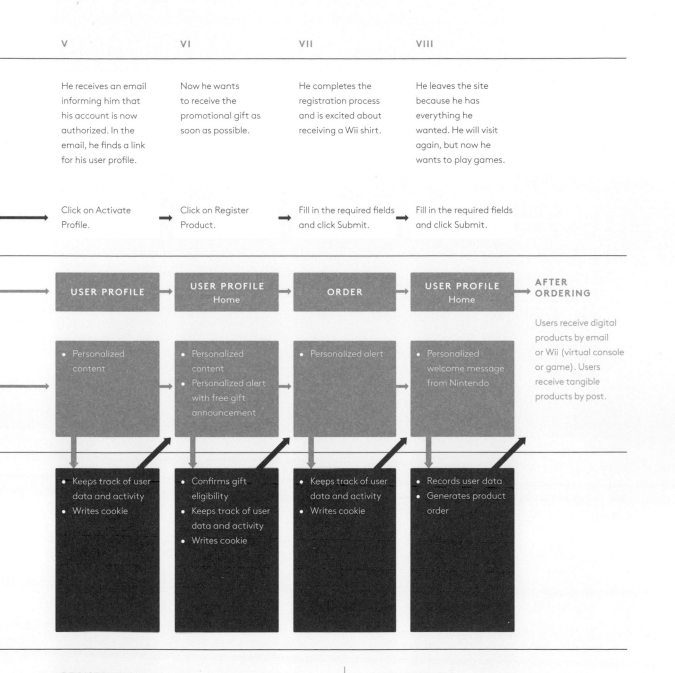

USER PROFILE

USER PROFILE
Home

ORDER

USER PROFILE
Home

AFTER ORDERING

- Personalized content

- Personalized content
- Personalized alert with free gift announcement

- Personalized alert

- Personalized welcome message from Nintendo

Users receive digital products by email or Wii (virtual console or game). Users receive tangible products by post.

- Keeps track of user data and activity
- Writes cookie

- Confirms gift eligibility
- Keeps track of user data and activity
- Writes cookie

- Keeps track of user data and activity
- Writes cookie

- Records user data
- Generates product order

1 REGISTRATION – If a user cancels the registration process, what alternative processes need to be available? Does the user need help, etc.?

2 AUTHORIZATION – There must be a landing page for parents who want to authorize an account.

3 AUTHORIZATION – A simple yet clear authorization system must be in place. What happens if registration is not approved after x days?

4 AUTHORIZATION – What can a young user do while waiting for their parents to give approval? How can the site entertain these users?

	MORNING	NOON	AFTERNOON	EVENING	NIGHT
WHERE?					
WHAT?					
WHO WITH?					
BENEFITS?					
PAIN POINTS?					

A DAY IN THE LIFE

This kind of template helps us to gain a better understanding of a user's daily routine, locate potential touchpoints and provide context-specific reactions to a user's needs.

A DAY IN THE LIFE

Depending on their purpose, user scenarios can extend over short or long periods. Describing a typical day in the life of the persona is another way of putting yourself in the user's shoes. You describe the places, activities and daily routine of a persona, including his or her thoughts, emotions and actions outside of the interaction with the brand touchpoint. Depending on what you want to know, different versions of this tool can be used. As an analysis tool, it is useful to describe a day in the life of the persona in the form of a user journey, in order to understand the brand touchpoints or a specific user behaviour.

A 'day in the life' can also be used to describe future scenarios, such as how a persona will deal with the issue of mobility ten years into the future. When would a persona use their own car or take the train and which interactions would take place? A 'day in the life' can be created in text form (usually about one A4 page) or as a chart showing a kind of daily schedule. You can also use photos or videos of a test subject, in order to gather unfiltered information on subjects' everyday behaviour and mental models (P. 74) .

SHADOWING

When we shadow, we observe a company's customers or employees performing their everyday activities and engaging in user experiences. We keep a low profile, rather like a private detective, and document our observations in videos, texts or photographs. The goal is to observe people first-hand and learn about problems directly, as well as seeing how people deal with them. Shadowing brings us closer to the subject than an interview, in which the description of experiences is often filtered. The goal is to understand a user's routine interactions with others and therefore find out how the design of an app could become part of this routine. Shadowing can therefore be used to discover services and product potential.

REVISITING PERSONAS AND SCENARIOS

Personas and scenarios are analytical tools. However, later in the BIxD process, we can evaluate content, functions and navigation systems, always keeping in mind the behaviour and needs of the persona. Personas and scenarios can help us to generate ideas for the design of an interactive product or service by predicting where a user may get stuck or become impatient (so-called pain points), or allowing us to understand what might motivate a persona to join an online community.

1.4

DEFINE
THE GOAL

THE TARGET MATRIX

At the end of the Discover phase, the documentation of the analysis results is complete. The findings of this phase can be presented to the client as an executive summary. For the next stage of the process, it's important to record your project's key objectives under three main categories – business, brand and user – in a target matrix (P. 91), which should then be discussed with the client. Often there are conflicting objectives that result from clashing stakeholder interests. For example, different company departments may be competing for space on the same website and all want their interests to be represented equally. In this case, you need to act as a moderator, prioritizing the goals and making recommendations for a solution.

THE PROJECT REQUIREMENTS DOCUMENT (PRD)

In technically complex projects developed using a linear process (PROCESS, P. 40), a detailed requirements analysis is carried out. The result of this analysis is called the project requirements document (PRD). This document has usually already been compiled by the client's IT department and serves as the basis for a tender, but often omits brand or user requirements. The Discover phase described here shows only the perspective of the design team. At the end of the Define phase, the metrics and requirements should be compared and combined. In agile project development, requirements can be added over the course of the project because, in principle, each sprint covers the essential four phases – Discover, Define, Design and Deliver – and a potentially shippable product is available at the end of each sprint. On an agile project, our concept developer puts the user stories straight into the project backlog, so that the stories can be incorporated into individual sprints by the developers. User stories represent the project requirements in a form that all team members can understand.

The most important elements in the PRD are:

1   CONSTRAINTS
These include technical system requirements, platform, browser versions or interfaces for existing systems, as well as time and budget restrictions, the working environment and other factors. We once created an installation for an ice cave, which had a constant temperature of -2°C and 98% humidity. A climate-controlled box was built to protect the computer and the projector. Another constraint was that the installation had to be built before the heavy snow season began because four to six feet of snow on the ground would have made it impossible to transport the hardware to the cave by sled.

2   FUNCTIONAL REQUIREMENTS
These are the functions that the system must offer, i.e. the things the system should be able to do. For example, the system should be able to learn how the user behaves in a certain situation and offer the user possible alternatives in the future. Functional requirements should be prioritized and subject to a feasibility assessment.

3   NON-FUNCTIONAL REQUIREMENTS
These include user experience factors such as look and feel, tone of voice, usability and performance. The non-functional requirements also include any cultural, political and legal issues that must be considered. For example, in the ice cave project mentioned above, we had to ensure that the installation was environmentally safe since it was developed as part of a campaign for clean energy.

> A requirement dictates *what* a system should be able to do, not *how* it should do this.

USER STORIES

It is not always easy for creatives to come up with the strictly formulated requirements and rules that the programmer needs to develop an app. Software requirements documentation demands strong technical skills and often entails significantly more effort from the UX designer. The main problem, however, is that creating the requirements may lead the UX or visual designer (or the client's product manager) to take the system's point of view, instead of viewing the app from the user's perspective.

For this reason, in agile software development (P. 43) we work with user stories. User stories are short, simply formulated descriptions of requirements from the user's perspective. They are less precisely formulated than traditional requirements and allow solutions to be altered later. User stories can be formulated informally but should contain three elements:

- the *role* of the user
- the *goal/desire*
- the *benefit* to achieving the goal

In practice, a user story might look like this:

> As the client [*role*] ordering a product, I want an information hotline to be available [*goal*] so that I can immediately call the service centre if something goes wrong [*benefit*].

CONCLUSION

Clients may want to save money during the Discover phase and argue that they have already done their own research, that a customer survey has been done and the target groups are known. However, a Discover phase is essential to allow the design team to understand the task, develop a feel for the client's business, become familiar with the user and empathize with the brand. The knowledge and experience gained here serves as a benchmark later in the project and can be compared to the developed solutions to check for thoroughness and accuracy.

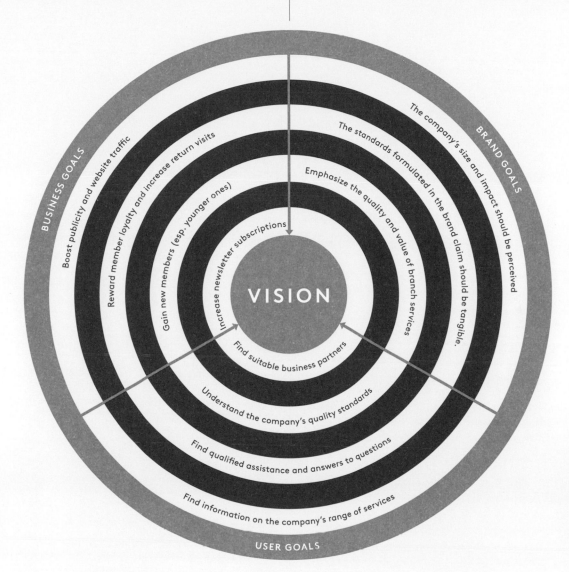

VISION

BUSINESS GOALS

Boost publicity and website traffic

Reward member loyalty and increase return visits

Gain new members (esp. younger ones)

Increase newsletter subscriptions

BRAND GOALS

The company's size and impact should be perceived

The standards formulated in the brand claim should be tangible.

Emphasize the quality and value of branch services

USER GOALS

Find suitable business partners

Understand the company's quality standards

Find qualified assistance and answers to questions

Find information on the company's range of services

BUSINESS GOALS	**BRAND GOALS**	**USER GOALS**
THE SITE SHOULD HELP THE COMPANY TO…	THE BRAND'S GOALS ARE TO…	AS A POTENTIAL CUSTOMER I WANT TO…
→ increase awareness	→ present its services	→ find information
→ promote member loyalty	→ make a tangible impact	→ find help and support
→ gain new members	→ make the brand claims tangible	→ understand quality standards
→ increase newsletter subscriptions		→ find business partners

TARGET MATRIX

A business commissions a new online presence. This diagram shows a possible target matrix. If the scope of the matrix is too broad, it is likely that you have identified requirements rather than specific goals.

SERVICE DESIGN

BRIAN GILLESPIE
CONTINUUM

Hi Brian, when I first met you, you were at a conference, giving a talk on service design. What is service design? Why do we need that term? And isn't designing services what interactive designers have always done?

It's interesting. The meaning and practice of service design has been changing and growing quite significantly in the past few years. Services have been designed for decades and a strong practice has grown up around the design of public services, for instance. What's new is how digital is impacting service design, the enhancement or replacement of traditional analogue services with innovative digital services. What is happening is that the tools and techniques and methods of service design that have been used for decades are merging with the tools and techniques of user experience design, and resulting in new hybrids and new ways to define and design services. I don't

typically call it service design, because I've always called it experience design, whether it is a product experience or a service experience. When I designed my first online shopping cart back in 1997, was I a service designer or was I a user experience designer? I prefer the name strategic design, as a broader description of what design can do.

I agree and actually prefer the term 'service system design' for when we design service systems across different digital touchpoints, rather than single touchpoint apps. adidas miCoach is a good example of that. You worked on that project when you were with Molecular/Isobar.

The term we used at Molecular at that time was 'brand as service'. Let me use the adidas miCoach system to explain what we meant by that. I could use Nike or other brands as examples but I'm a loyal adidas customer. One of adidas's promises as a brand is that they aspire to help customers achieve their impossible. adidas works hard at communicating this promise by describing and branding the individual product lines that they sell: shoes, shirts, socks, equipment, etc.. They also align some of the greatest athletes in the world with the products and create ad campaigns promoting these links, and also use other platforms such as events designed to inspire consumers to purchase and use the products. If people use the products over time, with a goal in mind, maybe they too can achieve their impossible. Consumers who buy a pair of high-end running shoes take a step in this direction but after that, whether they can achieve their personal fitness goals is entirely up to them.

miCoach changes all that. It has enabled adidas to think beyond traditional ad strategies, beyond simply communicating the attributes of the product. adidas is not typically viewed as a service provider. However, they are very much in the experience business, as providers and facilitators. In the non-virtual world, many of us have used the services of a personal fitness coach to help us achieve our fitness goals. The trained and experienced people who offer this service probably put a lot of thought into the design of that service. So the wonderful thing about miCoach is that it is possible to offer this service via a virtual personal coach. adidas is no longer relying solely on inspiring consumers by telling them how great their running shoes are. Now this complex and connected system of digital and analogue interfaces and touchpoints can help consumers achieve *their* impossible.

There is a synchronicity in the whole system that raises the delivery of the brand experience to a new level. It is that combination of products and service, delivered via multiple touchpoints, that really transforms the meaning of brands and service design, and so leads us to the idea of brand (experience) as service (experience). If my seemingly impossible goal had always been to run a 5k race, now miCoach can actively guide, inspire, motivate and train me to achieve that goal. The brand promise has actually been fulfilled. That is the beauty of a system like miCoach and the beauty of a brand like adidas. They have all the fundamental elements that make up a very strong brand: great products, great image, great history, and great reputation. And now this virtual-yet-real service experience comes along to take things to another level. It is no longer just about product, not just about experience, but also about personal transformation.

92

93

That is the next level that design agencies need to reach; to think in terms of making the full service ecosystem work.

With miCoach, it started out fairly simply. The ecosystem was just the runner, the gear and the website, but now that is expanding. The community aspect is growing, the mobile aspect is growing. The service platforms are expanding and the methods to really deliver on the service are expanding. Ideally, service becomes multidimensional and allows people to personalize the service. It's not a case of: 'Here's the service, take it or leave it.' Instead it's: 'Here's the system. Interact with it, and use it however you want to.'

What does that mean for the brand? Branded traditional services are not new. But now there are service systems where people personalize the system and can continue to change it.

There is a lot of fear in brands. Companies worry that they will lose control of the relationship and are not sure how to relate to empowered and influential consumers. Traditionally brands are used to talking to people but not used to being part of conversations. The interactive agencies have been aware of this changing landscape for some time and have been saying this.

It's not about talking at consumers, you have to talk with and trust your customers. It's about dialogue and sharing and conversation; it cannot be one-way traffic.

Agencies can help their corporate branding and design departments with the transition and help

them adjust. I don't think many companies are prepared for this shift. It takes time to re-shift your marketing department, to re-shift your brand communications, to re-shift how you organize yourself to deliver that new experience.

This shift is affecting agencies, too. Interactive agencies that used to be considered service providers can now become sounding boards and consultants for product and business management.

It really is changing. The design thinking movement, which has been emerging for more than ten years now, is having a global impact. Design thinking is very much about the aspect of the design process that tackles fuzzy, tricky, unclear problems, often called the Discover and Define phase. It is about the process of establishing a strategy or vision for innovation by design.

Business managers are being encouraged to expand their business thinking and become design thinkers. Schools and courses teach managers the methods. However the non-designer design thinkers still face the challenge of design *doing* and so must rely on design agencies. Should we be concerned that design agencies may get popped out of the strategy formation process and return to the days of simple tactical doing? I would hate to think that. How ironic that emphasizing the value of design thinking in the strategy process could result in its being taken over by business managers and shoving design managers back down the line and back into the past!

Agencies need to step up and be unafraid to talk strategy. It is within their power to lead the integrated thinking movement and great opportunities exist for innovating design consultancy.

What does a typical process look like? How do people work together in the process? How do you start? What is the role of strategy? And how do you, as a strategist, work together with the design team?

Process is messy. Process is never the same thing twice. Process is an ideal that everybody aspires to.

Process works best when approached as a flexible set of tools and techniques that are organized, timed and sequenced in a way that is intended to solve the design and business challenge in the most effective and efficient way. I typically like to keep the overarching process as simple as possible but encourage teams to develop expertise in tools and techniques we fcel will best help us to strategize and create great design.

I approach the strategic design process with the key activities typically described by most design thinkers or design strategists or innovation designers. Gather insights that drive understanding, that power ideas, that craft vision, that produce concepts, that are in turn validated,

that may lead to iteration, and then eventually requirements, full design, implementation, launch, and analytics. We divide our insight generation activities into two parts: one focuses on business insights, the other on customer insights. The business component is usually focused on business strategy and objectives of a company, the industry and the market in which they compete, the competitors with whom they compete, and last, but not least, the brand we're working with. The customer component is very much focused on design research. Ultimately our ideas and concepts look to form a marriage between the two, a platform upon which to build and grow relationships. That's the process driver.

Probably two of the most useful artifacts from the customer or user discovery work are personas and customer journeys. At Molecular, personas were a hugely important part of our work. To make sure that our personas were driven by both quantitative and qualitative data and insights, the teams that produced them included business strategists, user experience designers, and visual designers. The personas became beautifully crafted pieces of information design. When our clients were introduced to the personas, we knew we'd done well when they said things like 'I know this person, this is our customer'. We also knew that the design team had an excellent lens through which to imagine and create designs that would have meaning for end-users. At Continuum, the visual presentation of strategy is a great strength and critical to how we communicate ideas and concepts.

What is the set-up of business, UX and visual designers at Continuum? Who does what?

When I was at digital agencies the composition was invariably pretty simple: business, design (including UX design), and tech people. At Continuum, we have a much wider range of design disciplines that can tackle an incredibly broad range of analogue, digital and integrated omni-channel products, services and experiences. We value strong skills in each discipline but we also value the ability to cross disciplines and integrate each other's thinking. We also value the ability to take an idea all the way to market.

Our office has a very open design. Large open rooms with no interior walls or cubes. We have a very mobile staff. We mostly work on laptops, and only have mobile phones, which allows us to form teams for full-on projects or hold cross-team creative brainstorming sessions quickly. People move around a lot. They work in project rooms, from couches and coffee table spaces, and from meeting rooms. Mobility within the spaces provides a very creative, flexible and dynamic environment.

Brian Gillespie is Principal of Digital Strategy at Continuum in West Newton, Massachusetts.

GOOD PRACTICE

—

Service Design

NIKE+ ECOSYSTEM / YELLO ENERGY METER /
FLINKSTER / KAI THE COACH / NI MASCHINE / WITHINGS / SCRABBLE

NIKE+ ECOSYSTEM

Nike+ Ecosystem demonstrates how different digital – and digitally enriched – products can interact within a service system to create a lasting brand experience. From a brand perspective, the system perfectly complements the classic product line, featuring digital services that support athletes during training.

Nike+ was produced as a training system for runners, and consists of a wireless sensor, Nike+ running shoes, a wireless receiver for the iPod and an iTunes account. Over time it was expanded to include other sports

and various shoe designs, apps and devices for both amateurs and professionals. The Nike+ GPS app for smartphones allows users to record and evaluate runs and share them with others on Twitter and Facebook. Nikeplus.com serves as a central platform on which all data is available. The community's own currency, NikeFuel points, is used in conjunction with other gamification elements to promote motivation and monitor performance.

www.nikeplus.com

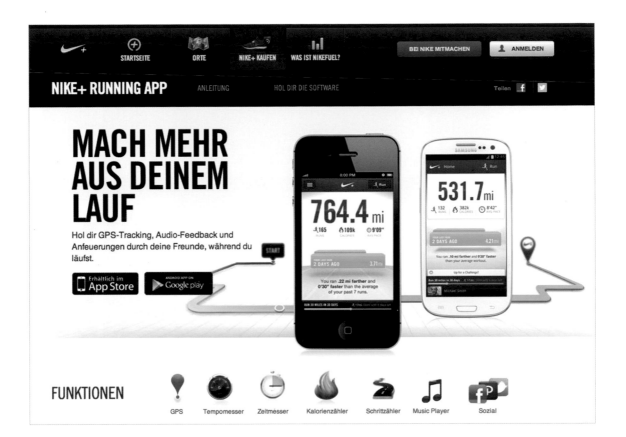

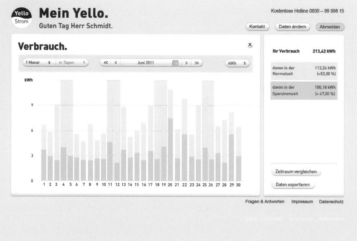

YELLO ENERGY METER
IDEO

It is a classic problem for the energy industry. How do you advertise an invisible branded product and make it stand out – aside from the price alone – within the market? Yello took on this challenge and boldly proclaimed: power is yellow. The Yello energy saving meter translates the brand message into a relevant meaning. Electricity supplied by Yello actually becomes visibly yellow, in the form of a meter box that stands out from the crowd. The hinged front fits over the grey housing and the illuminated digits shine through the translucent plastic to show how much energy has been used. These flickering 'vital signs' are a reinterpretation of the spinning discs of a traditional meter. The energy meter also matches other elements in the brand's service system. From the comfort of your own living room, you can track your energy use on a PC, smartphone or tablet.

www.yellostrom.de/privatkunden/sparzaehler

FLINKSTER

For some time now, the German rail network Deutsche Bahn has offered its customers a wider selection of mobile services. These include the cycle hire system Call-a-Bike and Flinkster, a car-sharing service, which replaced DB Carsharing in 2011. Using a smartphone, customers can locate nearby Flinkster stations or parking facilities and reserve a car. The cars are unlocked using a customer card. Billing is calculated per hour or half-hour depending on duration of use.

Despite using a separate brand name, the system itself uses the corporate branding of Deutsche Bahn, and so benefitted – especially during the start-up phase – from the reputation and reliability of the master brand. More important is the reverse effect: Flinkster complements the services offered by Deutsche Bahn and helps it to position itself as a modern way to travel beyond the train tracks.

www.flinkster.de

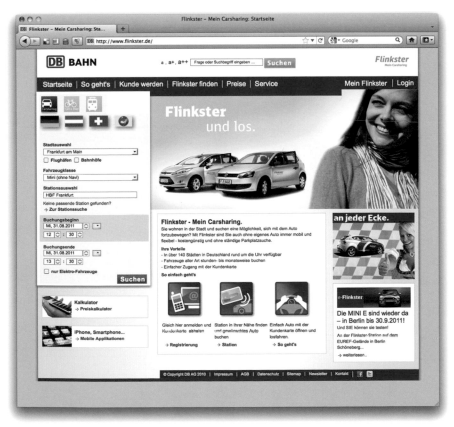

KAI THE COACH

THINK MOTO

Kai the Coach is a service design study for a system that replicates a personal fitness trainer. The aim of the study was to adapt the concept of *Men's Health* magazine into an innovative digital service. An interactive trainer combines interactive magazine content with organizational and community functions.

Kai the Coach was designed as a separately branded product that maintains a clear connection with the parent brand. The design focused on creating a contextually meaningful user experience. The various apps for smartphone, tablet and browser therefore offer a range of functionalities based closely on context of use. The core of the system is a set of cards containing facts and exercises. The tablet app is primarily used for information and motivation. In the gym, exercises are tracked using a smartphone app. The website offers easy-to-use features that allow users to compile training and nutritional plans.

Opposite, below: Borahm Cho, an employee at think moto, while bodystorming. Borahm is playing the role of Kai, the virtual personal trainer. In the background you can see the training schedule; on the table are event cards with workouts, recipes and editorial articles. Another employee took the role of the user.

NI MASCHINE
NI PRODUCT DESIGN DEPARTMENT
AND PRECIOUS

Maschine from Native Instruments is a 'Groove Production Studio' – a combination of desktop software and hardware controller. It unites the flexibility of digital music production and the hands-on feel of a physical control system. Maschine was acclaimed by both users and the press and has received many awards. The iMASCHINE app is a practical extension of the studio software for a smartphone.

Because of the small size of its screen and its limited capacity, the iPhone is not suited to being a fully functional digital music studio, but the advantage of smartphones is that they are always within reach, especially if you're feeling inspired when on the move. iMASCHINE was therefore developed as a 'musical sketchpad' on which users can record their

ideas anytime, anywhere. Results are immediately shared on the online music platform SoundCloud or transferred to the desktop software to be processed in the home studio. In order to ensure a consistent user experience, both the characteristic interaction patterns and the visual language of the Maschine brand were used for the app. The product design for Maschine was developed by an internal design team in NI's research and development department. Precious supported the interactive design and created the graphic user interface. From the beginning of the Maschine's concept design, the focus has been on the simultaneous development of software and hardware in order to ensure an integrated workflow for users.

www.native-instruments.com

WITHINGS

Withings specializes in developing healthcare products that can be connected to your PC or mobile device. Although the individual products are similar, they are not identical in their formal language, tone of voice, interface design or user experience. Instead, the brand focus is on a shared design philosophy of simplicity and easy integration into other systems.

Opposite, above: The Wireless Blood Pressure Monitor comes with a specially developed app for iOS. After checking blood pressure levels, all results,

including systolic and diastolic pressure and BPM, are stored on the device. The Withings app contains tools that can display morning and evening measurements separately.

Opposite, below: The Smart Body Analyzer is a scale that automatically transmits data via WiFi. On the accompanying smartphone, iPad or web app, graphs for weight, body fat mass and lean body mass for up to eight people can be stored and viewed.

www.withings.com

GOOD PRACTICE —— SERVICE DESIGN

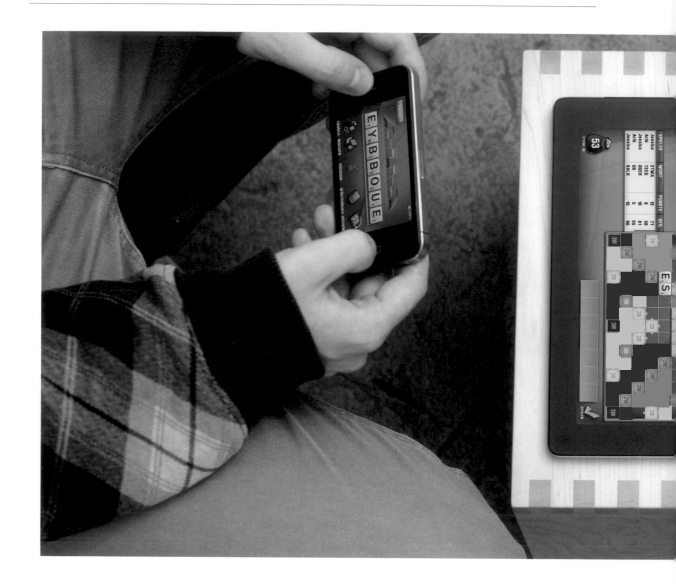

SCRABBLE™

ELECTRONIC ARTS

Electronic Arts has adapted the world-famous
board game SCRABBLE™ for consistent use across
many devices. However, SCRABBLE™ for iPad is a
particularly good demonstration of the potential for
multiscreen experiences through the connection of
multiple devices. The free SCRABBLE™ Tile Rack app
can transform an iPhone or iPod Touch into a rack for
a player's tiles. In Party Play mode, up to four players
can compete against each other and 'swipe' the tiles
from the iPhone or iPod onto the iPad game board.

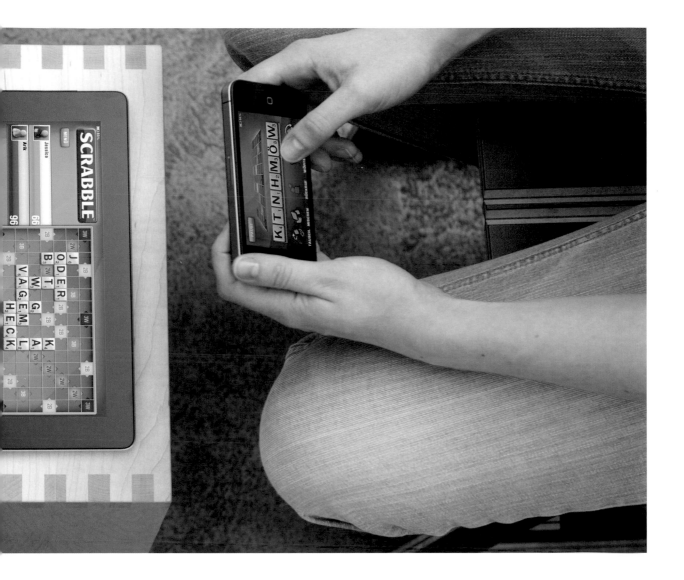

2

DEF INE

THE STRATEGY PHASE

2.4
DEFINE
THE METRICS

SET-UP / PROCESS ——— DISCOVER / **DEFINE** / DESIGN / DELIVER / DISTRIBUTE

2.2 PLAN THE BRAND EXPERIENCE

2.1 PLAN THE PRODUCT OR SERVICE

BRAND

2.3 PLAN THE USER EXPERIENCE

3
4
5
6
7
2
1
10
6
8

5   6   7

Now the stage is set! The strategic decisions made in the Define phase will determine success or failure. Those who put the work in now will find it easier to make decisions in the Design phase.

Developing digital brand and communication strategies requires the experience and skills of specialists. Nevertheless, visual designers should be included in the Discover and Define phases. Based on the business goals, a communication strategy for the chosen digital touchpoints must now be developed. Based on the brand goals, we will create the design principles: the so-called brand filter. With the help of user insights, we will develop guidelines for the user experience. And based on all the goals and requirements, we will define metrics for measuring success.

2.1

PLAN THE PRODUCT OR SERVICE

Before we develop a communication strategy for interactive media, we must first identify where and how users come into contact with the brand. These brand touchpoints are based on the user scenarios, which extend beyond individual apps, products or services to span the entire customer life cycle. The path that a prospective buyer or customer takes to reach this endpoint is called the user journey.

TOUCHPOINTS: WHERE AN AUDIENCE MEETS A BRAND

A touchpoint is anywhere that a potential customer comes into contact with a brand or company. As the number of media channels grows, so does the number of touchpoints. In the past there were print ads, TV ads and billboards. All of these are still available, but now there are also websites, apps, email newsletters, Facebook pages and more. But something else is also different: these new touchpoints no longer function in a single direction. Now the customer can contact the company – or other customers. For many companies, this is the cause of a deep-seated fear. Touchpoints are meant to positively influence the behaviour and attitude of users towards the brand, but how is this possible when users can publicly express their own opinions at any time? In this chapter we will address how a company can deal with the digital Moment of Truth (P. 126) and meet the challenges of social media.

☰ DIGITAL BRAND TOUCHPOINTS

▸ **WEBSITES** – including all browser-based apps such as corporate websites, product microsites, online stores and product catalogues, intranets and extranets, online advertising, social media, etc.

▸ **EMAIL** – newsletters, confirmations and other mails that can be opened in the client's mail app on mobile devices or PCs or with a webmail service.

▸ **DESKTOP APPS** – company apps, desktop apps for customers, kiosk apps, B2B apps, software products for professional users, etc.

▸ **MOBILE APPS** – apps for the iPhone, iPad, Android, Windows Phone 7, etc. that are controlled via touchscreen.

▸ **AUGMENTED REALITY** – apps in which a real image is enriched in real time with other information, either at home, on screen at the POS via a smartphone, or as an interactive city guide.

▸ **INTERACTIVE INSTALLATIONS** – installations for exhibitions and showrooms, controlled by specialized devices, touchscreens or gestures.

▸ **INTERACTIVE ENVIRONMENTS** – accessible spaces that are controlled directly through body gestures or indirectly by analysing sensor data; e.g. for corporate museums or showrooms.

▸ **INTERACTIVE OUT-OF-HOME MEDIA** – interactive or reactive billboards and streetlamps used for outdoor advertising or information; these include digital signage.

▸ **INTERACTIVE ARCHITECTURE** – interactive facades or entire buildings that respond to events from outside or inside the building.

▸ **OBJECTS AND HARDWARE** – the 'Internet of Things' includes fridges that can automatically re-order groceries, the Nike+ Sensor, or scales that send data to a virtual fitness trainer.

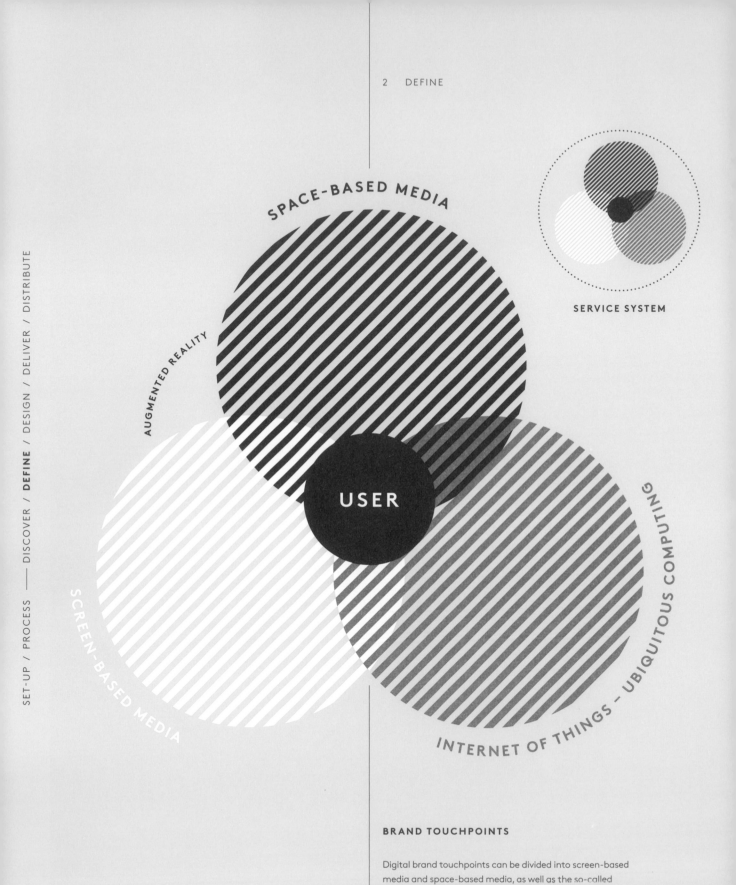

SET-UP / PROCESS —— DISCOVER / **DEFINE** / DESIGN / DELIVER / DISTRIBUTE

SPACE-BASED MEDIA

AUGMENTED REALITY

USER

SCREEN-BASED MEDIA

INTERNET OF THINGS – UBIQUITOUS COMPUTING

SERVICE SYSTEM

BRAND TOUCHPOINTS

Digital brand touchpoints can be divided into screen-based
media and space-based media, as well as the so-called
'Internet of Things'– intelligent objects that are capable
of new forms of direct and indirect interaction.

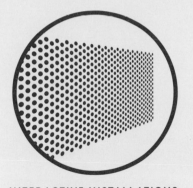

INTERACTIVE INSTALLATIONS

INTERACTIVE SPACES

INTERACTIVE ARCHITECTURE

INTERACTIVE OUT-OF-HOME MEDIA

AUGMENTED REALITY

DESKTOP APPS

MOBILE APPS

WEBSITES

EMAIL

INTELLIGENT OBJECTS

PORTABLES

WEARABLES

THE CUSTOMER LIFE CYCLE

The business relationship between a company and its customers has a life cycle: the so-called customer life cycle. This begins at the moment in which a potential customer first hears about a brand's product. It includes the moment in which interest is aroused and the purchase of the product or service is first considered. It continues through the acquisition and possession of the product or the use of a service. And it ends, in some cases, with the decline of interest – a phase of the customer life cycle in which the company must take care not to lose the customer.

In each of these phases, there are touchpoints that we can and should use in digital business strategy. Different methods of interaction suit different phases of the customer life cycle. The phases vary depending on the industry and also vary in length depending on the product. The automotive industry, for example, faces the challenge of maintaining contact with customers and positively influencing them during the very long purchase phase; several months may elapse between the day a car is ordered and the day it can be picked up. For other products (e.g. furniture), there is a very long possession and use phase in

which there is no occasion for additional customer contact – unless you are dealing with 'fans' who wish to stay in contact with the brand even when they are not purchasing anything. These loyal customers are not only repeat customers when deciding to buy a new product; they are also often advocates and ambassadors for the brand. Loyal customers and fans recommend a product, join brand-based communities and provide helpful tips for product improvement. We gain loyal users of a digital product or service when we create joy of use (P. 140).

2 CONSIDERATION
How do we communicate the product or service
benefit, in order to convince the customer to buy?

PURCHASE
How do we make the
buying experience easy,
pleasant, safe and
positive?

AWARENESS
How do we draw
attention to a brand and
its products or services?

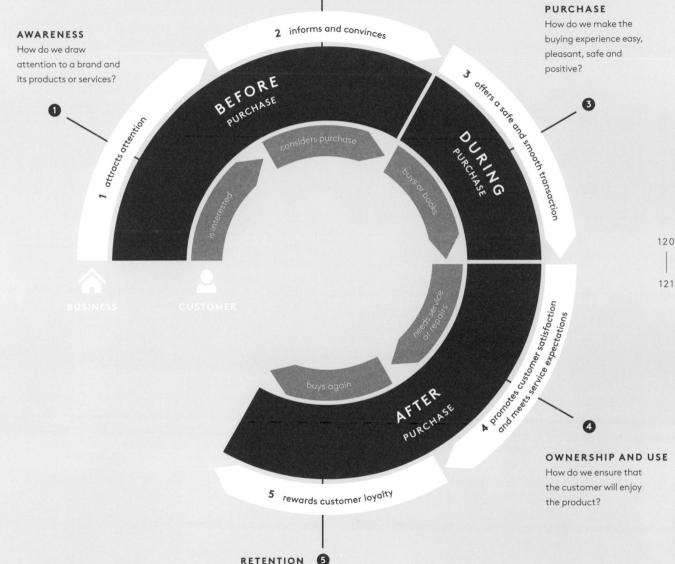

2 informs and convinces

BEFORE PURCHASE

DURING PURCHASE

AFTER PURCHASE

1 attracts attention

3 offers a safe and smooth transaction

considers purchase

buys or books

is interested

needs service or repairs

buys again

4 promotes customer satisfaction and meets service expectations

5 rewards customer loyalty

BUSINESS   CUSTOMER

OWNERSHIP AND USE
How do we ensure that
the customer will enjoy
the product?

RETENTION
What services can we offer to ensure
that the customer will choose the
brand, product or service again?

CUSTOMER LIFE CYCLE

A typical customer life cycle for a branded product or service –
from the perspective of both the company and the customer.
Depending on the product, the phases may vary in length.

ON THE MOVE
In conjunction with iTunes and the iTunes Store, the iPod was the first building block in the successful development of a now complex service system.

AT HOME
iTunes and iTunes Store are available on all platforms, allowing music and videos to be purchased and played everywhere. With iTunes, Apple not only supply the hardware and software for a personal media library, but also the logistics behind it.

ON THE MOVE
The iPhone and iPad have become key platforms in Apple's system. Not only are images, videos, music and personal contacts available on mobile devices, but, with iBooks and Newsstand, other services that are particularly relevant in a mobile context are as well.

THE CLOUD
iCloud stores all media files, including photos, music, videos and ebooks, and makes them available at multiple touchpoints.

AT HOME
Using the iLife suite, photo albums, music and videos can be created on laptops or desktops. Photo albums can be turned into books, printed to order.

AT HOME
Apple TV connects devices to the television and can stream video-on-demand services.

SERVICE SYSTEMS

Over time, Apple has created a service system incorporating all home media data; this includes not only hardware and software but also the logistics needed to download music, videos and e-books, to buy or print photo albums and ship them. Unlike its competitors Google and Yahoo, Apple consistently builds up its own system, without getting bogged down by buying up services that are later difficult to integrate.

DESIGNING AND PLANNING SERVICE SYSTEMS

Websites, mobile apps and other software are not only useful for brand communication. These are digital products whose complexity extends far beyond traditional advertising methods. Companies that provide their customers with digital apps would do well to see these as an extension of their classic product portfolio. Digital services combine multiple software products into a service system. The design of this type of system is called service design, and includes designing communication between people using a digital service, as well as the technical systems that make this communication possible, and the interfaces required.

The Branded Interaction Design (BIxD) process includes the essential steps you need to develop a digital service system. This includes the service's Discover phase with a stakeholder analysis, use cases and goals for the services, the Define phase in which a service is strategically defined as a solution for a particular problem, and the Design phase, in which the solutions are designed and worked out conceptually. Finally, the technical implementation and documentation follow in the Deliver phase, while the Distribute phase covers the ongoing development of the service.

SERVICE DESIGN SKETCHES

Before a service is actually designed and implemented, we first explore potential solutions in a concept study, implement the first interactions as prototypes and evaluate the user experience.

This so-called 'service design sketch' can be created within a week or two. For example, for a travel service, we took the roles of predefined personas, visited various travel agencies and documented our experiences as current-state scenarios. Using roleplay, we continued the scenarios and so developed approaches for a digital service that would span the entire customer life cycle. The potential solutions were illustrated in design sketches that were presented to the client. The service design sketch is the basis for an initial product development phase, which then passes through the entire BIxD process and finally becomes an ongoing service.

☰ PRODUCTS AND SERVICES

▸ The difference between a product and a service is not always clear. According to the common definition, products are tangible and can be retained – and thus patented; the product experience can be repeated; and the quality of data is controllable. Services, however, are time-limited and intangible, and thus difficult to patent; they are measured by the quality of experience and are difficult to repeat. Digital services often combine several software products into a service system. For online apps, the distinction is often difficult to make – which is why digital products and services are often discussed together in this book.

COHERENCE

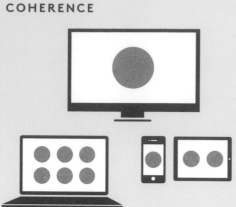

SYNCING

SCREEN SHARING

DEVICE SHIFTING

COMPLEMENTARITY

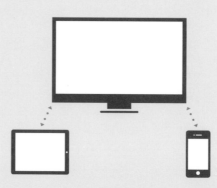

SIMULTANEITY

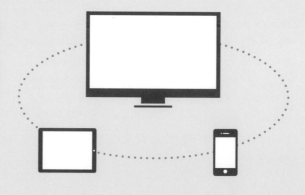

MULTISCREEN STRATEGIES

Six methods of designing digital apps across multiple screens. OS developers are now trying to expand their operating systems to include the potential for interaction and the creation of an overall user experience. OS interfaces can now incorporate the use of a keyboard, mouse, touchscreen, gesture and voice interaction.

MULTISCREEN EXPERIENCES

Digital service systems are often designed to be used at a variety of digital touchpoints and must therefore have cross-device and cross-platform functionality. Depending on the situation and context, users can use different terminals with different screen sizes. Four formats are currently dominant: smartphones, tablet PCs, laptops and desktop PCs, as well as internet-enabled TVs. In order to optimally design the user experience at each of these touchpoints and provide the appropriate functionality in each case, you need to predefine a suitable multiscreen strategy. Christophe Stoll and Johannes Schardt of Precious (INTERVIEW, P. 266) distinguish between six multiscreen design patterns:

1 COHERENCE

A digital product is designed coherently across multiple devices. Features and content are optimized and context-specific. An iPad is better for reading than an iPhone, while a TV is better for video playback. Another example is the digital notebook Evernote (evernote.com): its mobile app can add GPS locations to notes to record where they were made.

2 SYNCING

Cloud data storage allows you to sync content across multiple devices. For example, the page number of an e-book or the playback position of a video is synced so that you can start in the same place, even if you switch from one device to another.

3 SCREEN SHARING

This method of combining several screens into a single one is not yet widely used. It is useful for software that requires a lot of screen space, for example, for audio or image processing, so that menu bars or libraries can be outsourced from the home screen onto a second screen.

4 DEVICE SHIFTING

Device shifting allows you to take content from one device and use it in a new context on another device. Here, the content from one screen can literally be 'moved' to another, for example, a video from iPhone to a TV screen, as with Apple's AirPlay technology.

5 COMPLEMENTARITY

Screens are used to complement each other. Content and functionality on one screen are expanded by adding content and features on other screens. An excellent and appropriate example of this is SCRABBLE for the iPad with its Tile Rack app for iPhone (GOOD PRACTICE, P. 110).

6 SIMULTANEITY

A popular way to use two or more devices simultaneously is to use a smartphone app to accompany a TV broadcast. An example is the Heineken Star Player app, which viewers can use during a live football match to predict what will happen in the game and potentially win prizes (GOOD PRACTICE, P. 241).

SET-UP / PROCESS ——— DISCOVER / **DEFINE** / DESIGN / DELIVER / DISTRIBUTE

USER JOURNEYS

We can visualize the interplay of different touchpoints in the form of a user journey. Imagine that a broad-reach media push is required to raise awareness for a new product or relaunch a brand. On the internet, this could mean online advertising metrics, social media or viral campaigns. In the real world, outdoor media such as interactive billboards or billboards in high-traffic areas can be added to the marketing mix. Of course, a combination of these media can be utilized.

A user journey shows how users come into contact with different touchpoints over a period of time, what they do there and how the brand experience is intensified step by step. The time period that we assign for a user journey depends on the scenario. We could record the touchpoints of one persona throughout a single day, represent a user journey over the period of a specific ad campaign or visualize the long-term use of a complex service system.

Like many of the methods featured in the Discover and Define chapters, user journeys can be used both as an analytical tool to describe current-state scenarios and as a planning tool for future-state scenarios.

MOMENTS OF TRUTH

A brand touchpoint creates a 'moment of truth' that determines whether the brand will leave a positive, a negative or no impression at all on the customer. These situations and the user experience of them are not always predictable. The company cannot control whether a customer will rate a competitor's product higher on his or her blog. It can, however, react to these situations in a positive or negative way. At times like these, not only is the true quality of a product and a brand's corporate communications strategy revealed, but also its credibility and supremacy. Those who learn to accept criticism and deal with it actively have no need to be afraid of the truth. Although moments of truth at non-interactive touchpoints are hard to perceive, with interactive media there is often direct feedback in the form of blog posts, tweets or Facebook comments to which you can respond directly.

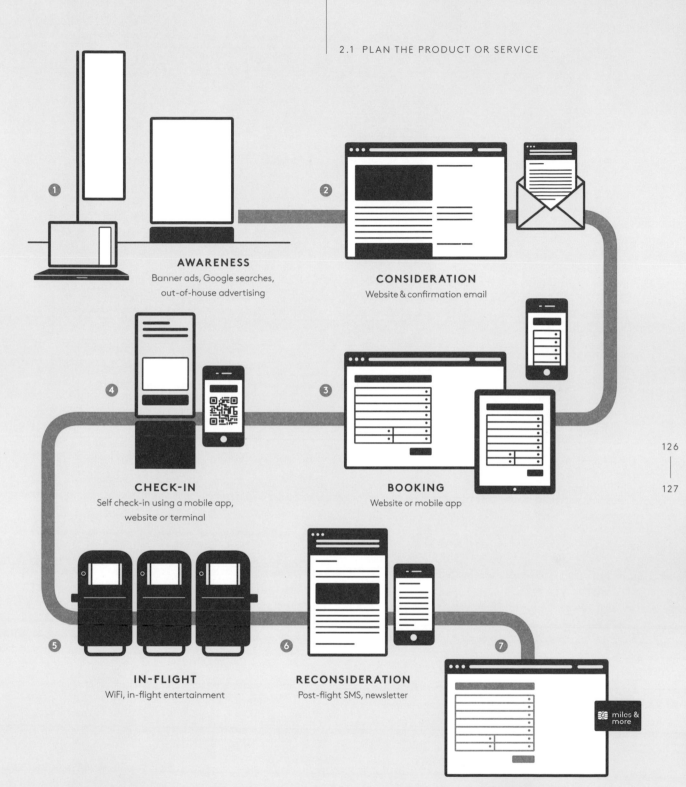

①

AWARENESS
Banner ads, Google searches,
out-of-house advertising

②

CONSIDERATION
Website & confirmation email

④

CHECK-IN
Self check-in using a mobile app,
website or terminal

③

BOOKING
Website or mobile app

⑤

IN-FLIGHT
WiFi, in-flight entertainment

⑥

RECONSIDERATION
Post-flight SMS, newsletter

⑦

RE-BOOKING
Customized area of website

miles & more

USER JOURNEY

This user journey shows the typical customer life cycle
of an airline, with all its digital brand touchpoints.

2.2

PLAN THE BRAND EXPERIENCE

Experience, intuition and an affinity for the product or the industry can all help in understanding a brand better (INTERVIEW, P. 214). Designers therefore need to be familiar with some branding basics. We need to know the background of a brand and be aware of its values, mission and positioning in the market. Defining brand filters allows us to check if we are on brand throughout the project, and helps us to present the design to the client in a convincing way.

BRAND POSITIONING

Brand positioning is a corporate strategy tool that we use to shape the unique identity of a brand. Most branding and strategy agencies have their own models for doing this, which will not be discussed here. In the BIxD process, however, it is crucial that we investigate, understand and evaluate all the elements of a corporate identity. In the Discover phase we should have already looked at the brand values, the brand vision and the brand benefits. These foundations, which nearly every company has defined for itself, nevertheless say little about how a brand behaves, what it looks like, what it says about itself and what it promises the customer – in short, they say little about what the brand means to its target group.

The Brand BIOS™ model presented below covers the four areas that make up the meaning of a brand, and which therefore have a direct effect on the design and creation of branded interactions. The four components cover the emotional (behaviour and image) and rational (offering and story) aspects of a brand. All four elements must positively influence the brand meaning in order to build a stable brand core. To ensure that these elements are relevant, we define brand filters, which not only can be used in brand communications but also serve as touchstones during product development (P. 137). These should be used alongside design thinking and lean management, to ensure and evaluate the continuous improvement of products (LEAN UX AND BIxD, P. 319).

1 BRAND BEHAVIOUR
Behaviour, values, attributes

Brand behaviour describes the behaviour of the brand both internally, towards its employees, and externally, when interacting with its customers. We describe a brand's behaviour using behavioural attributes based on the company's brand values. Ideally, we should have already analysed the brand personality in the Discover phase, viewing the brand as a person with traits that make it credible and authentic. Market research insights that describe the way a brand is perceived by its customers and non-customers are also invaluable here. The goal: awareness.

2 BRAND IMAGE
Corporate design and iconography

The brand image refers to the symbolic aspects of the brand, its iconography. The positioning of a brand ultimately relies on it being noticeable and recognizable. This includes visual representation in the form of a logo and corporate design as well as the architecture and even sound of the brand. We must know a brand's existing iconography if we wish to design branded interactions. An interactive designer should always have the brand handbook or style guide on hand. When working on brand development or repositioning, we initially visualize the brand using mood boards. The goal: uniqueness.

3 BRAND STORY
Myths and messages

The brand story tells the origin myth of a brand. Narratives are deeply rooted in human culture and help us to classify and remember things. Therefore, the message and competence of a brand are best conveyed through stories. These include founding myths and visions of the future, as well as stories about the brand's origin. The concept of Starbucks as the 'third place' – in addition to work and home – is true in the literal sense. The tale of how Adolf Dassler, the founder of adidas, personally screwed the studs into the boots of the victorious German World Cup team in 1954 continues to substantiate the brand's authenticity. The story often provides good ideas for the brand tagline (DESIGN, P. 173). The goal: credibility.

128
129

SET-UP / PROCESS ——— DISCOVER / **DEFINE** / DESIGN / DELIVER / DISTRIBUTE

4   BRAND OFFERING

The brand's promises

The brand offering refers to the quality, service or product of a brand – and thus the actual benefit to customers, and the thing that proves the reason why people should interact with our app. Unlike a pure advertising message, the brand promise can and should be immediately provable at the digital touchpoint and not merely stated. The more the brand offering is digitally tailored to the consumer, the sooner we achieve joy of use (P. 140). It is therefore important for the designer to know precisely what the brand offering is and to integrate it from a user perspective. The goal: relevance.

RESULT: BRAND MEANING

What the brand means to people

Today's brands need to do more than send out mass messages if they want to reach people and stay with them. Brands need a meaning, a unique, tangible, relevant and credible core, with which people feel connected. The meaning of a brand is tangible in the brand behaviour, visible in the brand image, told in the brand story and available in the brand offering.

THE BRAND

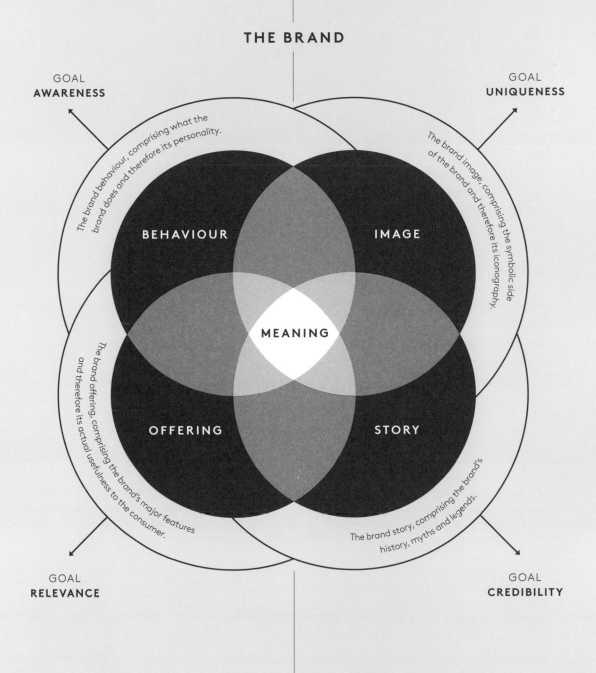

GOAL
AWARENESS

GOAL
UNIQUENESS

The brand behaviour, comprising what the brand does and therefore its personality.

The brand image, comprising the symbolic side of the brand and therefore its iconography.

BEHAVIOUR

IMAGE

MEANING

The brand offering, comprising the brand's major features and therefore its actual usefulness to the consumer.

The brand story, comprising the brand's history, myths and legends.

OFFERING

STORY

GOAL
RELEVANCE

GOAL
CREDIBILITY

THE BRAND BIOS™ MODEL

The brand model used by think moto shows the four elements that make up the brand meaning. In the Define phase, these issues should be defined for use in interactive communication.

BRAND POSITIONING WITHIN THE MARKET

When positioning a brand, product or service in the market, we define a target position within a previously determined space. A brand positioning graph (see opposite) can be compiled to show the brand in comparison with the positioning of its competitors. The trick of this technique is to find two or more evaluation criteria that define the brand and its unique features in the eyes of consumers, which can be used as the axes of the graph. These axes should be selected based on consumer insights obtained from qualitative and quantitative market research (DISCOVER, P. 51).

Products and companies with unique selling propositions (USPs) or compelling 'reasons to believe' stand slightly apart from their competitors. As designers, we need to know why a brand is popular and what the company's USP is – these can often be the source of a strong central theme.

BRAND POSITIONING BASED ON USER LIFESTYLES

Some agencies and consultants position brands using consumer typologies. These are based on the lifestyle categories used by institutions such as Sinus and SIGMA in their descriptions of social groups or milieus (P. 74). The categories are regularly reviewed and reflect changing social values. Positioning models based on user lifestyles use a values axis (from 'traditional' to 'progressive') and an axis that reflects social status (from 'working class' to 'upper class') or cultural orientation (from 'mass market' to 'elite').

Under some circumstances, however, this model can be restrictive; it excludes socially marginalized groups and says very little about certain behavioural typologies regarding the purchase or use of products. Nevertheless, it is a helpful marker because it is easy to understand and apply to products, product aesthetics, visual branding, terminology and other issues of taste, which can vary according to social status. It is therefore reasonable to compare competitors in terms of their visual communication. Brand names, taglines, colours and tones of voice can all be categorized according to user lifestyle and compared with each other.

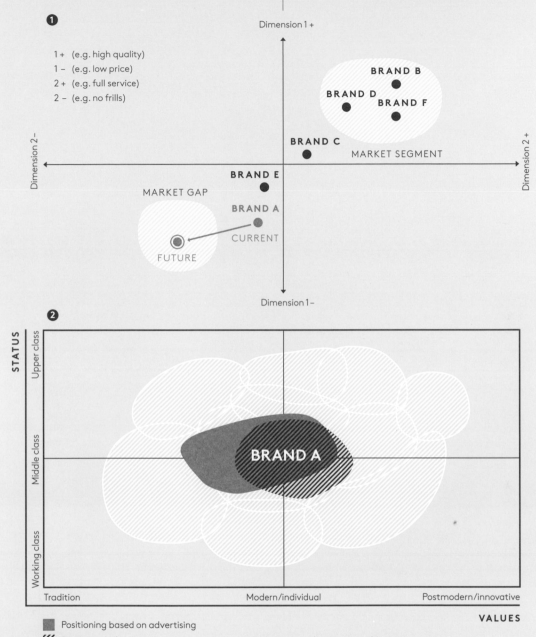

❶

1 + (e.g. high quality)
1 – (e.g. low price)
2 + (e.g. full service)
2 – (e.g. no frills)

Dimension 1 +

Dimension 2 –

Dimension 2 +

BRAND B

BRAND D   BRAND F

BRAND C   MARKET SEGMENT

BRAND E

MARKET GAP

BRAND A

CURRENT

FUTURE

Dimension 1 –

❷

STATUS

Upper class

Middle class

Working class

BRAND A

Tradition   Modern/individual   Postmodern/innovative

VALUES

▨ Positioning based on advertising

▨ Positioning of customers based on consumer analysis = most buyers are in this group

1 BRAND POSITIONING GRAPH

A brand positioning graph distinguishes brands from one other and can be used to visualize a strategic repositioning. The brand positioning graph can be used for analysing a current state and for describing a target future state. The desired shift in positioning is shown with a vector arrow.

2 BRAND POSITIONING BASED ON LIFESTYLES

Positioning based on user lifestyles clearly shows whether the brand positioning matches a real-life consumer lifestyle. This kind of positioning is based on social milieus or lifestyle models.

SET-UP / PROCESS —— DISCOVER / **DEFINE** / DESIGN / DELIVER / DISTRIBUTE

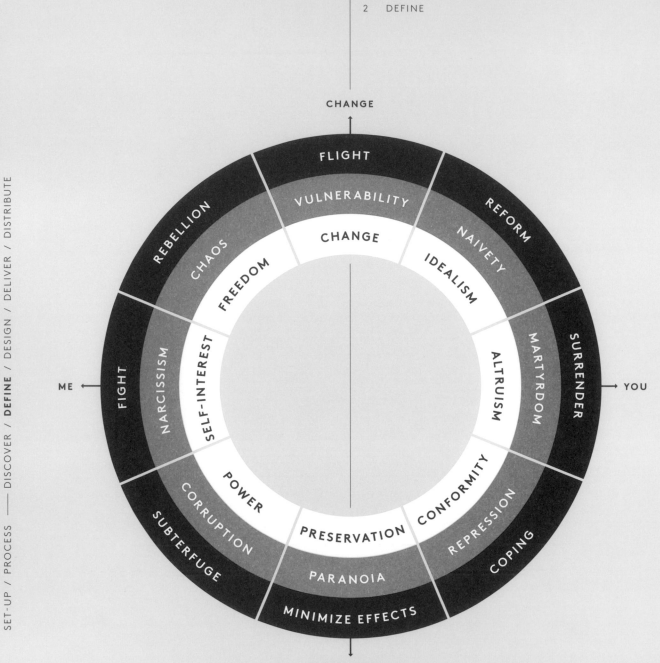

CHANGE

FLIGHT

VULNERABILITY

CHANGE

REBELLION

REFORM

CHAOS

NAIVETY

FREEDOM

IDEALISM

NARCISSISM

MARTYRDOM

SELF-INTEREST

ALTRUISM

ME ←

FIGHT

SURRENDER

→ YOU

POWER

CONFORMITY

CORRUPTION

REPRESSION

SUBTERFUGE

PRESERVATION

COPING

PARANOIA

MINIMIZE EFFECTS

PRESERVATION

BEHAVIORAL ARCHETYPES™

Behavioral Archetypes™ are designed to be a lexicon of human behaviour. The inner ring shows an archetypal behaviour in its most basic form. The middle ring shows what happens when we exaggerate this behaviour. The outer ring shows negative behaviour archetypes: the behaviours we exhibit when things are beyond our control. Each segment includes up to 40 specific behavioural patterns. © Leo Burnett Worldwide.

USER LIFESTYLES VS. BEHAVIOUR

Brand positioning based on user lifestyles is relatively straightforward (because it is empirical) and is easy for clients to understand. However, this is also its weakness. Since it is based solely on socio-economic factors, it is not detailed enough for positioning digital products and services. If we want to create not only a brand message but a memorable experience as well, we need to know more about potential users and their behaviour, which can vary greatly depending on context. Human behaviour is less dependent on socio-economic factors than on needs (intrinsic) and events (extrinsic). It does not matter if these needs or events are real or imaginary – behaviour is always an emotional response, and is influenced by personality traits, goals and values, self-image and the practical knowledge that is available in a particular situation.

BEHAVIORAL ARCHETYPES™

At Leo Burnett, brand strategists take a different approach to brand positioning (INTERVIEW, P. 152). Leo Burnett's HumanKind philosophy includes several tools for planning behaviour-based communications solutions. These include Behavioral Archetypes™, a lexicon of human behaviour based on two basic questions: 'How do we behave towards ourselves and towards others?' and 'What do we do in order to get or change things in life?' The model is based on eight behavioural archetypes, each of which can be divided into between thirty to forty distinct behaviours. Behavioral Archetypes™ are used at Leo Burnett to answer four strategic questions:

1 What are people doing now with regard to a brand?
2 Do we want to reinforce or change this behaviour?
3 If we wanted to change this behaviour, what would we change it to?
4 Can we change it through advertising, or does the brand need to change its own behaviour first?

These archetypes can be found in people's buying behaviour in some product categories. Leo Burnett developed a series of consumer journeys that clearly illustrate the different behaviours in different categories (P. 346).

SET-UP / PROCESS —— DISCOVER / **DEFINE** / DESIGN / DELIVER / DISTRIBUTE

BRAND FILTER AND REASONING

BEHAVIOUR ATTRIBUTES		
HUMAN	**SIMPLE**	**CUSTOMER-FOCUSED**
LOOK & FEEL, TONE OF VOICE — **INSPIRATIONAL** Fresh, urban, appealing to the target group	**STRIKING** Easily recognized visual elements and message	**INVITING** Show proximity and accessibility, integrate social media
INFORMATION ARCHITECTURE — **USER-FOCUSED** Rather than product or company-centred	**MODULAR** Modular page layout with clear zoning of content	**SIMPLE** Use contemporary interaction techniques, e.g. swiping
USER-FRIENDLINESS & NAVIGATION — **JOY OF USE** Create navigational flow, an element of style	**REDUCED TO THE ESSENTIALS** Short pathways, clear call-to-action	**GOAL-ORIENTED** In the style of street signage
USE & INTERACTION — **PLAYFUL** Playful elegance, not pure playfulness	**PRECISE** High-performance, fluid and clear with animations	**MEDIA-ORIENTED** What is playful yet precise on an iPad is not necessarily so on a PC

BRAND FILTERS

Brand filters are used to confirm that brand values are reflected in the digital brand experience. They ensure that brand positioning is maintained in all areas of an ongoing project (interaction, visual design, navigation, etc.). Courtesy of Simyo.

BRAND FILTERS AS GUIDELINES FOR INTERACTIVE DESIGN

Positioning according to user lifestyles and Behavioral Archetypes™ can help you to get a feel for how branded interactions look and behave and which functions they should offer. To prevent these starting points from getting lost in the design process, we need to set guidelines that we can use later for reference. These guidelines and touchstones are called brand filters.

Brand filters are criteria based on specific aspects of UX and visual design, derived from the behavioural attributes that we created for the Brand BIOS™ (BRAND POSITIONING, P. 128). These attributes are used to filter all ideas relating to the brand and user experience – everything that does not fit is discarded. In addition to working with personas, I believe that brand filters are the best way to keep a project on brand, while being able to provide the client with a valid basis for argument. Those who regularly use brand filters will, in many cases, be able to avoid time-consuming discussions with the client over matters of taste.

VISUAL BRANDING AND MOOD BOARDS

Using brand filters as a basis, we can move on to visual branding. The visual brand language is the design vocabulary for the project, and the brand filter is used to decide whether each element is the right fit. It would be wrong to leave visual branding choices to a focus group – even if marketing managers sometimes suggest this in order to safeguard themselves against decisions by the board. Good design is not a matter of taste and can't be democratically decided. A focus group will never take into account the many demands of the brand, user and business perspective that are relevant to a design decision.

Early suggestions for visual branding are outlined as mood boards. A mood board is a collage of images, screenshots, colours, typography, shapes, initial layout ideas, illustrations and patterns. Mood boards can be analogue or digital creations, but it always makes sense to keep them handy for reference during later phases. They are discussion points for the design direction stage (DESIGN DIRECTION & DETAILED DESIGN, P. 176) and they set the tone for later design work. Audio samples and video clips can also be used to capture the brand's tone of voice and to make sure the design team and client are thinking in the same direction.

SET-UP / PROCESS ———— DISCOVER / **DEFINE** / DESIGN / DELIVER / DISTRIBUTE

PLAN THE USER EXPERIENCE

'To be really successful on a long-term basis, customer experience needs to be seen as ... the sum-totality of how customers engage with your company and brand, not just in a snapshot in time, but throughout the entire arc of being a customer.'

ADAM RICHARDSON, *Understanding the Customer Experience*

Brand filters give us a tool to ensure brand fit throughout the design process. They should therefore be used when developing an overarching user experience concept. UX planning during the Define phase is an important step for any digital product. We take the user scenarios from the Discover phase and make them more concrete by giving our personas realistic tasks and imagining how they will deal with these in the future (USER JOURNEYS, P. 126). Using these future-state scenarios, we can develop an access concept for a website or service system or define behavioural patterns for a digital app in a way that will bypass potential pain points from the outset. In addition,

CONCEPTUAL MODEL

The conceptual model is based on the brand and lays down the basic concept for the whole digital project.

CORE CONCEPT
METAPHOR

CONCEPTUAL
MODEL

BRAND FILTER
ATTRIBUTE

USER BEHAVIOUR
USER STORY

we should now know enough to structure the content to fit the needs of users, develop a navigation system and create a draft sitemap. We should also prioritize and discuss content and functionality with the client, in order to divide the project into multiple stages of implementation if required (e.g. if time and money are limited).

CONCEPTUAL MODELS

The conceptual model is an extension of the core concept to form a functional and feasible metaphor or a procedural approach, which in the case of branded interactions must be based on the brand. The model itself is not as easy to express in a phrase or a sentence as the core concept, but represents the fundamental idea behind the app or site. The conceptual model can be viewed as a structured form of brainstorming or as a precursor to sitemaps and process flows (DESIGN, P. 173). It can be represented in the form of a map or told as a story.

VISUALIZING CONCEPTUAL MODELS

The conceptual model can be visualized in the form of a concept map. Concept maps are a preliminary version of sitemaps and create a provisional hierarchy of content based on the pre-existing features of a website or app. Concept maps include both content and features that affect the behaviour of an app, but unlike a mind map, they are not randomly ordered but clustered and visualized in a way that shows key ideas, overlaps and potential navigation paths.

THE JOY OF USE PYRAMID ———

Concept maps provide a basic set of categories that can be used to organize an app's content and functionality. In a way, the concept of 'joy of use' is a similar organizational model. The brand experience pyramid (opposite below) is based on the assumption that users link the experience they have when interacting with a website with the brand itself. In the simplest terms, the brand experience *is* the user experience. Brand values and principles must therefore be reflected in all aspects of the user experience. The objective is the optimal emotional consumer response to the brand.

Brands accomplish this goal through multiple steps that are based on the famous 'hierarchy of needs' formulated by the social psychologist Abraham Maslow. First of all, an app should serve a basic need, i.e. offer a specific function that allows a user to perform a particular task online. In a second stage, a brand should communicate these benefits in a way that draws attention to itself. The third and fourth stages of the joy of use pyramid customize the content and functions of an interactive offer, emotionalizing it so that a personal bond is formed with the brand and transforming occasional users into loyal users. In general, it is necessary to develop a consistent user experience across all phases of the customer life cycle so that all touchpoints align with each other.

MASLOW'S HIERARCHY OF NEEDS

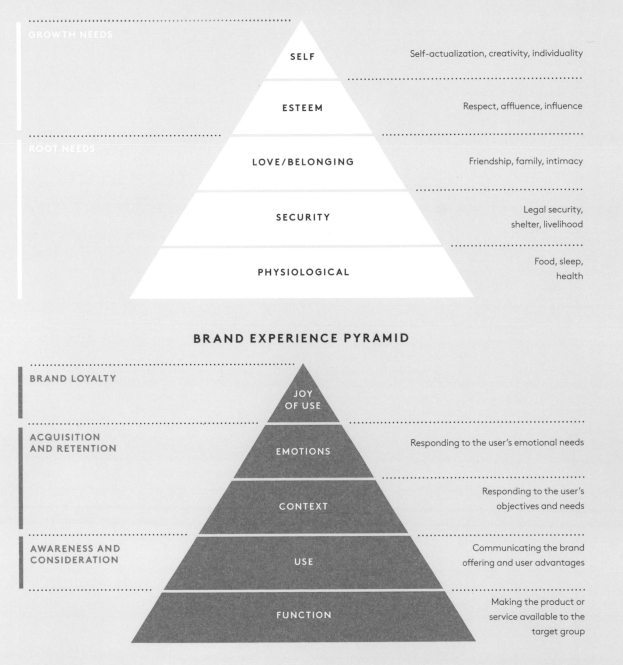

GROWTH NEEDS

ROOT NEEDS

SELF — Self-actualization, creativity, individuality

ESTEEM — Respect, affluence, influence

LOVE/BELONGING — Friendship, family, intimacy

SECURITY — Legal security, shelter, livelihood

PHYSIOLOGICAL — Food, sleep, health

BRAND EXPERIENCE PYRAMID

BRAND LOYALTY

ACQUISITION AND RETENTION

AWARENESS AND CONSIDERATION

JOY OF USE

EMOTIONS — Responding to the user's emotional needs

CONTEXT — Responding to the user's objectives and needs

USE — Communicating the brand offering and user advantages

FUNCTION — Making the product or service available to the target group

BRAND EXPERIENCE PYRAMID (JOY OF USE)

Maslow's traditional hierarchy of needs (top) has been adapted for use with branded interactions to create this brand experience pyramid. The labels on the left show the relevant stage of the consumer life cycle. The more the consumer is drawn in and accommodated emotionally, the faster we attain joy of use and therefore brand loyalty.

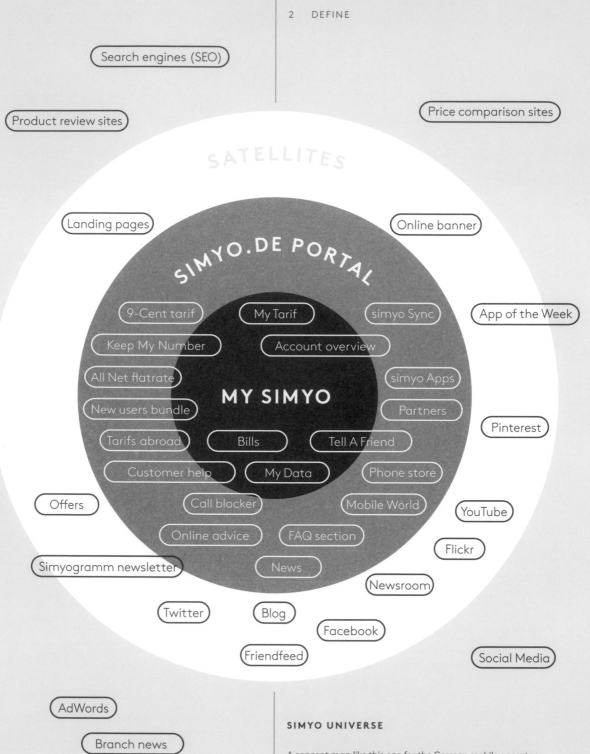

Search engines (SEO)

Product review sites

Price comparison sites

SATELLITES

Landing pages

Online banner

SIMYO.DE PORTAL

9-Cent tarif   My Tarif   simyo Sync   App of the Week

Keep My Number   Account overview

All Net flatrate   simyo Apps

New users bundle   Partners

Tarifs abroad   Bills   Tell A Friend   Pinterest

MY SIMYO

Customer help   My Data   Phone store

Offers   Call blocker   Mobile World   YouTube

Online advice   FAQ section   Flickr

Simyogramm newsletter   News   Newsroom

Twitter   Blog   Facebook

Friendfeed   Social Media

AdWords

Branch news

SIMYO UNIVERSE

A concept map like this one for the German mobile operator Simyo shows an overview of the brand's various online presences and apps. The inner circle shows pages and apps accessible from the customized area of the website. The intermediate circle shows the public content of simyo.de. The outer circle shows satellites: touchpoints that are controlled by the brand but lie outside the central website. Reproduced with the kind permission of Simyo.

NAVIGATION PATHS

In website or mobile service design, the navigation path describes how different user groups can access the site's content. First the target group segments are divided into user types. Content and functional requirements (user tasks) are taken into account, but so are the user's expertise, experience and knowledge of the product and its technical features. The navigation path includes:

- all target group hits on the company homepage, whether through visual or textual signals that address the users or via a direct detection of the users (cookies or login)
- hits on subsites for specific products, submarkets or target groups (so-called verticals)
- hits via landing pages and microsites for specific products and services
- click-throughs from other services or sites

If the brand or product architecture is complex, the navigation path may also be complex. A good example are international companies that are active in various markets in different areas of business, under a master or monolithic brand name. The Linde Group, for example, targets different audiences (physicians, engineers, craftspeople) in different fields (healthcare, industrial gases, plant construction) in different markets (Australia, Botswana and Brazil).

In addition to these, the parent corporation has its own target groups, including the press, competitors and investors. This complex situation means a web landscape that includes more than 160 web presences. Linde's navigation path solves the problem by first separating the target groups of the parent company from the individual markets (P. 336). On the market level, customers and potential customers can quickly find the right website via a map and a teaser.

SITEMAPS AND CONTENT MAPS

With all the organizational principles discussed above, it is important to use the brand filter to establish whether the principle reflects the brand and its underlying values. A range of basic organizational principles are possible, for example:

- **EXPLORATIVE**: The user must actively discover the content within a relatively free structure.
- **ADAPTIVE**: The structure adapts to use.
- **HIERARCHICAL**: A classic tree structure; the wording is important here.
- **MATRIX**: The content can always be reached through two access points.
- **SEQUENTIAL**: A linear sequence of content is particularly useful in narrative forms.

We visualize the complete structure of a website or software app using a sitemap, which is a handy tool for page-based apps because they can do more than simply reflect the structure. They can also:

- reflect a hierarchy of content
- include navigation and menu items
- indicate how many templates/page types are needed and which types (as a list)
- visualize closed areas of content (which aspects can be customized, which areas are available only after login, etc.)
- define where sites are physically located and how they are linked

- reflect further expansions, such as in the case of a rollout in various markets

Sitemaps can also reflect the status of the project or be used for estimating costs, since they should clearly show which pages will be created as wireframes and/or layouts.

Jesse James Garrett's Visual Vocabulary is very useful when compiling a sitemap.
→ bit.ly/RNt0ra

USER TASK FLOWS ————

Although not intended for this, sitemaps may include some chronological sequences. In order to model an entire process from start to finish, however, another tool is needed. For this, information architects use task flow diagrams of the kind used in software modelling. Process flow diagrams can be used when complex processes with several decision steps need to be modelled. User task flows visualize the interaction steps required by a user to execute a previously defined use case (PERSONAS, P. 79).

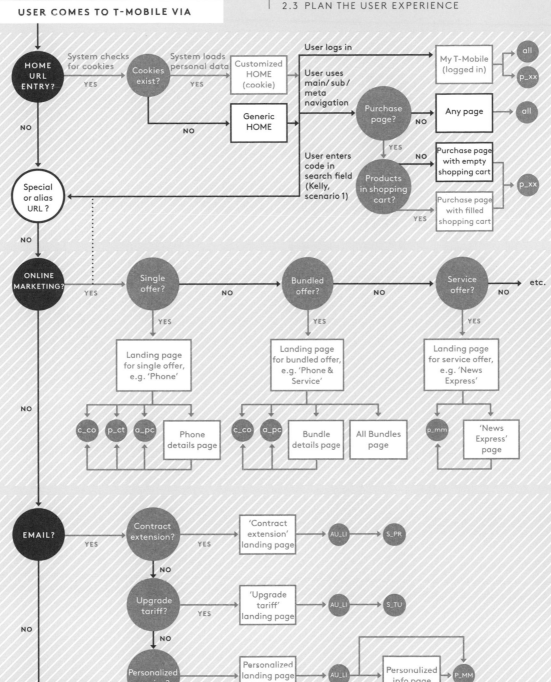

USER COMES TO T-MOBILE VIA

URL ENTRY

HOME URL ENTRY? → System checks for cookies / YES → Cookies exist? → System loads personal data / YES → Customized HOME (cookie) → User logs in → My T-Mobile (logged in) → all / p_xx

Cookies exist? NO → Generic HOME

Customized HOME (cookie) / Generic HOME → User uses main / sub / meta navigation → Purchase page? → NO → Any page → all

Purchase page? YES → Products in shopping cart? → NO → Purchase page with empty shopping cart

Products in shopping cart? YES → Purchase page with filled shopping cart → p_xx

User enters code in search field (Kelly, scenario 1)

HOME URL ENTRY? NO → Special or alias URL?

Special or alias URL? NO

ONLINE MARKETING

ONLINE MARKETING? → YES → Single offer? → NO → Bundled offer? → NO → Service offer? → NO → etc.

Single offer? YES → Landing page for single offer, e.g. 'Phone' → c_co / p_ct / a_pc / Phone details page

Bundled offer? YES → Landing page for bundled offer, e.g. 'Phone & Service' → c_co / a_pc / Bundle details page / All Bundles page

Service offer? YES → Landing page for service offer, e.g. 'News Express' → p_mm / 'News Express' page

ONLINE MARKETING? NO

EMAIL MARKETING

EMAIL? → YES → Contract extension? → YES → 'Contract extension' landing page → AU_LI → S_PR

Contract extension? NO → Upgrade tariff? → YES → 'Upgrade tariff' landing page → AU_LI → S_TU

Upgrade tariff? NO → Personalized service? → YES → Personalized landing page 'MM Special' → AU_LI → Personalized info page → P_MM

optional depending on service offered

EMAIL? NO

GOOGLE

SEARCH RESULT? → YES → Detail page

144
—
145

TASK FLOW

Task flow diagrams such as this example from T-Mobile represent the central processes of a website as a sequence of user and system interactions.

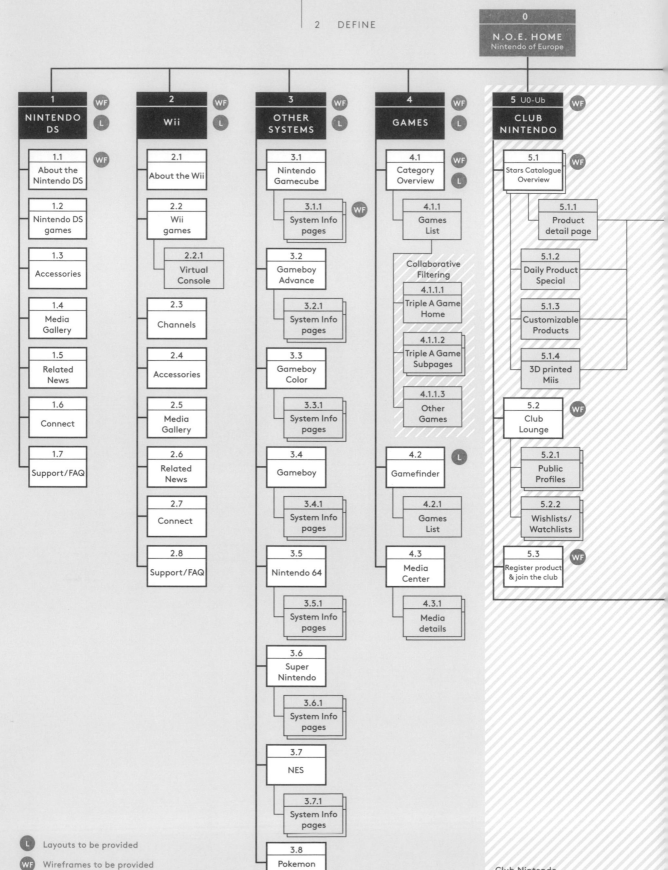

SET-UP / PROCESS —— DISCOVER / **DEFINE** / DESIGN / DELIVER / DISTRIBUTE

0
N.O.E. HOME
Nintendo of Europe

1 WF L
NINTENDO DS

1.1 WF
About the Nintendo DS

1.2
Nintendo DS games

1.3
Accessories

1.4
Media Gallery

1.5
Related News

1.6
Connect

1.7
Support/FAQ

2 WF L
Wii

2.1
About the Wii

2.2
Wii games

2.2.1
Virtual Console

2.3
Channels

2.4
Accessories

2.5
Media Gallery

2.6
Related News

2.7
Connect

2.8
Support/FAQ

3 WF L
OTHER SYSTEMS

3.1
Nintendo Gamecube

3.1.1 WF
System Info pages

3.2
Gameboy Advance

3.2.1
System Info pages

3.3
Gameboy Color

3.3.1
System Info pages

3.4
Gameboy

3.4.1
System Info pages

3.5
Nintendo 64

3.5.1
System Info pages

3.6
Super Nintendo

3.6.1
System Info pages

3.7
NES

3.7.1
System Info pages

3.8
Pokemon Mini

4 WF L
GAMES

4.1 WF L
Category Overview

4.1.1
Games List

Collaborative Filtering
4.1.1.1
Triple A Game Home

4.1.1.2
Triple A Game Subpages

4.1.1.3
Other Games

4.2 L
Gamefinder

4.2.1
Games List

4.3
Media Center

4.3.1
Media details

5 U0-Ub WF
CLUB NINTENDO

5.1 WF
Stars Catalogue Overview

5.1.1
Product detail page

5.1.2
Daily Product Special

5.1.3
Customizable Products

5.1.4
3D printed Miis

5.2 WF
Club Lounge

5.2.1
Public Profiles

5.2.2
Wishlists/ Watchlists

5.3 WF
Register product & join the club

Club Nintendo
(not available in B-markets)

L   Layouts to be provided

WF Wireframes to be provided

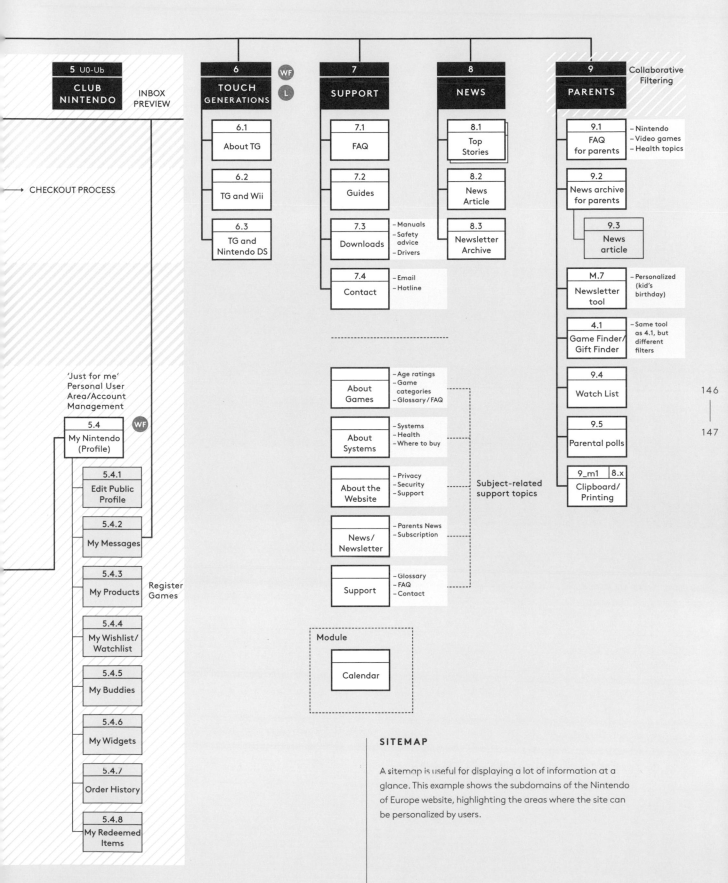

5 U0–Ub
CLUB NINTENDO

INBOX PREVIEW

→ CHECKOUT PROCESS

'Just for me'
Personal User
Area/Account
Management

5.4 WF
My Nintendo
(Profile)

5.4.1
Edit Public Profile

5.4.2
My Messages

5.4.3
My Products

Register Games

5.4.4
My Wishlist/ Watchlist

5.4.5
My Buddies

5.4.6
My Widgets

5.4.7
Order History

5.4.8
My Redeemed Items

---

6 WF L
TOUCH GENERATIONS

6.1
About TG

6.2
TG and Wii

6.3
TG and Nintendo DS

7
SUPPORT

7.1
FAQ

7.2
Guides

7.3
Downloads
– Manuals
– Safety advice
– Drivers

7.4
Contact
– Email
– Hotline

About Games
– Age ratings
– Game categories
– Glossary / FAQ

About Systems
– Systems
– Health
– Where to buy

About the Website
– Privacy
– Security
– Support

News/ Newsletter
– Parents News
– Subscription

Support
– Glossary
– FAQ
– Contact

Subject-related support topics

Module

Calendar

8
NEWS

8.1
Top Stories

8.2
News Article

8.3
Newsletter Archive

---

9 Collaborative Filtering
PARENTS

9.1
FAQ for parents
– Nintendo
– Video games
– Health topics

9.2
News archive for parents

9.3
News article

M.7
Newsletter tool
– Personalized (kid's birthday)

4.1
Game Finder/ Gift Finder
– Same tool as 4.1, but different filters

9.4
Watch List

9.5
Parental polls

9_m1 | **8.x**
Clipboard/ Printing

146
—
147

SITEMAP

A sitemap is useful for displaying a lot of information at a glance. This example shows the subdomains of the Nintendo of Europe website, highlighting the areas where the site can be personalized by users.

SET-UP / PROCESS ——— DISCOVER / **DEFINE** / DESIGN / DELIVER / DISTRIBUTE

DEFINE
THE METRICS

'The designer does not need a pile of information to do thorough work, but relevant information used in the decision making and implementation processes.'
GUI BONSIEPE

THE METRICS CATALOGUE

After the kick-off workshop (P. 56), the analysis and planning results are compiled into a metrics catalogue. The metrics are evaluated and prioritized according to their cost and their relevance to the business, the brand and the user. To come up with a relatively objective initial evaluation, I use a fairly simple formula. Business benefit, brand benefit and user benefit each receive a priority rating between 1 and 3 (1 = essential, 2 = important, 3 = optional). A rating is also given for cost, which is doubled. The cost element is not always easy to predict, especially with actions you have not previously performed. Therefore, in the cost assessment, I always factor in feasibility and experience. The sum of the individual ratings is then divided by five. The result determines the final priority ranking, which is then discussed with the client.

In addition to the ratings and ranking, the metrics catalogue includes:

- **DESCRIPTION** of the metric
- **TARGET** – what the metric is intended to measure
- **TARGET GROUP** – or in the case of multiple target groups, the primary target group
- **POSSIBLE COSTS** – if these can already be estimated; effort, complexity
- **TIMING** – when should the measurement be done?
- **RESPONSIBILITY** – who should obtain the measurement? (The client may specify who is responsible in-house.)
- **SUCCESS CRITERIA** – how will you verify if goals have been achieved?
- **SUGGESTED SOLUTIONS** for potential implementation
- **LINKS** to examples

The metrics catalogue can be structured to match the phases of the customer life cycle (P. 120) or represented as a timeline in order to create a roadmap for communication. The individual task groups should be recorded using a project management tool, which also highlights any tasks that are mutually dependent.

MEASURING SUCCESS

To check whether metrics have been achieved or not, we define key performance indicators (KPI). This information should be presented in a way that is concrete and factual, for example:

- We have 10% more community members than last year.
- We reduced calls to the telephone hotline by 30%.
- We are among the top three Google hits for the keyword 'xyz'.

Sometimes agencies receive performance-related pay. There is nothing wrong with this in principle. On the contrary: when suitable tracking and testing mechanisms are provided, it is instructive to see for yourself what works and what does not. However, the performance metrics should be clearly defined in advance, because only then can you judge whether the goal is achievable and whether you wish to be measured against it. In any case, before every project, you should ask yourself at what point the project can be deemed successful.

METRICS CATALOGUE

PROJECT / METRIC	DESCRIPTION	GOAL	TARGET MARKETS	PRIMARY TARGET GROUP	EFFORT	COSTS
CUSTOMER LIFE CYCLE PHASE 1 — AWARENESS						
SEO Search engine optimization	→ In cooperation with individual countries, a list of relevant searches for all target markets should first be created. The site must then be optimized for the relevant search engines.	Top 3 in search engine rankings for predefined search terms.	All	A B C	1	One-off fee: around £XXX for all European markets
SEM Search engine marketing	→ Via sponsored links and keyword advertising, a permanent presence in Google and other search engines for relevant searches must be achieved.	Increased visibility and top ranking in AdWords and sponsored links for relevant search terms.	All	A B C	2	Fees: £XXX Media budget per quarter: £XXX
Online opinion mining and management	→ Online opinion mining should include monitoring of social media sites (forums and blogs). Close tracking allows for early intervention in discussions.	Recognize negative and positive input and actively manage these.	All	B C	2	Estimate: £XXX per month

BUSINESS BENEFIT	BRAND BENEFIT	USER BENEFIT	PERFORMANCE METRIC	PRIORITY	RECOMMENDATION	CLIENT NOTES	POSSIBLE SOLUTIONS
1	1	1	For x% of search terms, traffic increase of y%	1	Immediately seek cost-effective measures to increase referrals.		Optimize metatags, sitemap, images… Define list of search terms…
2	1	2	For x% of search terms, traffic increase of y%	1.8	Immediately seek new SEO package. A monthly media budget should be ringfenced.		Research available offers…
1	2	2	Hard to measure. Avoidance of failures counts as success.		Implement by the end of the year.		

METRICS CATALOGUE SAMPLE

For each metric, the catalogue contains a description, a priority ranking, estimated cost and more. The priority ranking is calculated by giving a rating from 1 to 3 for business, brand and user benefit, plus a rating for cost (counted twice). These are added then divided by 5 to create an average, which serves as the basis for discussions with the client.

THE CREATIVE BRIEF

A few years ago, I believed that as a creative director, the brief was a crucial and necessary document– not only for marketing use but also for branded projects – and provided a link between strategy and design. Today I find its brevity and reduction of everything to a few key points rather problematic.

I now believe it is more important to develop a collective vision with the team (including developers) based on interdisciplinary research (which should ideally include the client). This is the only way to ensure that everyone knows what is going on over the course of the project. The strategist is then no longer in the role of policing the design team, but instead a curator on a joint journey of discovery (INTERVIEW, P. 152).

However, on advertising projects, or if the strategy has been completed before the project starts, a creative brief can be helpful. It is usually an internal document that gives the creative team a framework during the idea generation phase and allows them to check whether an idea is on strategy or not. It contains the project objectives and the main findings of the Discover and Define phases and the initial ideas that were collected during the first two project phases.

✓ A CREATIVE BRIEF IN 9 BASIC QUESTIONS

▸ What should we do?
  ⟶ TASK
▸ Why should we do this?
  ⟶ BACKGROUND AND MOTIVATION
▸ What are we trying to achieve?
  ⟶ GOAL
▸ Who are we speaking to?
  ⟶ TARGET GROUP
▸ What does the target group think of…?
  ⟶ CURRENT TARGET GROUP POSITIONING
▸ What should they think instead?
  ⟶ FUTURE POSITIONING
▸ How do we reach them?
  ⟶ TOUCHPOINTS
▸ What do we tell them?
  ⟶ CORE MESSAGE
▸ How do we achieve this?
  ⟶ CONCEPTUAL MODEL
▸ What should we start thinking about?
  ⟶ RAW IDEAS

HUMANKIND AND DIGITAL BRAND STRATEGY

ALEXANDER WIPF
LEO BURNETT

Alex, you are head of strategic planning at Leo Burnett Germany and lead a team of strategic planners from various disciplines: brand strategy, digital strategy and shopper marketing. Your personal background is in information architecture and design. Why is this a good starting point from which to tackle integrated brand strategy?

Even the most traditional agencies have long recognized that digital media have changed people's behaviour fundamentally and that the old advertising solutions no longer work. While many agencies did not want to admit to these changes, it was becoming clear that traditional agency services alone – using mass media to bombard people with the messages until they buy the product – would not be profitable in the future. Therefore, at Leo Burnett it made sense to have someone on board who had qualifications in both fields – brand strategy and user experience strategy – in order to create a team of strategists. This team not only practised brand management in the form of communication strategies ('What does the brand say?'), but also in the form of experience strategies ('What does the brand do, what experiences does it create?').

Our new business model is to help brands do something instead of just saying something.

What are the challenges for the agency?

First, the agency's area of expertise must logically expand and shift, even with regard to brand strategy. Brand strategy is now communications strategy and experience strategy. For example, we now need user experience strategists and shopper strategists working on strategy and experience designers and packaging designers working on design. It is not enough to say that 'offline' and 'online' disciplines should be integrated; we also need different tools. Instead of praising 'integrated communication' for the umpteenth time, we need to become experts in human behaviour. Second, if we want to help brands to 'do' something, rather than just 'saying' something, then we also need to make marketing a service *for* the people, and not just a tool for manipulating people. That's why we have stopped using military-style marketing terms: target, brief, positioning, territory, launch, campaign, leakage, impact. This may seem a rather esoteric thing to do, but when you look at the language we use to discuss the job and how hard it is to break away from it, you soon see that something has gone wrong somewhere. Even if agencies claim otherwise, when the consumers have the final say, marketing cannot be a war.

How can we bring our products to people if we think of them as 'targets' and 'bomb' them with our messages?

You said you want to create brands that will not only say something, but also do something. Can you explain your 'HumanKind' approach in more detail?

The HumanKind approach is our answer to today's brand challenges. Our goal is to provide a qualitative difference in the lives of people in small ways and perhaps also in larger ones. This can be something as simple as helping people save time and money or helping them at the right moment or giving them control over a complex situation; or just by entertaining them, giving them a new impetus to relax, or being committed to something that people believe in. If a brand does this credibly, it becomes popular and therefore commercially successful. To encapsulate this kind of popularity, we have redefined the 4Ps of marketing (product, price, placement, promotion) and are focusing on the new 4Ps: popularity = people + purpose + participation. In other words: qualitative difference in people's lives = insight into actual human behaviour + brand tasks instead of brand promises + experiences, not just messages.

And how do you approach the target group?

If we look at the product and marketing innovations that have occurred since the rise of the web, which also brought other significant changes, then the foundations for this were rarely traditional target group descriptions based on socio-demographics, motivations, opinions and attitudes. These descriptions are still useful, but they usually only provide us with the basis for communication ideas (e.g. the brand wants to tell me something and wants to change my perception). This is because human behaviour is much more complex and unconscious than questionnaires can capture. This is why the personal, social, structural and environmental forces driving human behaviour are so important. By using these, brands can create new interaction ideas based on a human context (USER JOURNEYS, P. 126). This is no longer true just for brands whose business model is obviously digitally based (like Google or Apple), but for all brands.

In the client's brief we can read what the brand wants, how it defines itself, what the business goals are, and how the target group perceives the brand and rates it on awareness, likeability, etc. But before we do this, we need to ask: how do people actually live today? What are their positive and negative experiences? What behaviours do they display? In other words: what can we observe without interpretation? After that come other questions. Which of these behaviours are relevant to the brand's business? Where do interesting tensions between people and their surroundings arise and where can the brand support people's behaviour or change it?

How do you find out how people behave, and where do you find a mechanism for creation and design?

We not only explore motivations and settings as in the past, but the actual behaviour of people in different contexts, at multiple touchpoints and in multiple product categories. For the purposes of idea generation, it's much more inspiring to observe people as they actually behave on a specific 'journey' within a product category (awareness, consideration, purchase, use, loyalty) across all relevant channels, instead of simply asking

people about their attitudes towards brands or just looking at a specific channel. In this situation, designers are extraordinary insight-generating tools, because they are accustomed to deriving their ideas intuitively or consciously from experiences. This means that in addition to classic market research, we use digital tools employed in information architecture and experience planning, such as personas and scenario designs, task analysis, customer journeys. These work just as well for brand strategy as for the design of digital channels.

A good example of this is the Fiat Punto Evo, in which the entire campaign is based on the behaviour of young people on the web: they prefer to look for information and experiences via social media and are reluctant to visit brand websites. Instead of asking the old mass media question: 'What do we have to say to people so that they go to our website and book a test drive?', we ensure that the brand takes relevant content to them, wherever they are. In this way, the brand deals with them on an equal footing on their digital home turf (Facebook, Wikipedia, Flickr, YouTube), rather than forcing them to do something they don't want to do. This social media strategy, based purely on behaviour, went on to become the communication strategy for all other media (outdoor, print, catalogue and trade advertising).

With behavioural strategies, it soon becomes clear what specific role each channel will play, rather than simply broadcasting a message across all media. So instead of changing people's behaviour

154

155

SET-UP / PROCESS ——— DISCOVER / **DEFINE** / DESIGN / DELIVER / DISTRIBUTE

('Go to our website!'), we change the brand's behaviour – and adapt it to people's behaviour.

What tools do you use?

By focusing on behaviour, we have created new tools and devices for design in order to understand the personal, social, structural and environmental driving forces of human behaviour at a more fundamental level. For example, we examined the behaviour and expectations of 5,600 people using over a hundred product categories in order to make assessments about the role brands can play for people with their communication and their experiences (RISK/REWARD™, P. 64). In other words, what are the opportunities and obstacles that brands face in fulfilling this role?

Brands and marketing often make the mistake of trying to be something that the behavioural dynamic will not allow.

This leads to mismatches and messages that aren't credible. Think of an insurance product (purchase type: Burden) that promotes the delusion that retirement is a simple and straightforward topic. It can also lead to questionable and empty brand experiences; for example, a detergent brand (purchase type: Routine) may decide it wants to be on Facebook – just because the target group

and competitors are there. Or an ice cream brand (purchase type: Entertainment) may decide to sponsor a fashion event, just to create interest. So the question is not only 'Who and where are my people?' but also 'What behavioural dynamics dominate this category and how can I give my brand a credible role?' That's why we created a lexicon of human behaviour that describes basic behaviour patterns and their underlying tensions. It helps us to become experts in human behaviour, rather than lumping people together under target group descriptions. In this way I can also define a direction for the brand, design and advertising, which will do this behaviour justice. Our kind of insights benefit not just classic TV campaigns, but also the design of websites, integrated campaigns, store and packaging designs and product innovations (P. 135).

Alexander Wipf is Head of Strategy at Leo Burnett Germany and a member of the Global Strategy Board of Leo Burnett Worldwide.

II

GOOD PRACTICE

——

Brand Design

TAGESSCHAU.DE / SWISSCOM /
TOYOTA IQ FONT / MIT MEDIA LAB / GOOGLE / NOKIA N9 /
THE CHALLENGES OF MOBILE INTERFACES

TAGESSCHAU.DE

Youth-oriented TV channels such as MTV were quick to embrace digital design trends in their on-screen branding. However, a greater testament to the prominence of digital channels is the fact that when German public broadcaster ARD overhauled its corporate design in 2011, a mobile app icon became the main logo for its daily news show *Tagesschau*, a sixty-year-old institution, along with its sister programmes *Tagesthemen* and *Nachtmagazin*. This reflects that *Tagesschau* is no longer purely a TV format, but available online and in app form for a range of devices, offering a wealth of extra content.

www.tagesschau.de

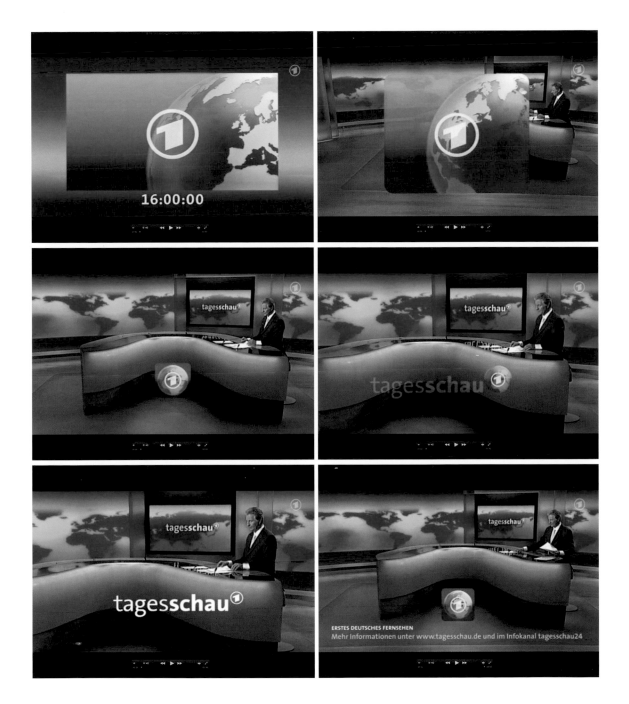

swisscom

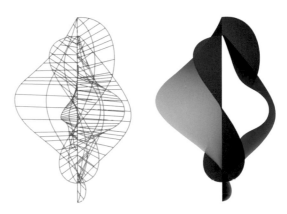

SWISSCOM
MOVING BRANDS

Swisscom is the market leader in the Swiss telecommunications sector. In 2008, a revised brand identity was created to reflect the company's expansion from telecoms and IT into media and entertainment. Central to this new corporate identity is Moving Brands' 'Life Form', a logo made up of both fixed and variable elements.

The Swiss people's traditional trust in Swisscom is represented by the logo's fixed longitudinal axis. The morphing outer layer, however, emphasizes the company's adaptability and progressiveness. The Life Form can be animated or viewed as a static element from different angles.

www.swisscom.ch

TOYOTA iQ FONT

HAPPINESS BRUSSELS

For the launch of the Toyota iQ, a compact city car with sleek design and advanced technology, Belgian agency Happiness – in collaboration with Pleaseletmedesign and the software developer Zach Liebermann – designed a typeface that represents the car's agility. The design process was unusual enough to be featured in the campaign. First, a sequence of movements was designed for the car to follow. Four coloured dots were added to the roof of the car, allowing each letterform to be tracked by a camera as the car moved. The making-of video was distributed through social media and linked to the Toyota website, where the font could be downloaded and a test drive booked.

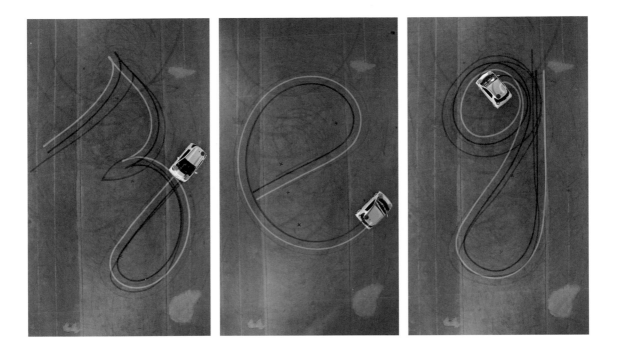

Hello I'm the iQ font

abcdefghijklmnopqrstuvwxyz

ABCDEFGHIJKLMNOPQRSTUVWXYZ

0123456789

. , : : ! ? + = @ & ( ) / - # " "

Lorem ipsum dolor sit amet, consectetur adipisicing elit, sed do eiusmod tempor incididunt ut labore et dolore magna aliqua. Ut enim ad minim veniam, quis nostrud exercitation ullamco laboris nisi ut aliquip ex ea commodo consequat. Duis aute irure dolor in reprehenderit in voluptate velit esse cillum dolore eu fugiat nulla pariatur. Excepteur sint occaecat cupidatat non proident, sunt in culpa qui officia deserunt mollit anim id est laborum.

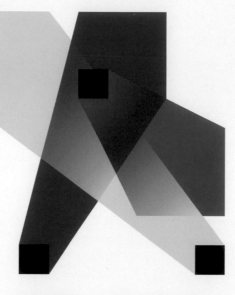

MIT MEDIA LAB

MIT MEDIA LAB

MIT MEDIA LAB

MIT MEDIA LAB

MIT MEDIA LAB

MIT MEDIA LAB

MIT MEDIA LAB

MIT MEDIA LAB

MIT MEDIA LAB

MIT MEDIA LAB

MIT MEDIA LAB

MIT MEDIA LAB

MIT MEDIA LAB
THE GREEN EYL

The focus of the visual identity of MIT's Media Lab is a generative logo consisting of three shapes that are connected in ever-new combinations by an algorithm. The underlying idea is that the three elements represent the individual skills and contributions of the researchers at the MIT Media Lab. The resulting logo variants form a continually redefined vision for the future. Each person and each department receives a unique personalized version of the logo that can be used on business cards or personal websites. The design kit also includes specially developed animation software, which generates motion graphic versions of the logo for use in the lab's video content.

GOOGLE

A stripped-down interface with a single search box and a catchy name and logo: this is branded interaction on a global scale. The word 'Googling' is now synonymous with online searching.

Opposite, below: Branded interaction on a smaller scale. The number of search results is visualized as the number of Os in the Google logo: a small but significant interface detail connects the brand with its benefit perfectly. The elongated logo then entered the real world on the wall of Google's Amsterdam office.

Opposite, above: Google Doodles bring joy of use to an everyday digital commodity. Variant Google logos for special events were introduced shortly after the founding of the tech company in 1998 and have become a major brand signature. The doodles add the 'human touch' and demonstrate familiarity, regional expertise and timeliness, core values of the company. Interactive doodles have been featured since 2010.

1 2 3 4 5 6 7 8 9 10   **Next**

From Grotesque to Humanist (see Peter Skillman interview, P. 326)

Nokia Sans.
Condensed forms.

Nokia Pure.
Seamless motion.

168
|
169

NOKIA N9

As a manufacturer of mobile devices, Nokia had longstanding difficulties keeping up with Apple and Windows software engineers when it came to operating systems. With Nokia N9 and the MeeGo operating system, it succeeded in making what chief designer Peter Skillman calls a leap from 'Grotesque' to 'Humanist' (P. 326). The product design of the Nokia N9 matches the visual language of the elegant MeeGo operating system and does not require any back or home buttons, thus optimizing the size of the touchscreen. Navigation is entirely swipe-controlled.

swipe.nokia.com

THE CHALLENGES OF MOBILE INTERFACES

Mobile devices pose new challenges for interactive designers. In contrast to websites, where users may enter a site on any page, app icons and loading screens must serve as homepages. The space for traditional branding is restricted – a logo on each side is neither useful nor necessary. Instead, brand recognition lies in the details. The page layout, the use of colour and small 'disruptive' elements, such as its Prime service, make a shopping page on Amazon unmistakable.

The Memo feature on the Amazon iPhone app (opposite, above) is another demonstration of how device-specific functions can be used. Users can photograph a product with their phone and Amazon will show its availability or suggest an alternative.

Another challenge arises when several brands must co-exist in a single app. On the left, we see a Nokia Lumia with Windows Phone 7 (as the icons at the bottom show), running an app by Burger King that makes use of Microsoft Bing mapping software.

3

DES IGN

CONCEPT AND VISUALS

172

—

173

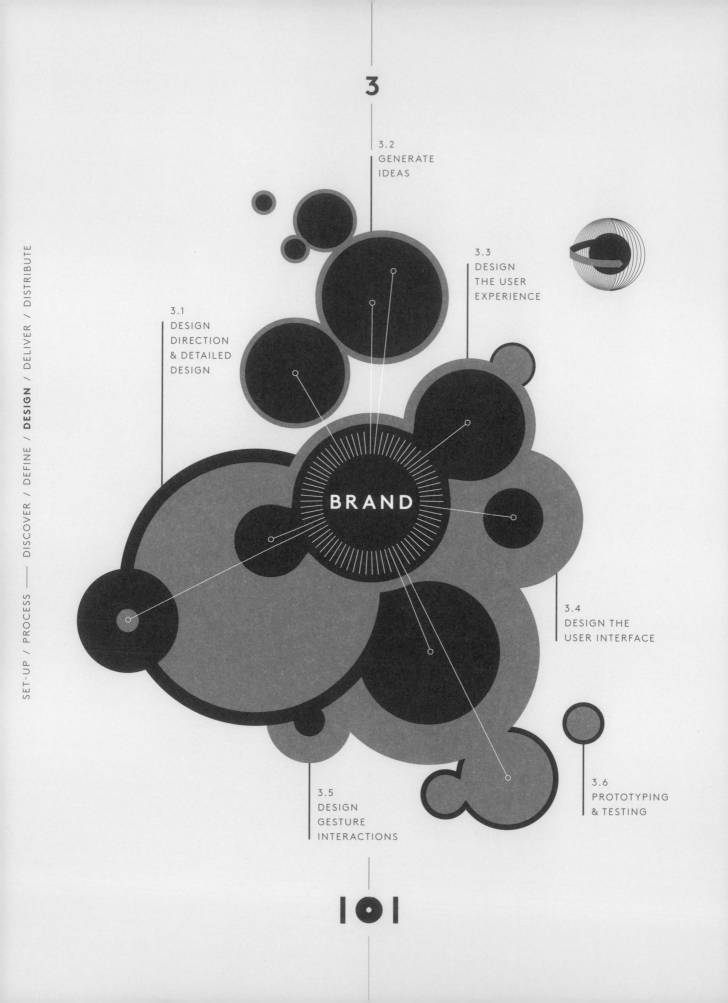

SET-UP / PROCESS —— DISCOVER / DEFINE / **DESIGN** / DELIVER / DISTRIBUTE

3.2
GENERATE
IDEAS

3.3
DESIGN
THE USER
EXPERIENCE

3.1
DESIGN
DIRECTION
& DETAILED
DESIGN

BRAND

3.4
DESIGN THE
USER INTERFACE

3.5
DESIGN
GESTURE
INTERACTIONS

3.6
PROTOTYPING
& TESTING

*Time to get serious.
The strategy has been approved
and the course has been plotted.
The Design phase is the moment
everyone has been waiting for.*

Looking at designs and trying out prototypes is
generally more interesting than reading strategy
documents, which is why a lot of clients grow
impatient before the Design phase begins. But if
you've done some solid groundwork in the first two
phases, you'll have a much better understanding of
what the final product should be like. This chapter
describes the methods used in the Design phase.
It starts with creative brainstorming techniques
before moving on to user experience design and
visual design, before discussing prototyping
and testing.

3.1

DESIGN DIRECTION & DETAILED DESIGN

'The detail is the design.'

CHARLES EAMES

In the Design phase, the creative and conceptual direction and informational architecture are defined based on the strategic guidelines and, when appropriate, the creative brief. The phase concludes with a comprehensive design and concept document that will serve as a template for production. The Design phase is divided into two stages. The first stage involves establishing the design direction, which is presented to the client for approval. The second stage is the development of the detailed design, which is fully documented.

THE DESIGN DIRECTION PRESENTATION (DDP)

The design direction stage concludes with the design direction presentation (DDP). The DDP takes the form of an extensive review, in which the client approves or rejects the design direction based on sample layouts and, if relevant, a prototype. In order to avoid any nasty surprises, however, a review with the client's project manager should take place before meeting with the client. The look and feel of the design should already have been presented in the form of mood boards. In addition, the feasibility of the design is tested in a meeting with the developers.

The design direction presentation takes place when the following aspects have been established:

- the core creative concept
- the structure in the form of a sitemap or content map (DEFINE, P. 113)
- the content concept
- the navigation system and interaction paradigms
- the visual language
- the key design elements

The DDP for a corporate website, for example, could include the following:

- a summary of the user experience strategy
- the brand filter and the creative design principle
- the strategic basis behind the design
- the sitemap and the list of required modules and templates (this can be expanded over the course of the project)
- wireframes and screen layouts for around five to seven key pages (e.g. homepage, About page, profile page for customers, etc. The number of pages will depend on the complexity of the project.)
- the navigation system and interaction principles
- a click-through prototype that demonstrates the basic behaviour of the app and can be used for early usability tests

For projects where time is of the essence and the client's team is familiar with the subject, you can agree with the client that there will not be a separate DDP presentation. In this case, the DDP only serves as a comprehensive check to confirm the status of the project. Documents such as sitemaps, wireframes, task flows and layouts are developed later. However, creating a prototype at this point is always a good idea. Not only does it make the user experience tangible for the first time, but it can also act as an early usability test that can be incorporated into the DDP.

THE DETAILED DESIGN DOCUMENTATION (DDD)

After the design direction has been approved, all other templates are turned into wireframes and then designed as layouts. If the tech provider is willing – and the client agrees – you can follow an agile work process (PROCESS, P. 40). In this case, the project is divided into smaller self-contained task sets that are implemented in iterations, gradually expanding on the original prototype. The results of feasibility and usability tests can be incorporated into the concept and design documents at an early stage. Whether you use an agile work process or not, the detailed design documentation (DDD) records all design-related decisions and, in the event that a waterfall process is used, serves as a production basis for the development team.

SET-UP / PROCESS —— DISCOVER / DEFINE / **DESIGN** / DELIVER / DISTRIBUTE

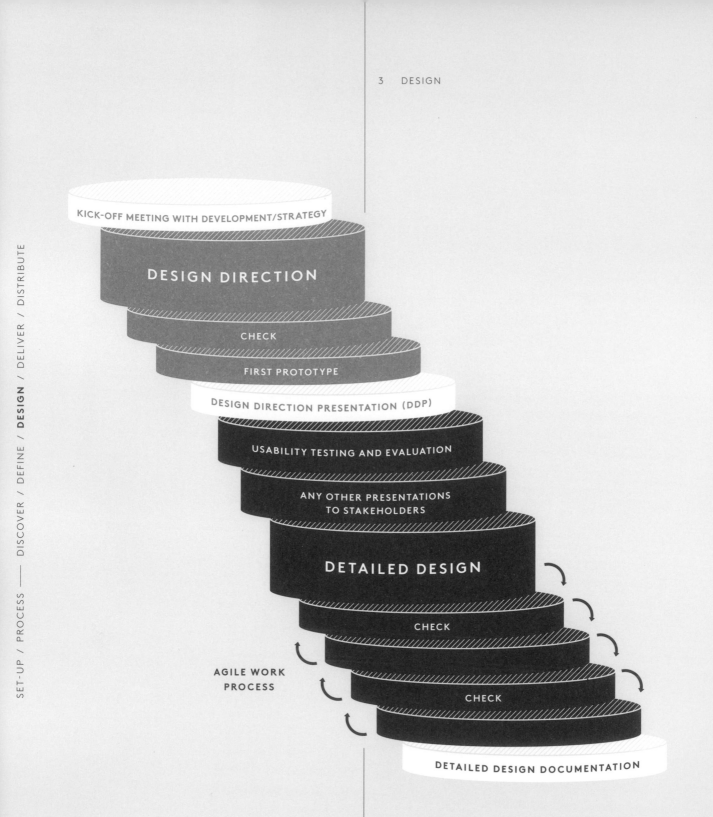

KICK-OFF MEETING WITH DEVELOPMENT/STRATEGY

DESIGN DIRECTION

CHECK

FIRST PROTOTYPE

DESIGN DIRECTION PRESENTATION (DDP)

USABILITY TESTING AND EVALUATION

ANY OTHER PRESENTATIONS
TO STAKEHOLDERS

DETAILED DESIGN

CHECK

AGILE WORK
PROCESS

CHECK

DETAILED DESIGN DOCUMENTATION

DESIGN PHASE

The Design phase is made up of the design direction and detailed design stages. For most projects, an agile work process should be followed in the detailed design stage.

WHAT THE DDD INCLUDES

1   ALL USER EXPERIENCE DOCUMENTS

- personas and user scenarios
- the final sitemap
- all templates and modules as wireframes
- a module and template list makes it easier to determine which module matches which template
- user task flows and access paths, documented in diagram form using standardized notation methods such as UML (Unified Modeling Language)
- any other design documents, e.g. on role concepts or personalization strategies, usually in the form of text documents

2   ALL VISUAL DESIGN REQUIREMENTS

- all layouts and states for the required templates and pages (usually as Photoshop or Fireworks documents, including layers and effects such as shading, gradients, etc.)
- the most important style rules (typography, colour codes, measurements), e.g. in the form of an A3 style guide poster

3   IN ADDITION
(depending on the project type)

- text and image samples to show tone of voice
- animation and navigation prototypes that visualize dry concept documents clearly (and which also specify the quality standards for the implementation)
- sound design and, if necessary, additional documents and prototypes to illustrate specific project features

A note about team composition in the Design phase. During the design direction stage, it's best to work with a small, experienced team of UX and visual designers (in most cases a senior user experience designer and a design or art director under the guidance of creative directors are usually sufficient). In the detailed design stage, the team size can be enlarged, as the major design decisions will have already been made and can be passed on relatively easily. It is important that the design lead remains involved in the process.

PRESENTING THE DESIGN

After the design is complete, it should be presented both internally and externally. If possible, the design lead should make the presentations, as no one else is in a position to speak as passionately and accurately about the chosen design strategy and its effect on the brand. If the trust of the brand managers has been earned over the course of the project, they will ask the designer for support in any case.

A presentation to the company board or other departments must be well prepared. The ultimate aim is to summarize the main findings and decisions and present the results in a way that is as logical and strategy-oriented as possible. Arguments concerning colours, shapes or other matters of taste should be deflected into a goal-oriented strategic discussion. The exact content of the presentation and the methodological steps that are discussed must be decided on a case-by-case basis with the lead project or brand manager. However, the use cases from the Discovery phase should help to tell a story that describes the context, the target and the product use. Videos or clickable demos will make a presentation more tangible and memorable.

BIxD presentations for international companies may involve travelling to other company locations. This is a chance for designers to learn about the corporate culture in those countries and the opinions and possible reservations of the local employees and to respond appropriately to these. Discussions with international partners may lead to new requirements that will need to be considered later in the rollout (PLAN THE ROLLOUT, P. 307).

3.2

GENERATE IDEAS

Good ideas can emerge anywhere at any time. But if you have to keep to a project plan, anywhere and any time is not always the best option. Furthermore, having an idea is one thing, but the real work begins when ideas are tested, evaluated and 'sold' – i.e. when they become a reality. Idea development is a process, and most designers are familiar with it. Nevertheless, too little time is often spent on idea generation, either because of the pressures of the project or because you believe you've already found the right approach. This is counterproductive because your goal should always be to find innovative solutions (although only if these are better than conventional approaches). In the BIxD process, the discovery of ideas occupies a central place.

We often find that lots of concept and design ideas emerge earlier, during the Discover and Define phases. We collect these, sort them and stick them up as Post-Its on the same project wall where our mood boards and personas are displayed. These early ideas can lead to the generation of other ideas in the Design phase.

When we talk about idea generation, two kinds of ideas are needed, depending on the focus of the project. A *core creative concept* is crucial for advertising apps and campaigns and often has already been developed in the Define phase as part of the strategy. For digital products and services, ideas that offer an *innovative on-brand solution to a problem* are more important. For service systems, the requirements tend to be mostly fixed. How can we simplify the checkout process? How can we deter a user from ending the query when asked his or her age? How can we get users to actually scan the QR tag in a book at some point? How can we make the initial set-up of a service exciting and entertaining? We find concrete answers to these and other questions through brainstorming and other idea generation methods, some of which are summarized here.

SOURCES FOR A CORE CREATIVE CONCEPT

Good concepts come from one of four strategic values: brand, product, target group or competitors.

THE CORE CREATIVE CONCEPT

For digital apps and campaigns, a core creative concept serves as a unifying focus for the design and development process. During the Design phase, it can – along with the brand filters – be used to check whether content and functions make sense. But beware: if you decide to work with a core concept, all the features and design ideas you develop must be checked to make sure they reflect the concept. After all, a concept can only be effective if it is used consistently and clearly and stays on strategy throughout.

CREATIVE METHODS

The creative techniques that we use to find ideas depend on the project's theme and on the size and composition of the team. The process usually begins with traditional methods such as brainstorming. Sometimes this is not enough, however, because brainstormed ideas always remain somewhat abstract. In these cases, methods such as roleplay or 'What if...?' questions can help to probe deeper into a subject.

Effective brainstorming requires preparation. The most important insights from the Discover phase and the phrasing of the central question need to be printed out and pinned to the wall of the creative space. Brainstorming is not something you should do on a computer. Instead, flip charts, Post-Its, presentation cards, A3 paper, pens and highlighters should be kept on hand. Brainstorming should take place in a closed space that contains no distractions. The goal of brainstorming is to break away from everyday thought patterns. Insights and information gathered in the Discover phase are therefore useful not just for strategy reasons but to provide relevant associations. Wild suggestions and spontaneous ideas have to be given a chance, so criticisms, censorship and snap judgments are all forbidden during brainstorming sessions. A warm-up phase involving fast word association or doodles can help to clear heads and hands. A brainstorming session should always have a set time limit.

BRAINSTORMING

The most commonly used methods are brainstorming and brainwriting: freeform methods of word association that are written down. They are primarily used to develop a lot of new ideas in a short space of time, which can then be grouped and prioritized. A useful variant form is the '6-3-5' method. Six participants are each given a sheet of paper, which is divided into three columns of six rows, resulting in 18 boxes. Everyone writes down three ideas, then after five minutes, the sheet is passed clockwise. The next person thinks about the first three ideas and tries to expand on them. This is done until all six participants have contributed to every sheet. This results in up to 108 ideas (6 participants × 3 ideas × 6 rounds) in 30 minutes.

'It is disturbing to think how many situations are incompletely understood because attempts at explanation persist in using well-tried familiar patterns which ought themselves to be re-examined.'

EDWARD DE BONO

☰ 9 RULES FOR BRAINSTORMING

1 Stay on topic.
2 Defer judgment – no blocking!
3 Go for quantity – lots of ideas are better than just good ideas.
4 Encourage wild ideas.
5 Build on the ideas of others.
6 Be visual.
7 Only one person talks at a time.
8 Number your ideas.
9 In a brainstorming session, everyone must be on the same page.

	IDEA 1	IDEA 2	IDEA 3
TEAM MEMBER 1			
TEAM MEMBER 2			
TEAM MEMBER 3			
TEAM MEMBER 4			
TEAM MEMBER 5			
TEAM MEMBER 6			

THE 6-3-5 METHOD

Six team members each come up with three ideas in five minutes. These are then passed on to another team member. After six rounds, the 6-3-5 method will have produced 108 ideas in around 30 minutes.

OTHER METHODS

1 MIND MAPPING

Mind mapping is primarily useful for getting an overview of a complicated subject. Every aspect of the topic is written down to form a roughly organized diagram or map. Mind mapping can be done alone or in a group. The initial focus of a mind mapping session is not relevance, but digital mind mapping tools offer functions and symbols that can be used to highlight or connect different areas. A quick mind map can also be created digitally in a meeting and then circulated to the participants afterwards. There are also online mind mapping tools that allow people work collaboratively.

2 STORYTELLING

If you're looking for a core creative concept, it is helpful to think of the product's benefits and promises in terms of a story. Storytelling makes a value proposition tangible, makes decisions easier to understand, and can also helps with evaluating service concepts. Storytelling is usually done by using existing personas, who become the main characters of the story. The story can also be told by a famous brand advocate, in the form of a testimonial. When selecting a suitable figure, ask yourself: 'Which celebrity would best embody the promise and how would he or she do this?' Even if the story is not shared later, people will sense that there is a story underlying the branded interactions. There may be elements in the

product that resonate emotionally and reflect the core creative concept. Storytelling is a good way to incorporate the unexpected and tap into your team's pool of experience. It can therefore be a useful method to employ with clients or focus groups. Before coming up with a story, however, it's a good idea to start by discussing an example of a modern fairytale with the focus group, such as *Pretty Woman*.

ⓘ **RECOMMENDED READING ON STORYTELLING:**

A classic book on storytelling is Joseph Campbell's *The Hero with a Thousand Faces* (1949). The book laid down the basic structure of human myths and influenced many modern filmmakers and authors. In his 1928 study, *Morphology of the Fairy Tale*, the Russian Vladimir Propp examined one hundred Russian folk tales and discovered that they were all based on a single plot structure consisting of 21 narrative units.

⟶ bit.ly/TIhPQZ

3   WHAT IF...?

The question 'What if...?' is useful in many fields, particularly when discussing potential problems. In the BIxD process, it can aid in anticipating user behaviour: 'What if Persona A is in this situation and contacts the call centre; what information would be needed to help that person and what questions would we ask?' or 'What if access to an interactive trade-show installation is blocked because of the high volume of visitors?

The same question can also be helpful during the creative process. Here, depending on the task, it can help to think outside the box and deliberately exaggerate: 'What if you clicked on a button in the app and got thrown out of the building?' Key functions and features of digital services can be explored in detail: 'What if the in-store app could be controlled using motion gestures instead of a touchscreen?' Unusual scenarios can also be considered: 'What if there were no more cars?' or 'What if all everyday objects were connected to the internet?'

4   AUTOMATIC WRITING

Storytelling and 'What if...?' exercises can be done in groups, with team members noting down ideas in the form of doodles or text. In my experience, an interesting way to do this is to use automatic writing. Automatic writing was a literary method used by the Surrealist movement to unearth subconscious images and feelings that were as spontaneous and uncensored as possible. At think moto, it works like this. Starting with a clear task or question, a group of five to seven members are given exactly three minutes to describe a situation without lifting their pens. Although this might be difficult at first, once you open yourself up, you can quickly get into the flow.

Automatic writing can also be used to describe a 'day in the life' (P. 87). In this exercise, you imagine what a day in the life of Persona A would look like. This method is mainly used to explore future-state scenarios or to generate new product and service ideas. It allows you to see which touchpoints are relevant to the persona, along with where and how the persona may come into contact with the brand.

5 ROLEPLAY

Roleplaying games are good for testing user scenarios that have been developed using personas. Here, one team member (or more) takes over the role of the user, while another (or more) plays the system. It is important to keep the brand personality in mind. We find out how the system should behave (in the sense of brand behaviour), and can also discover potential pain points for the persona. Props can help to make the scenario more believable.

While developing the concept study for Kai the Coach (P. 104), we imagined that the iPad app was a real personal trainer, and gave him a name and a specific personality. The roleplay focused on asking questions. What would Kai do? How would he motivate me? How would he assign me my exercises or work with me to create a training plan tailored to my needs? Roleplay can be set up like a kind of improvised drama. The setting, the action and the roles are assigned in advance (Who plays the customer? Who plays the system? Who plays the company employees...?) and then we watch what happens.

CROWDSOURCING CAN BE USED FOR:

- collective development of ideas
- co-creation: shared development of content and design
- prototyping and testing

CROWDSOURCING

Brainstorming and idea development don't have to be restricted to the design team. If a deeper knowledge of the content is required, it's a good idea to get the client involved. However, not everyone is comfortable with brainstorming sessions, since successful brainstorming means not being afraid to sound silly. Potential consumers, the future users of the app, can also be integrated into the process. To do this, face-to-face meetings aren't always required. Ideas can be generated through competitions, online communities and the integration of so-called lead users. These are users whose needs have not yet been discovered by the majority of the market for a product or service. The needs of lead users define the future direction of brand development and so they are often involved in the quest for innovation. This can be done in workshops, in which participatory design methods can be used, or via online platforms for discussion and collaboration.

You can also choose to ask all your questions in an open forum and invite your users to generate solutions. In this case, however, you should be aware that you are completely relinquishing control – and that competitors may well be watching if you're conducting the discussion in a public space.

SELECTING AND FILTERING IDEAS

Whatever methods you use, at the end of a brainstorming session it is time to sort through the ideas and filter them for the brand. Different approaches can be used to do this. In the case of brainstorming, Post-Its or keywords are put forward by a team member, sorted and grouped together, and then evaluated using a points system. Each team member is given up to 10 points to award, either as Post-Its or on a flip chart. Whether they give all the points to one idea or distribute them between multiple ideas is up to them. The scores are added up at the end.

For storytelling methods or automatic writing, the central ideas need to be filtered first. Terms will often been mentioned that refer to basic human needs. We note these down in abstract form first, then develop them into specific ideas. Courage is required, because the connections you find may

initially seem very far removed from the core of the brand or product. For instance, in a brainstorming session for a sports shoe brand, it emerged that many runners see running almost as a religious act. A lot of the basic motifs came from religious terminology, and all of the descriptions contained – in one form or another – the idea of self-flagellation followed by redemption. This provided a strong image for a core creative concept.

RATING AND COMMUNICATING IDEAS

Before we present the idea or solution to the client, we need to make sure that it's clear, creative, innovative and feasible. To assess whether an idea will work, a little more conceptual work may be needed. Some marketing directors like to choose three big ideas, which are developed in rough and turned into mock-up designs. We can evaluate these mock-ups using personas and the metrics catalogue (DEFINE, P. 113). The ultimate goal is to convince your client, and this may not be easy if the client lacks imagination or wants exactly what their competitors have, only a little different. This kind of 'me too' thinking is hard to combat, especially if there are no up-to-date results to validate the new approach. These three tactics can help to get the client on side.

1   VISUALIZING IDEAS

Using mock-ups and sketches to design or build physical models helps both the client and the whole team to visualize the final result. In addition, early prototypes can serve as initial feasibility or UX tests and will hopefully prove that an idea works.

2   TELLING A STORY

A picture often says more than a thousand words, so visualizations are important. But a well-told story can stimulate stronger mental and emotional connections, activating your listeners' in-built scripts (MENTAL MODELS, P. 74) and encouraging them to think ahead. A picture sequence or video that relates the idea in story form can be more effective than a PowerPoint presentation. But take care: the story must be well told and actively engaging, or the results could be more embarrassing than effective. It's worth finding out what the client's expectations are before you begin. Sometimes a PowerPoint presentation is enough.

3   INVOLVE AS MANY PEOPLE AS POSSIBLE IN THE IDEA PROCESS

A wider range of perspectives can make the idea generation process richer, as long as the meeting is well moderated and everyone obeys the basic rules of brainstorming. If you're developing user-centred products and services, it therefore makes sense to get the focus group and potential users involved in the generation of ideas. The advantage this gives you later is simple: an idea developed in a participatory way is often easier to sell.

When evaluating ideas, you should work closely with the client from an early stage and remain open to any counter-arguments. The client will often be more aware of existing constraints, so designers should not take the rejection of their ideas personally.

✓ THE CORE CREATIVE CONCEPT IS RIGHT IF:

▸ it's on strategy and can be applied to the relevant brand touchpoints (PLAN THE PRODUCT OR SERVICE, P. 116)

▸ it's on brand and passes the brand filter (PLAN THE BRAND EXPERIENCE, P. 128)

▸ it's relevant to the interests of the user (PLAN THE USER EXPERIENCE, P. 138)

TOUCHPOINTS

Can the idea be translated to all touchpoints?

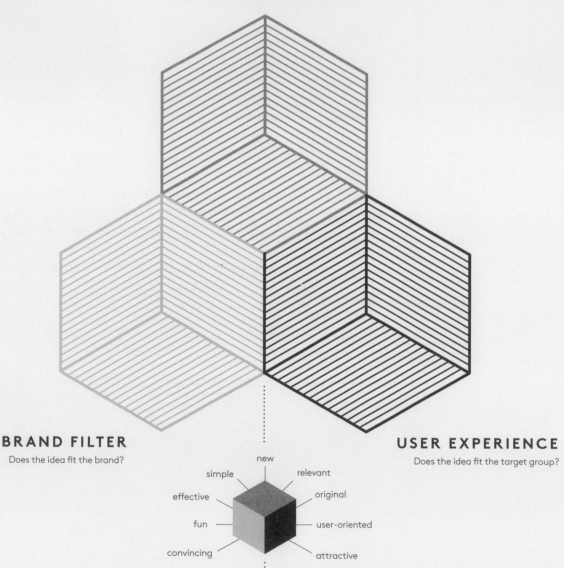

BRAND FILTER

Does the idea fit the brand?

USER EXPERIENCE

Does the idea fit the target group?

new
simple
relevant
effective
original
fun
user-oriented
convincing
attractive

CORE CREATIVE CONCEPT

CORE CREATIVE CONCEPT

A core creative concept provides a basis for the visual design of the interface and a story or conceptual model for the UX design. But it must reflect the target group and the brand, and be applicable to the relevant touchpoints.

3.3

DESIGN THE USER EXPERIENCE

Information architects, interaction designers, UX designers, service designers – the vast array of job titles can be confusing. Strictly speaking, information architecture refers to the structure and hierarchy of content, while interaction design (IxD) relates to features such as navigation or access. In the early years of the discipline, information architecture referred to the design of both the functions and content of interactive systems. In recent years, UX design has emerged as the new umbrella term. Service design, in contrast, refers to the design of complex services across multiple touchpoints.

When using the methods presented here, it is important to keep your goal in mind along with possible patterns to achieve it – or to consciously break away from these. Wireframes can encourage inexperienced information architects to do nothing but shift around boxes and arrows. In the worst cases, content can be invented simply to fill a void, without there being a strategic rationale behind the decisions. Everything you do should be either anchored in the brand, the business or the user.

190
|
191

'Creating an interface is much like building a house: If you don't get the foundations right, no amount of decorating can fix the resulting structure.'

JEF RASKIN, *The Humane Interface*

SET-UP / PROCESS —— DISCOVER / DEFINE / **DESIGN** / DELIVER / DISTRIBUTE

BUILDING PAGES FOR SCREEN-BASED APPS

Websites and mobile apps are designed as a set of static screens or pages. These screens can be sorted into different types: for example, homescreens or content screens. The basic model for a specific screen type is called a template. Each template includes containers with a predefined number of modules and elements that are arranged in a particular pattern. Several modules can be combined within a container. A single module, such as a product teaser, is made up of elements: e.g. product name, product image, price, order button.

A module can be used in multiple templates, but context is key. A shopping cart module, for example, can be used across all templates so you can always see the products you've already selected. A service module should be offered if users require help. A module, in turn, consists of individual elements, e.g. images, text, headings, links. The UX designer describes templates, modules and elements using wireframes, whose graphic look is determined by the visual designer. In the case of websites with a high proportion of customized pages, many different modules may appear on a single template. Conversely, many modules will appear on more than one template. To document these relationships, it is helpful to make a list of modules (GAP ANALYSIS AND MODULE LIST, P. 276). The hierarchy and the behaviour of modules and elements is defined in the detailed design documentation. Interactive elements are also usually explored using user scenarios. The graphic identity of modules and elements will eventually be regulated by the style guide (CREATE A STYLE GUIDE, P. 256).

WIREFRAMES

Wireframes are schematic sketches for screen-based apps. They show the structure, content and function of a page or templates, as well as the hierarchical relationship between different modules and elements. Wireframes can vary in complexity and are sketched or created with specialist software. In the early Design phase, I prefer to sketch or doodle on A3 paper. You can then add Post-Its to a doodle in order to experiment with different content modules, creating a sort of early prototype (PROTOTYPING & TESTING, P. 226). You can also buy pre-printed iPhone or iPad sketchbooks or download printable templates, to ensure that your sketches always have the right proportions.

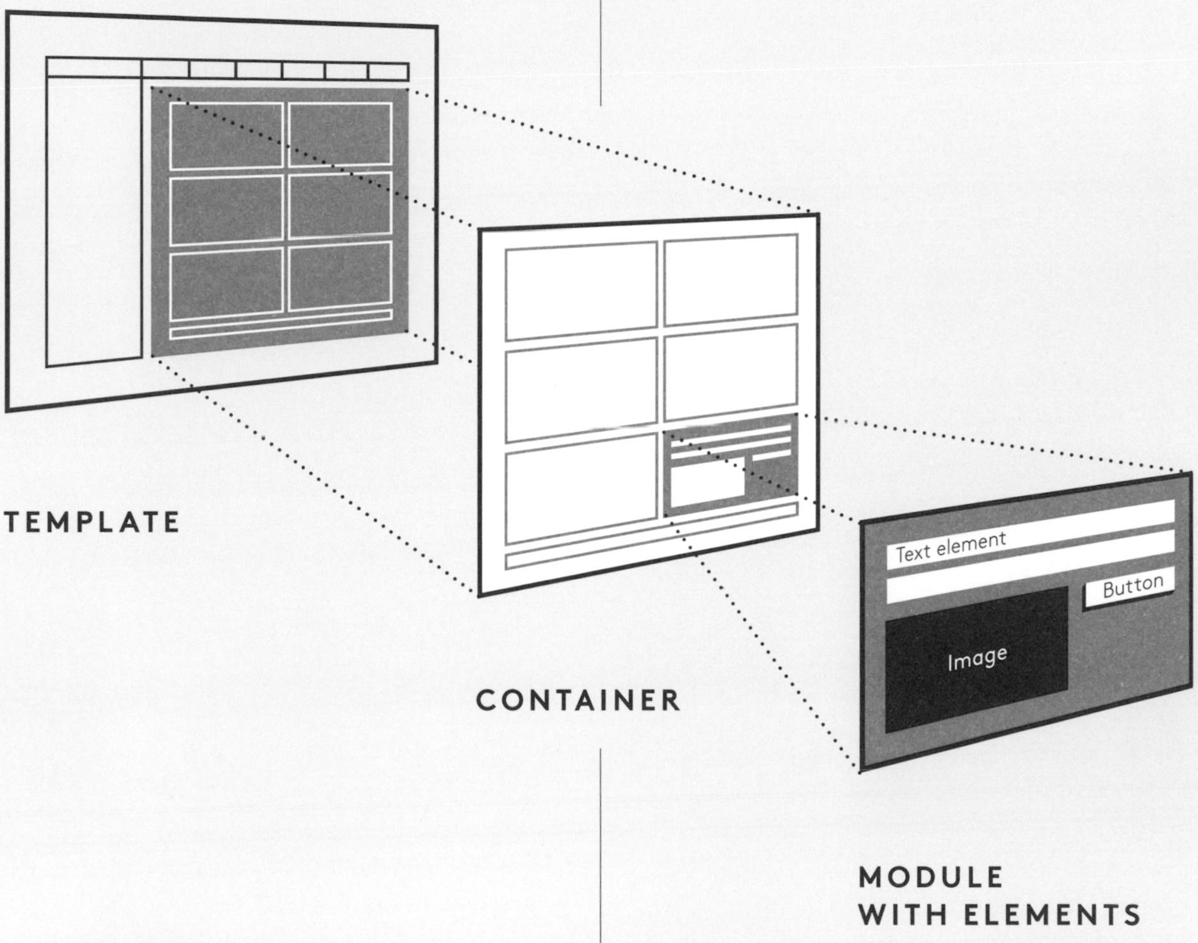

TEMPLATE

CONTAINER

Text element

Button

Image

**MODULE
WITH ELEMENTS**

A BASIC WIREFRAME STRUCTURE

A template includes multiple containers, which, in turn, hold modules. Modules are made up of elements such as images, text or interaction elements.

SET-UP / PROCESS —— DISCOVER / DEFINE / **DESIGN** / DELIVER / DISTRIBUTE

Many UX designers work from the start with specialist software such as Visio, OmniGraffle, Axure or the online-based Pidoco. Some of these tools allow you to export clickable wireframe prototypes (sometimes called black/white prototypes), which you can use for initial usability testing and to illustrate task flows.

Wireframes are created by the UX designer and may be aimed at different target groups:

- **CLIENT**: In communication with the client, they can help clarify content and functional issues at an early stage.

- **VISUAL DESIGNER**: They serve as a framework for the visual designer working on the layouts.

- **DEVELOPMENT TEAM**: They provide the dev team with accurate descriptions of the functions that need to be programmed.

Dan M. Brown rightly warns against seeing wireframes as a one-stop solution for presenting design concepts, performing usability tests, determining requirements and more. Wireframes are expensive to produce, so you should give plenty of thought to the level of detail you need. Basically, the more agile the development process, and the closer the cooperation with the development team, the less documentation is required and the less detailed wireframes can be. While the wireframes should be described in as accurate and detailed a way as possible for technical implementation, it is important when working with the visual designer to test possible layout solutions together. Wireframes also have the disadvantage (especially when communicating the client) that they suggest a finished layout. If the visual designer sticks too closely to this predetermined design, the final layout will never be as innovative as it could be because the designer's imagination will be stifled. You should therefore make sure that a wireframe mainly dictates the hierarchy and function of the modules and elements from a UX point of view. How these are implemented visually is then determined by the designer. However, choosing the right form of user interaction or the right information design is best done as a team, in my experience.

I would like to highlight one aspect that is often neglected. As design documents, wireframes must reflect the chosen strategy. We therefore develop a target matrix for the main pages of a website or app, based on the requirements from a brand, business and user perspective, in order to test potential conflicts and evaluate them. It's also important to keep the brand filters (P. 137) in mind. Do the chosen navigation and UI design fit the brand and the core concept? How aggressively or defensively is the content presented and what is its hierarchy from a user or business point of view? Are we talking to separate target groups in different ways?

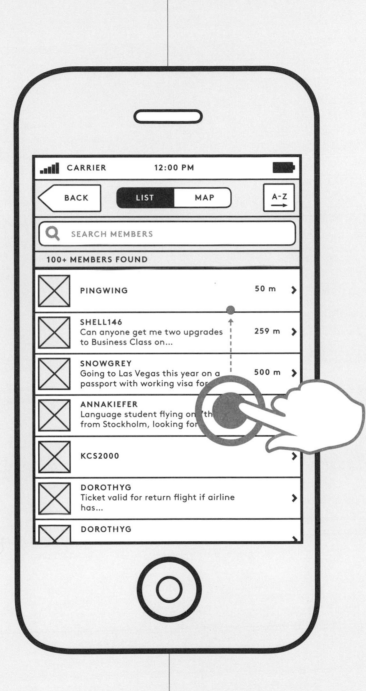

WIREFRAME FOR A TOUCHSCREEN APP

A sample wireframe for an iPhone app. Touchscreen
interactions are represented using pictograms.

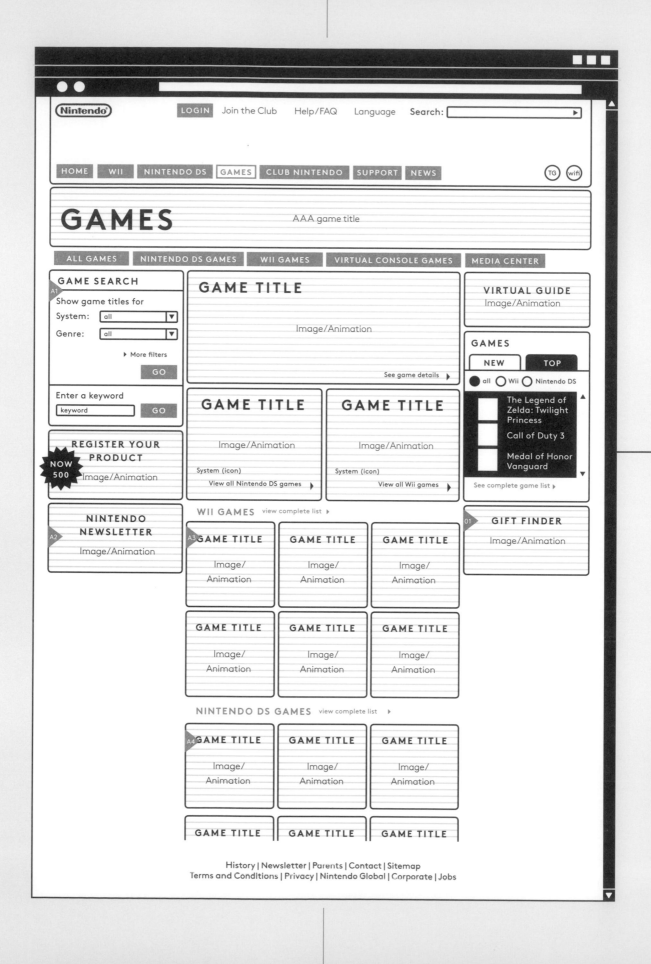

WIREFRAME

PAGE TYPE | GAMES

PURPOSE

A gateway to the world of Nintendo Games, with a focus on the Wii and Nintendo DS. The page includes animated game teasers, videos and mini-games.

CORPORATE AND BRAND REQUIREMENTS

The Games page must provide the user with a full overview of the games Nintendo has to offer. This site is primarily aimed at buyers; the information must therefore be presented in a clear and user-friendly way. The games wizard should also be located here, based on features that both new players and experienced players use to find games.

COMMENTS AND NOTES

The game teasers are presented in order of promotional importance. The content begins with a header/key visual, which refers to a AAA game, followed by a striking teaser module that refers to another AAA game. This is followed by two standard game teasers and then smaller games. Using a headline and anadditional link, the standard game teaser is used to guide the user to either the Nintendo DS or the Wii section.

UX AND USABILITY REQUIREMENTS

This page must feature content accessible to a broad range of different users. To meet these varied requirements, the games can be accessed in various ways. Below is a search field for advanced users, several teasers for immediate access, a list of new games with top ratings and a wizard (Gift Finder) aimed at parents and other buyers.

 GAME SEARCH
Advanced game search, see module list for more details.

NEWSLETTER
Slot for newsletter teaser:
If.user.registered & newsletter.not subscribed TINA NEWSLETTER 01.show
else TINA NEWSLETTER
01.hide

WII GAMES
The database automatically creates a list of current Wii games. The list is not based on collaborative filtering.

 NINTENDO DS GAMES
The database automatically creates a list of current Nintendo DS games. The list is not based on collaborative filtering.

GIFT FINDER TEASER
Content: image, headline, claim [optional]
Actions: Gift Finder.click page {ID tbd.}.load.

SAMPLE WIREFRAMES FOR A WEBSITE

Wireframes are diagrams that show the workings of individual webpages. Links on this page define the requirements from the perspective of the brand, user and business. The key in green describes the page functionality.

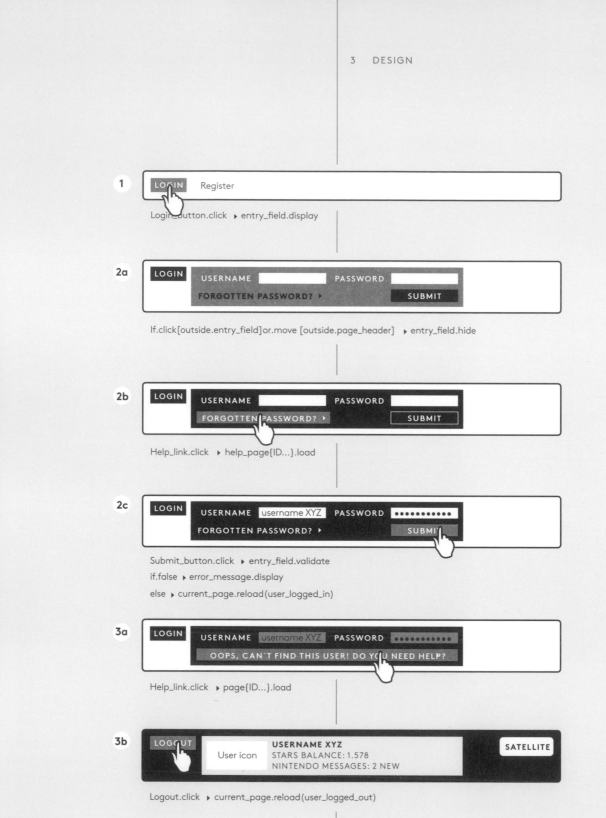

1

Login_button.click ▸ entry_field.display

2a

If.click[outside.entry_field]or.move [outside.page_header] ▸ entry_field.hide

2b

Help_link.click ▸ help_page{ID...}.load

2c

Submit_button.click ▸ entry_field.validate
if.false ▸ error_message.display
else ▸ current_page.reload(user_logged_in)

3a

Help_link.click ▸ page{ID...}.load

3b

Logout.click ▸ current_page.reload(user_logged_out)

WIREFLOWS

Pseudo-programming codes, such as Interface Object
Notation (ION), allow dynamic status changes within
modules to be described.

WIREFLOWS

Wireframes are good for describing static states, and so are ideal for developing and documenting page-based screen apps such as online magazines, corporate websites, online stores, mobile apps and many types of software. However, the more dynamic the content on a single page, the more important it is to describe the processes and behaviour rules for the individual screen objects. This is particularly vital for pages that are built using a high degree of customization or personalization, as well as for pages that use technologies such as AJAX to dynamically update content.

This is where wireflows are useful. Wireflows are a combination of wireframes and process flows. Wireflows focus on an individual module from the page template and describe its different states and rules in the form of a process diagram. The format of this description may vary. For the relaunch of the Nintendo of Europe website discussed above, we chose to use a kind of pseudo-code, which closely resembles Interface Object Notation (ION), presented at the IA Summit 2007 in Las Vegas by Kevin Silver and Chris Rivard.

WIREFRAMES FOR RESPONSIVE DESIGN

Static wireframes and wireflows have long been used to describe the functionality of websites and software apps. But with the ever-growing number of devices with varying screen sizes, resolutions and forms of interaction, a new paradigm for online apps has emerged. Responsive design means creating sites whose layouts change to fit the way they are viewed, either by querying the specific device ('adaptive') or using a scale of percentages ('fluid' or 'liquid'). The technical requirements for this are a fluid grid and flexible images. In UX design this means that we need to anticipate different screen sizes and describe how the layout will behave. It makes sense to take different contexts of use into account (e.g. mobile or desktop), rather than simply thinking of the mobile app as a reduced-size version of the desktop app.

Find out more about responsive design at:
→ bit.ly/1hj81rp

STORYBOARDS

Wireflows are used to document the behaviour of modules, especially if these include complex functions. However, for interactive movies or apps with more linear processes, classic storyboards can be sufficient. This is often true of sites built with HTML5, Flash or Silverlight, which do not have a page-based structure. Storyboards take the form of a sequence of doodles or wireframes. Their schematic nature means that the client can easily view them as placeholders, thus leaving the visual designer with sufficient room to design.

Most of us are familiar with storyboards as way of visualizing film scripts. They show a series of events over a period of time as a sequence of images. Storyboards are useful for describing animations or interaction sequences that are fairly linear. You can, however, also use them to illustrate app screens. The doodles must show perspective, movement, composition, setting and so on. To illustrate a sequence of separate screenshots (e.g. a guided tour), wireframes can be placed in a row. Storyboards are also useful for interactive projects in public spaces, describing user scenarios and showing the gestures that can be used to interact with the installation, architecture or object.

Storyboards can also be useful for illustrating a user scenario as a chain of actions (USE CASES AND USER SCENARIOS, P. 83). Storyboards of this type not only make it easier to describe technical operations but are also helpful when discussing which elements of a scenario work and which do not.

UX DESIGN PATTERNS

The methods discussed above are used to organize information within websites, mobile apps or software interfaces. Design patterns are used to help design to meet user expectations. This is most important when users lack the time or willingness to deal with new interaction paradigms. In an online shop, knowledge portal or library system, users should be able to search through large quantities of information quickly and find what they need. For example, we expect the main navigation on websites to be at the top or on the left, and the login and search fields at the top right. However, it doesn't always make sense for brands to stick to these standards, especially if the pattern doesn't match the interaction principle or the brand filters. In this case, it may make more sense to deliberately disregard users' expectations and surprise them with new patterns of interaction.

STORYBOARD FOR A SERVICE SCENARIO

The following sequence illustrates a user journey for a digital travel service across multiple touchpoints.

BEFORE THE TRIP: VISIT TO A TRAVEL AGENT

At the travel agent's, Norman the customer and John the agent work together to find out what Norman and his girlfriend Maya want from their vacation.

John finds a list of suitable destinations, so that, at the end of the conversation, Norman has a good overview. However, he is yet not ready to make a final decision.

TRAVEL AGENT

▼

BEFORE THE TRIP: RESEARCH AT HOME

That evening, sitting on the couch, Norman shows John's suggestions to Maya on his iPad. Both look at websites and offers for the suggested destinations and sift through the recommendations of others. Norman and Maya adjust their trip profile accordingly.

TABLET

200
—
201

▼

DURING THE TRIP: DIARY FUNCTION

During the trip, Maya posts her experiences on Facebook. And because it is so easy, she connects to Facebook with the travel app, which brings together Norman's photos and their travel details to create a chronological record of their holiday.

SMARTPHONE

STORYBOARD

As in filmmaking, storyboards are often used to plan animation sequences. However, they are also suitable for describing a chain of interactions with a system. This example illustrates various user scenarios for a digital travel service. Illustrations by Jordi Trost.

SET-UP / PROCESS —— DISCOVER / DEFINE / **DESIGN** / DELIVER / DISTRIBUTE

GAMIFICATION

Gamification refers to the use of game elements or game-like processes in non-game contexts. It includes rewards and motivational elements such as points systems or other incentives such as collecting badges and medals, as well as playful patterns of interaction. The goal of gamification is usually increased user engagement, leading to a more intense and sustained contact with the brand. But this is only possible if the chosen game elements fit the brand and contribute to a better user experience. Gamification is difficult to add later in the design process and should be inbuilt from the beginning to ensure that the game elements form a credible part of the overall design, generating a willing suspension of disbelief. When designing gamification processes, the same guidelines apply as for storytelling (P. 185).

The rule for successful gamification is: do not force it. Gaming is an end in itself and should never be a prerequisite for achieving other user objectives. It is frustrating if users have to achieve something to make any progress. Small hidden elements known as Easter eggs, either as time-fillers while waiting or as an end in themselves, can intensify the bond, if they fit the brand. A good example are short hidden games with easily attainable goals,

or unlockable characters such as those that appear in the Nintendo game world.

Points and badges are probably the most common form of gamification. They create incentives to use an app regularly and also bring out a user's competitive spirit. In some cases, the incentive may even lie outside the app. With the Nike+ running app (P. 98), a key motivational and control mechanism is telling friends about a completed run via Facebook or Twitter.

Gesture control can encourage the urge to play. The pinch gesture for zooming (TOUCH GESTURES, P. 222) is one example of a playful approach. When you see someone using Google Maps on the iPad or iPhone for the first time, they generally zoom in and out – at least if the map loads quickly enough. The iPhone's multiple sensors can also be utilized in playful ways: for example, shaking the iPhone to select an object at random, or 'bumping' it against another phone to transfer data. With the iPhone app Kouyou (www.kouyou.de), Japanese maple leaves with messages on them can be blown out into the world via the iPhone's microphone, while the Explore mode allows users to find messages that have landed near their location.

3.4

DESIGN THE USER INTERFACE

Ugliness doesn't sell, said Raymond Loewy in the 1950s. What sounded plausible then has since been proven and can also be applied to the aesthetics of digital products and services. Attractiveness is a success factor when it comes to creating interest and promoting user motivation (and therefore frequency of use).

A less obvious factor is the influence of design on a digital app's usability. This is known as the aesthetic usability effect. Experiments show that attractively designed products or services are perceived as more user-friendly, regardless of whether they really are. The greater the tension in the situation of use, the truer this statement becomes, because people who are relaxed and entertained are more forgiving of inconveniences. An attractive design can actually defuse critical use cases.

THE FIRST DRAFT

The strategic planning and design of digital apps have already been discussed in the previous sections. Now we focus on the aesthetics of user interfaces. Before the first visual design is created, the following are needed: brand filter, mood boards and, if appropriate, a core concept and basic wireframes for two or three of the app's main screens. Any material provided by the client should also be looked through. Good picture material is vital. If the images supplied are looking outdated or no longer reflect the brand positioning, you should make this known as early as possible and suggest looking at new stock photos or organizing a shoot.

In some cases, this is crucial, as some ideas live or die based on their visuals. For the fashion brand Y-3, the company's web presence became the key touchpoint for a trend-conscious target group in the 2000s. Their innovative web specials presented the clothes in striking ways, making use of interactivity and unusual angles. To make this possible, the company's agency, Neue Digitale, organized a private shoot exclusively for the web every season.

If a strategy has been determined, the first draft of the visual design should reflect this. If you can justify your design using the brand filters and goals defined in the strategy, your design direction presentation will be more convincing and you may avoid arguments over matters of taste. For websites and mobile apps for smartphones and tablets, three to five main pages are designed at the design direction stage (P. 176). For example, these could include the homepage, a landing page and a content page, along with page headers and footers and the navigation system. All the pages should be designed more or less at the same time, since you need to show individual elements in different contexts and states (e.g. large teaser with image, small text-only teaser in list form, etc.). The pages and templates chosen for the DDP should establish around 70% of the visual vocabulary.

As the project progresses, it's helpful to print out the layouts and pin them up alongside each other, making it easy to see all the templates at a glance. You can then evaluate the page composition (within the page hierarchy and as part of a click path), make elements and modules match up and check for brand consistency. With larger teams, it is the responsibility of the UX lead or creative director and strategic planner to decide how much detail the DDP should include for each project and client. If you're working in very close cooperation with your clients, they may already know a lot about the project's status.

☰ FIRST DRAFT CHECKLIST

Do we have everything we need to begin the visual design process?
- brand filter (P. 136)
- mood boards (P. 137)
- core creative concept (P. 182)
- wireframes and draft sitemap (P. 192)
- source material from the client (images, text, videos, icons, diagrams)

⊜ IMAGE CHECKLIST

Images for use in digital branded projects:
- Choose a format and page ratio. Vertical-format images, like those used in catalogues, are not suitable when working with widescreen platforms.
- Check that all photos and other imagery are up to date. A website relaunch always means a brand update.
- Check the brand filter: select images that fit the brand and create the look and feel you want.
- Select images that match the site or touchpoint. Where could images be used to deepen the brand experience?
- Select angles and details. Is there enough space to add text? Would the detail work as a small-scale teaser?
- Check that existing picture licences cover the web and apps.

MULTIPLE OPTIONS

The number of different designs you present to your clients depends on the type of project and the clients themselves. Some clients expect 'Big Ideas'. Others just want good advice. Basically, the more strategy-led the process is and the more strategic guidelines exist from the Define phase, the clearer your direction should be. Likewise, the more

innovative the project, the greater the room for potential solutions. However, if you are planning to offer multiple alternatives for evaluation, it's important to test them first to establish if they will work. I have seen agencies and clients get lost in endless design processes that were too driven by personal taste, leading to designs that eventually chosen more or less at random. So be careful. You can quickly find yourself speaking in terms of what you like and don't like, and losing sight of the strategic goal. If the target brand positioning has been established, not every option can be the right one.

The only sensible case for presenting multiple designs is when you want to show different positioning possibilities. In this case, you can emphasize a specific brand filter and present variations that fit along an axis from 'mainstream' to 'edgy', for example. The design must still pass all the brand filters, but particular elements can be emphasized to exploit any leeway you have.

GRID AND PAGE CONSTRUCTION

In the draft stage, we develop the layout grid for our design. The grid is the backbone of a graphic interface, and dictates the basic structure of the final design. It's not built from scratch, because the UX designer has already created sample wireframes of key pages or screens. The question you should ask is: what grid do I need based on these pre-existing wireframes?

By looking at the various templates and modules used in the wireframes, the visual designer can see how flexible the grid needs to be. Two- and three-column layouts are often used for websites and are good for presenting a lot of text. Four or more columns are suitable for overview pages that include photos, graphics or teasers. Grids based on an even number of columns look harmonious, but can lead to a loss of focus if the content presentation is too symmetrical. It makes sense for the underlying grid to be based on a multiple of the columns you need so that variations are possible. A basic 12-column grid is useful because it can be turned into a two-, three- or four-column layout.

The fundamental difference between an onscreen grid and a printed layout is obvious. Websites and mobile apps can be viewed on lots of different devices at a range of screen sizes, so the appearance of the layout on every screen can't be fixed. In most cases, a flexible system called a fluid grid (or liquid grid) can help. With a fluid grid, a website viewed on a smaller screen adjusts to the width of the browser by, for example, displaying columns beneath each other instead of side by side. However, check the requirements first: a fluid grid is not always essential.

'Design is a relationship between form and content.'

PAUL RAND, *Conversations with Students*

Here are some basic rules:

FIXED GRID

- easier to design and technically less complex to produce
- ideal when a fixed screen size is specified, for example with POS kiosk systems or corporate intranets that share a single computer environment

FLUID GRID

- necessary if the layout will be viewed on different devices, such as PCs, tablets and smartphones (WIREFRAMES FOR RESPONSIVE DESIGN, P. 199)
- more complex to plan and design

The brand should also be taken into account when deciding on a particular layout grid. As design tools, grids themselves can also be branded. The Japanese fashion brand Uniqlo regularly uses its square logo as a basic building block for its page layouts. With its Uniqlo_Grid web app, the brand offered its customers an interface that they could log onto and create their own designs based on the brand logo, which were then displayed in Uniqlo stores.

LOOK AND FEEL

Based on the grid, the positions and the relative sizes of an app's main usable areas can be determined. These include the headers (with navigation and logo), the content area, the margin or sidebar (if any), and the footer. The intended look and feel of an app can also influence the choice of grid:

- How much empty space do we need?
- How will the corporate colour be used?
- Is the content presented against a background image or texture?
- Is there a core concept or metaphor that should be used as a key element?
- What is the feel? How easy, open, static, flat or spacious do we need it to be?

When considering these issues, we mustn't lose sight of the existing corporate identity. Working digitally doesn't mean that everything has to be completely reinvented. Instead, we need to achieve visual autonomy in the new medium that expresses the brand and distinguishes it from its competitors. If the company has never used dividing lines offline, then you should also avoid them online, even if this means finding another way of separating different elements, e.g. using blank spaces. A brand often has a visual vocabulary that can be transferred to other media. For the relaunch of the Nintendo of Europe website,

for example, we derived the shape of buttons and teasers from the Wii console interface.

PAGE STRUCTURE

The look and feel takes form when the first page layout is design, based on the wireframes and grid. The information architecture is not carved in stone at this point, so the visual designer can still – within reason – experiment by moving modules and elements around and reprioritizing them in cooperation with the UX designer. Aspects of the layout such as reading direction, proportions and module organization can be designed to fit user expectations (UX DESIGN PATTERNS, P. 200) or may choose to deliberately break away from them. In some cases it's even worthwhile to give aesthetic considerations precedence over usability.

Sites that have been designed with 1:1 wireframes often look mechanical, sketchy and visually inconsistent. Most wireframes are adjusted after the rough design draft. It is important for the visual designer to keep the strategic goals in mind. Displaying the target matrix in a single central location can help with this (WIREFRAMES, P. 192). Only a visual designer who's focused on the goal can really sell the design to the team and the client. A few years ago, information architects and other UX specialists had a hard time getting clients to understand the value of their work, but the situation has now switched. In my experience, it is now much harder to convince clients to go down a new aesthetic route than to sell them two extra rounds of usability testing or an A/B split test.

TYPOGRAPHY

Typography is one of the most important brand building blocks. Many companies have their own in-house font, which makes them recognizable at first glance. A distinctive font can convey the brand just as effectively as other imagery. Most type designers today also create web fonts that can be used in online apps. For Word or PowerPoint documents, a typeface must be used that is available on all computer systems, including those of the client and the media. However, embedding corporate fonts into webpages is no longer an issue. When a brand's house font is also available as a web font, this does not mean it should be avoided; nonetheless, it's a good idea to test the font first on all current browsers. Windows still has issues with the clear rendering of fonts, but many web fonts are now also suitable for use as text fonts. If not, you should choose a similar font from the set of system fonts.

HEADER, LOGO, NAVIGATION

In many cases, the first aspect of a site or app that you will deal with is navigation. Most websites include a header at the top of the page, which also contains the logo. This ensures that a page can quickly be identified while surfing or clicking through open browser tabs. For software or mobile apps, however, a header is not required since the user must open the app deliberately. In these cases, identification is done via the app icon and a start or loading screen (THE CHALLENGES OF MOBILE INTERFACES, P. 170).

The logo is the brand's symbol. In the past, the rules for logos were clear. A logo had to be unique, simple and permanent, and had to work at different sizes and in different environments. Its job was to communicate the source behind a product, poster or letter as clearly as possible. In traditional advertising, this usually meant making sure the logo was large, but much has changed since then. A logo should still be unmistakable, but this no longer means static and unchanging if the brand is using active media. Interactivity and animation can also be incorporated into logo design. At the same time, using a logo across digital media involves certain limitations with regard to colour, size, resolution, etc. When designing or revising a logo, an experienced agency will consider all these media and allow for a range of user scenarios.

An important design step is the development of the navigation system. A basic idea for this is often included in the UX design, but now needs to be validated visually. This normally means using elements such as button shapes and house fonts to achieve visual independence and brand fit. The aim of the navigation design should not only be to make content easy to find. Colour, shape, animation and interactivity can all enhance the brand experience. The brand's strategic orientation can also have a significant impact on the choice of navigation. For example, the car manufacturer Audi's website placed its main navigation down the right-hand side, clearly distinguishing the brand from its competitors and emphasizing its core value of innovation.

Designers have much more leeway when it comes to navigation on touchscreens. Touchscreens bring eyes and hands together. In many situations, you could even omit conventional navigation altogether and use intuitive swipe and tap gestures (P. 222), encouraging users to discover content for themselves.

FORM FOLLOWS FUNCTION: VISUAL CATEGORIES

When the basic areas of a page are defined, it is important to categorize the functions and types of content and design them consistently. Knowing your target group is crucial. How large, elaborate and playful can interaction elements be for the target group? Which operating paradigms is the target group familiar with? Older people, children and inexperienced users have specific requirements that need to be considered. The device plays a role too. Menu items on a mobile touchscreen need larger buttons than menu items designed to be selected with a mouse. Context of use is also relevant. Interfaces that are used on the move or in agitated and stressful environments need to be simpler and more fault-tolerant than interfaces used in the office or at home on a desktop PC. And last but not least comes the question: what kind of branding can be used here?

In order to meet these varied requirements, visual categories for the different elements of an interface should first be defined. To keep track and stay consistent during the Design phase, all the modules can be compiled into a single document that can be hung on the wall as a style guide poster (P. 261). This poster also serves as a good initial basis for the final style guide.

SET-UP / PROCESS —— DISCOVER / DEFINE / **DESIGN** / DELIVER / DISTRIBUTE

INTERACTION ELEMENTS

Interaction elements are buttons, links and any other recurring elements in an interface. However, the type of interaction will not always be the same. This distinction must be reflected visually. Using a consistent design for each category makes understanding easier, creates recognition and shortens the learning curve. Interaction elements can also be branded, as Google demonstrates: to show the number of pages of search results that have been found, it uses a stretched-out 'Gooooogle' logo (P. 167).

However, proceed carefully when reworking brand-typical colours or shapes. This can quickly get fanciful or distracting and may even affect usability. Colour coding, for example, usually creates a hierarchy of elements. If it's justified in functional terms, you can incorporate the brand colours into this, but you should be aware of anypossible consequences.

CONTENT AND FUNCTIONAL MODULES

Containers, modules and page elements have already been described in the previous chapter (BUILDING PAGES FOR SCREEN-BASED APPS, P. 192). The documentation for a BIxD project should determine the elements that a module consists of. The task of the visual designer is then to codify the function of a module in a visual way. Which elements can be branded? How can we use colour, contrast, typography, icons, illustrations and other visual language in a way that serves both the brand and the function? In addition, the multiple states and contexts of a module must be considered. For example, if you want to include a teaser for a price comparison tool on the site's homepage, you could use a sidebar module with very basic functionality that performs the price comparison directly. However, the complete module with a full range of functions is featured on its own subpage. A list of modules (GAP ANALYSIS AND MODULE LIST, P. 276) can help to determine whether you have all the modules you need and which templates they can be combined with.

- **PROCESS BUTTONS**
  to initiate a process such as purchase
  or registration (e.g., the 'Checkout'
  button in the online store)
- **ORDER BUTTONS**
  (e.g. with shopping cart symbol)
- **BUTTONS OR LINKS FOR SERVICE
  FEATURES**
  (e.g. product comparisons, call-back
  function, zoom function)
- **PROGRESS BAR**
  For ordering or registering processes or
  online surveys; displays the remaining
  and/or completed steps in a process
- **CALL-TO-ACTION LINKS**
  These address the user directly and are
  visually highlighted to 'activate' them
  (e.g. 'REGISTER NOW!')
- **CONTENT LINKS**
  are mostly underlined (e.g. for links in
  the body text or 'Read more...' at the
  end of a teaser)
- **FORMS**
  for registration or customer inquiries
- **SOCIAL ICONS**
  to 'Share', 'Vote' or 'Like' a product
- **OTHER ELEMENTS**: e.g. **PAGE
  NUMBERING, SORTING, DISPLAY
  OPTIONS**

- **PLATFORM MODULES**
  for start pages or product
  presentations
- **CONTENT MODULES**
  e.g. articles, product lists, videos
  (these can be extremely diverse)
- **TEASER MODULES**
  These can be divided into promotional
  teasers, teasers for product cross-
  selling and up-selling ('Related
  Products'), product carousels, etc.
- **FUNCTION MODULES**
  comparison and consulting tools,
  callback, search, etc.
- **EDITORIAL MODULES**
  ('Top 10 products')
- **FEEDBACK MODULES**
  e.g. error messages, instructions,
  tool tips
- **DISRUPTIVE ELEMENTS**
  to highlight product teasers
  or other content

METAPHORS

The goal of BIxD is to make interaction as natural as possible and for it to reflect the brand as much as possible. An understanding of mental models (P. 74) can help us to present complex processes to the target group in a clear and simple way. The principle of a metaphor is simple: it involves creating a connection between something new to the user and something already familiar. However, working with metaphors can also involve risks. Using well-known imagery may, under some circumstances, restrict your message.

In addition, the same things are interpreted differently in different cultural environments, which may effect the brand. This usually happens when metaphors are too concrete. The infamous Clippy, the animated paperclip in Microsoft Word that annoyed users from 1997 to 2007 with its unwanted suggestions, became a prime example of the infantilization of the user by Microsoft products. A better question would have been: what should a digital assistant look like and how should it act if it is giving me instructions on how to use a system – but only if I request this?

UX design lead Albert Shum describes his work at Microsoft:

'At Microsoft I had the unique opportunity to bring in new ideas and pursue a fundamentally new approach. For me, whether something was technologically feasible was only secondary. I was more interested in what users really wanted in order to bring their lives, their jobs, their social circles and their hobbies together.'
ALBERT SHUM

Microsoft has learned from this. The Metro interface, the mobile operating system for Windows Phone 7, was inspired by signage and navigation systems from urban spaces – street signs and pictograms. Interface elements should be easily and quickly recognizable, like signs on the road or at train stations and airports. UX designer Albert Shum and his team have used this metaphor consistently without making specific graphic references to their source of inspiration. The conceptual parallels between Windows Phone 7 Metro interface and Nokia's MeeGo interface operating system are discussed in the interview with Peter Skillman (P. 326).

'Simplicity has to be designed. In order to design something, you need to know exactly what you are dealing with and what you intend to achieve.'

EDWARD DE BONO, *Simplicity*

SIMPLICITY

In my daily work as a consultant and designer for interactive media, clients often give me the following 'requirement': 'Users should find the content they need within three steps.' The three-step rule has become commonplace, like having no more seven items in a menu or Jakob Nielsen's decree that links must be blue and underlined. All of these staples of web usability are successful because they are so simple – three and seven are easy figures to remember – and all of them were devised with the best intentions, but they are not always right. When an experience is reduced to a rule or a truism, there is always a risk of losing sight of the actual goal. The rule becomes an end in itself. To stay with the example of web usability, the client's *real* goal should be: 'Users should be able to find the content they are looking for.' This should lead to the requirement: 'Provide navigation that lets users find the content they want easily.' In some circumstances, you can get rid of classic menu-style navigation entirely. Searches and indexes, filters or a clever personalized messaging structure may – in the right situation – be a much better match for the brand personality and mindset of the user than the three-step rule.

Dieter Rams's 'less but better' approach can also be applied to the visual design of interfaces. If one element lacks prominence, it is almost always better to take emphasis away from the competing elements than to give this item more. Unfortunately, companies are often dubious about techniques such as this. All departments want to remain equally prominent and feel that access to content should be offered twice rather than one time too few. In these cases, if necessary, we should use persuasion based on prototypes and testing. Simplicity is not something that is easy to manufacture. Simplicity is the result of decision-making and strategy. On the road to a solution, a thousand attractive-looking possibilities may present themselves, but must be rejected if we are not to lose sight of our actual goal.

DIGITAL FIRST

DAVID LINDERMAN
HI-RES!

Hi David. Hi-ReS! has done a lot of work for clients in the fashion, music and lifestyle industry, and has always focused on video and motion design. How has that changed over the years?

I wouldn't say things have changed all that much, maybe stylistically a little, but what I've noticed since I came here is that storytelling remains the biggest element of every project that we do.

I can't think of any successful projects that don't include some form of storytelling.

Motion graphics or animated elements play a big part in that, by creating the illusion of space or depth and setting a mood, and also by simulating a psychological state or situation that will really bring users inside the site, rather than just looking at it. The Hi-ReS! experience is never pure information. It's more about creating a state of immersion inside a bigger conceptual strategy connected to a particular brand.

What developments do you predict for the future?

We see the digital perspective as being increasingly integrated into the basic brand message and no longer being just a supporting channel alongside above-the-line campaigns for TV and print. A concept or brand experience that starts with an interactive idea can easily be applied to other media and channels. The other way around can be much more difficult to pull off successfully. For years, interactive designers have always been at the bottom of the industry food chain. Until recently, we've always been at the end of the conceptual chain too, kind of like 'We've got a great TV ad, now make a website for it.'

Now we're seeing clients coming to us before the big idea is nailed down, and working on that big idea from a digital perspective first, before TV or print.

An idea originally conceived for Facebook can easily be part of an outdoor or print media campaign to make it part of a bigger social event, leaving a footprint beyond the web. The only way to do that is to have an idea that works interactively in people's minds, that involves them intellectually or entertains them, through dialogue or another form of participation, rather than just passive viewing. A lot of our work is getting much broader, going way beyond websites. Social media is even more extreme: it forces us to think interactively from a purely conceptual standpoint with less importance attached to visual bells and whistles.

Can you give an example of a project with an interactive core that was expanded to other media?

Probably the best one is *The Lost Experience* that Hi-ReS! did in 2007, before social media became a mainstream popular thing. It used blogs, search results and microsites to create a virtual experience based on the TV show *Lost* and to create a bigger sense of audience participation by involving people in a quest that involved digital channels that we use every day, such as Google searches or blogs, but in

a different way. Telling a story that used these channels as tools created a deeper immersion that was less visual and more of a mental experience. That's one of the finest examples, in my opinion.

Another project is one we did in collaboration with Syzygy Germany, called *Jägermeister Hausbesuch* (Jägermeister At Home; P. 243). Before this, the Jägermeister digital world was primarily fantasy-based, with an immersive 3D world crafted from Jägermeister legends (the stag logo, 'Ice Cold'). But Jägermeister At Home was all about reaching a slightly older audience and focusing on relaxing at home and 'active unwinding'. The project brief was demanding, because it asked us to find a way to challenge some long-held perceptions of the brand and position it for a new audience. We had to use real-life situations and bring groups of friends together to actively pursue a shared goal.

Jägermeister At Home was a break from the brand's traditional gimmick-driven communications (stags talking on a bar wall, for example) and a conscious move towards honest, real-life interactions with Jäger fans, their friends and community. It began in Germany by searching for interesting people with unusual hobbies and visiting them, celebrating their community and throwing a party for them and their friends; in essence, giving Jägermeister fans a voice – 'I have something to say about what I like to do and I want to share it' – and connecting each smaller story to the larger overall concept. Instead of planning a big TV ad, we used an interactive platform and found a format that could be constructed from many smaller elements that were quicker to make and didn't require the huge film crew or production budget needed for a longer on-going campaign.

This format was partly inspired by a trend we see happening as a result of the new way in which we consume stories online. YouTube has had an enormous influence on the way we watch and enjoy video or motion content. Since YouTube, shaky home video has come to represent a new kind of 'honesty' in films and documentaries, and a way of telling a story within a different context. Audiences now have a tendency to question flawless-looking film productions, depending on their message, because they immediately identify them as some sort of advertising or contrived event.

Did Jägermeister take your ideas further? Did you give them something to keep working with?

A lot of the responsibility for re-addressing the brand image and positioning in 2011 and 2012 fell on digital communication and finding answers to some really interesting questions. How does Jägermeister interact with its fans? How can we speak to new subcultures and genres without alienating old fans? Or something as simple as 'What does Jägermeister sound like in Manhattan? Brooklyn? Atlanta? Denver? Or San Francisco?' How do we create interaction that embodies this brand, and explore what it is by stimulating the imagination of our audience rather than simply blasting them with a single message? It is a big step for Jägermeister, because they've never done anything like this before.

Okay, let's talk about the process behind it all. What competencies do you have here at Hi-ReS!?

It's hard to define in terms of the classic roles of design or advertising. Most of the designers and technologists at Hi-ReS! are multidisciplinary by nature and, more often than not, work on their own creative pursuits (e.g. music, photography or film) when they're not in the studio. In the best cases, this passion is reflected in their project work. Producers also often come from a creative field as well. Proportionately, we have relatively few developers (but very good ones!) and there are few concrete distinctions between job roles. It's very much a hands-on experience here with a lot of sharing and pooling of talent on projects.

Do you have concept developers?

No, that's totally the job of the creative team here. We typically start with a theme or a core concept for a proposal before gathering references from various sources (usually not advertising or web work, however) and writing a treatment for those ideas (much as you would for a film) and painting a picture, or story, to communicate this bigger idea.

At this point, do you talk about brand? Do you try to lay down brand guidelines for a project or do you just allow the feel to come through?

We don't spend a lot of time on brand guidelines here. We're fortunate enough to be able to trust our intuition and feelings and I think that's why our clients keep coming back. That's also why

I love working here. Following brand guidelines slavishly often results in very formalized work.

As a creative director you have to feel what a brand is. Reading a client project brief means learning to read between the lines.

Even bad briefs can often give you a feeling for what they're not saying, so you can ask the right kind of questions to find out what a project is really about and where its core strengths and personality lie. We rarely look at corporate style guides. We're more interested in the company's history, in asking questions, in talking to them. Hearing about the directions they've already tried, testing them with some ideas about what might be possible. It's more of a learning experience than a reading experience. But I also think that a large part of what we do is about authorship and the unexpected. When we're finished with a project, we've often gone beyond the initial brief or explored new territory.

I think it works that way if you're very experienced. But when you have to hand over to other agencies or other departments in the company, you have to make sure that what you feel as a creative director is also felt by the person who has to deal with it.

A lot of what we're doing now is content in its own right, but part of a bigger identity. We're often asked to move something in a new direction and try and find something unique and innovative that still fits a particular brand or project positioning. Brand identity today has to be flexible to adapt to changing technological and social trends. We need more recognizable personalities, not more Pantone colour systems and standardized typography.

I think this attitude creates something like authorship, a signature style that can be felt in Hi-ReS! projects. Have you ever felt as if this authorship conflicted with a client or a brand?

'Do we follow the brief, or do we turn it upside down?' is a common in-house conflict that typically surfaces during new pitches. Sometimes you understand the brief right away and the direction is quite clear, but there are many more occasions where it is more like: 'Actually, this is all wrong. What they really need is....' There's no better time to question your direction than before you begin. It's a great way to guarantee that you don't end up doing something you hate and most of our clients admire the courage to question the initial brief.

On the other hand, we've also had a lot of good ideas that never saw the light of day. It's a pity, but life goes on. There are a lot of personal ideas that are put into each project and everything that gets produced here has some soul in it. I think that's what you meant when you mentioned authorship. The sense that somebody actually cared.

David Linderman is Creative Director at Hi-ReS! New York.

3.5

DESIGN GESTURE INTERACTIONS

SET-UP / PROCESS ——— DISCOVER / DEFINE / **DESIGN** / DELIVER / DISTRIBUTE

Gesture interaction design is now a part of the daily routine for BixD designers. Gestures such as touching a surface or reading body movements via video tracking and sensors can be used to control digital apps. With gesture interaction, new design issues emerge that were once only relevant to disciplines such as industrial design or architecture. These include questions such as: how far away is the user from the interface? What is the interface made from? What ergonomic form underlies a physical object? What is the use situation with regard to traffic, noise level, lighting conditions? Cultural aspects should also be taken into account. What gestures have already been learned from other apps? Which gestures may have a hidden meaning? Are there any fears related to touching surfaces? Is there a general reluctance towards gesture interaction in public spaces?

GESTURES FOR TOUCHSCREENS

In the realm of digital media, we are undergoing a change that will leave PCs as we have known them for the last two decades looking like rough prototypes. The grey box on the table is already gone from most households and has been replaced by mobile devices like notebooks, tablets and smartphones. Interaction with digital media has been fundamentally changed by this. The most important input devices are no longer mice and keyboards, but touchscreens. These do away with the separation between display and interaction, allowing surface objects to be manipulated directly.

Another design challenge is to make full use of the range of networked devices. PCs, laptops, smartphones, tablets, e-readers and interactive TV have access to a shared cloud database. Each can be used to access digital products and content, and each has special properties that make it more suitable for some user scenarios than others. The challenge for brands is to make optimum use of these features when designing interactive screens and to develop an appropriate multiscreen strategy (MULTISCREEN EXPERIENCES, P. 125).

Our job as interactive brand designers is to create meaningful media networks from the diverse range of digital touchpoints, networks that are not homogeneous, but which work together in the interests of the brand and offer users the added value of interaction. Of course, for all devices, we must ensure that the chosen form of gesture interaction fits the brand and the goal.

5 TIPS FOR GOOD TOUCHSCREEN INTERACTION DESIGN

1 **Think big enough:** Even with small touchscreen displays (e.g. smartphones), individual elements must be large enough to be selected.

2 **Consider readability:** Information should not be placed directly beneath the touchscreen surface since it will hidden during the interaction.

3 **Keep it simple:** The complexity of the gesture should correspond to the task. Always consider the context of use. An app used while walking must be relatively easy to use.

4 **Design for the medium:** before using buttons or links from the point-and-click world, always consider if there is a better gestural solution.

5 **Make it fault-tolerant:** What is true for visual branding also applies to gestures. Different actions require gestures that are significantly different. If they are too similar, errors can easily occur.

SET-UP / PROCESS ——— DISCOVER / DEFINE / **DESIGN** / DELIVER / DISTRIBUTE

BRANDS IN THE AGE OF THE INTERNET OF THINGS

The new world of touchscreens is only one part of the paradigm shift. A second has been quietly taking place but can already be perceived in some areas. On one hand, there is digitally enriched interaction with real spaces (e.g. facades, architecture and installations); on the other, there are an increasing number of objects that items that are barely even recognizable as digital media, but that are nonetheless connected to digital networks. These allow a more natural, physical form of interaction via a range of sensors.

The so-called Internet of Things, also known as ubiquitous computing (TOUCHPOINTS, P. 116), includes 'intelligent' textiles and clothes (so-called 'wearables'), interactive objects, toys and household devices that can respond to their environment or 'learn' through use. In the field of consumer electronics, more than half of all devices can already connect to the internet*. Many household appliances can now be controlled via mobile apps (YELLO ENERGY METER, P. 101), while the networking of cars or bicycles has enabled new service concepts such as car-sharing (FLINKSTER, P. 102).

ⓘ * Figure courtesy of GFU Consumer and Home Electronics: www.gfu.de

The interconnected nature of our world is driven by touchscreen devices but also makes new types of interaction possible. Interactive shop windows, billboards and city lights react to free gestures that no longer require an input device. Free gestures based primarily on camera-based tracking technologies in enclosed spaces work even better. In brand experiences such as the Famous Grouse Experience at the Glenturret Distillery in Scotland, visitors interact with a floor projection that tells them about the history of whisky in a playful way.

FREE GESTURES ———

Free gestures open up a new realm of potential interaction, but also create new usability hurdles. For example, there's no clearly defined way to signal whether and how you can interact using free gestures. With Kinect, an add-on for the game console Microsoft X-Box for gesture interaction, the gestures are almost always illustrated on screen, but instructions of this kind are not always possible in public spaces. Public spaces also present other challenges (INTERVIEW, P. 224).

Free gestures are a new challenge for interaction designers. Body movements must be described; borrowing from dance notation can sometimes be helpful here. Some gestures are already becoming standardized, and the two pages overleaf show how we record these gestures at think moto. There is another crucial change, however. Since the screen is no longer the medium *for* which we design, it is also no longer the medium *with* which we design. For interaction designers, this means getting up and moving around the room. For developers, this means getting away from the code on the screen and picking up physical tools, as well as making use of an ever-increasing variety of sensors, which in turn allow access to a huge range of data.

⊜ ADVANTAGES OF FREE GESTURES

- Free gestures are a natural form of interaction, allowing digital or mechanical objects to be directly manipulated.

- Free gestures are suitable for use in public spaces (shop windows, airport, museums) because they do not require any (ugly) visible hardware.

- Free gestures are fun: a new playful and physical way to use interactive media that invites people to try things out and explore.

FROM GUI TO NUI

User interfaces that are controlled via touchscreens or free gestures and camera tracking are just one part of a paradigm shift, which can be described as 'from GUI to NUI'. NUIs (natural user interfaces) are any user interfaces that can be operated without additional aids such as a mouse or keyboard. 'Natural' refers to the way in which people interact with the app – i.e. it is the use that is natural, not the interface itself.

Multitouch interfaces such as smartphones, tablets or touch tables offer the potential for natural interaction, but this is not always explored; for example, standard mouse-interaction patterns are used on touchscreens. Designers should try to free themselves from click-and-point design patterns and aim for the most direct interaction possible. The same applies to hands-free gestures for interacting with hardware such as Microsoft Kinect. In addition to gesture control systems, NUIs include voice-operated apps such as Apple's Siri or Microsoft's TellMe. Voice control can be used in situations where gestures aren't possible or would not be safe, e.g. while driving or in home aids for people with physical disabilities.

220

221

TOUCH GESTURES

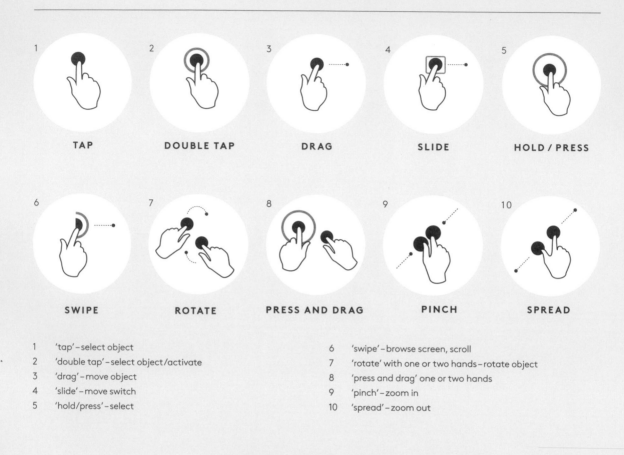

TAP	**DOUBLE TAP**	**DRAG**	**SLIDE**	**HOLD / PRESS**
SWIPE	**ROTATE**	**PRESS AND DRAG**	**PINCH**	**SPREAD**

1   'tap' – select object
2   'double tap' – select object/activate
3   'drag' – move object
4   'slide' – move switch
5   'hold/press' – select

6   'swipe' – browse screen, scroll
7   'rotate' with one or two hands – rotate object
8   'press and drag' one or two hands
9   'pinch' – zoom in
10 'spread' – zoom out

MOBILE GESTURES

READ QR	**BLOW INTO MIC**	**USE CAMERA**	**BUMP**	**SHAKE**

SYMBOLS FOR GESTURE INTERACTION

These gesture symbols can be downloaded as
OmniGraffle stencils at: www.thinkmoto.de/gestures
They are published under a Creative Commons
licence and may be used for your own documents.

BODY GESTURES

1	'wave' – activate, move, scroll
2	'one arm out / hands on hip' – pause or stop
3	'turn head / nod' – vertical / horizontal scrolling / browse
4	'pinch / spread' – shrink / enlarge
5	'lean left' – move object or dodge
6	'thumb up' – confirm selection
7	'clap' – activate / deactivate
8	'standing / arms down' – disable, initialize
9	'step left / right' – move left / right
10	'jump' – select object or skip
11	'lift left / right leg' – avatar turns left / right
12	'stand on one leg' – scroll right / left

GESTURE INTERACTION

PROFESSOR MICHAEL ZÖLLNER
HOCHSCHULE HOF

Michael, you work as a designer, researcher and lecturer in the field of experimental interfaces. What practical applications does gesture interaction have?

Unlike touch interaction, the use of gesture interaction can be used at a distance from the object or image. An arm's length is often not sufficient to recognize content and interact with it at the same time. It's most useful for abstract and indirect interaction, where movement and behaviour are recorded but not broadcast or displayed.

When do gestures work and when don't they?

Gestures work best when they are natural and obvious. First of all, however, users need to become aware of gestures as a form of interaction. This is not yet the case, since most users have almost never, if ever, used this kind of interaction. A few years ago, children were still being taught not to touch anything in museums and not to touch the TV with their fingers. This has changed dramatically through the ubiquity of touchscreens like the iPhone or iPad. Touching displays is now a given and lots of people know the pinch-to-zoom gesture. The widespread use and standardization of gestures has therefore become a good foundation for natural user interfaces. Microsoft's Kinect may become an ambassador for this, just as the iPhone was for multitouch interaction.

However, an important component is missing from gesture interaction: touch. Of course, this is not necessary when dancing or training with Kinect, but holding an imaginary steering wheel to control a racing game feels unnatural and difficult. Activating and manipulating virtual objects also feels awkward. The Nintendo Wii and Playstation Move, however, incorporate a tactile component and a real representation of the virtual object in the form of the gesture controller. But when they are used for installations in public spaces, these controllers have a tendency to disappear rather quickly!

What are the main considerations when designing gestural interactions for brands?

As with all new interactive technologies, it is important to carefully consider whether use of the app is intended to improve a situation (i.e. is it problem-driven?) or whether it's a me-too campaign attempting to publicize the brand by using the latest technologies (i.e. is it technology-driven?). If it's the latter case, it can create user irritation and even have a negative effect on the brand.

This is particularly true in the field of augmented reality (AR) apps, in which an AR presentation is often chosen in preference to classic display formats despite its poorer suitability, simply for the sake of using the feature. It's also important to pay attention to the public image that gestural interaction creates. The user must not feel silly when 'physically' interacting with the brand.

What technological knowledge do designers need to design gesture interactions?

The designer should be open to new technologies in order to learn how to use them well. Having a greater understanding of technology's potential as well as its restrictions is an advantage over simply being able to use predefined interfaces.

What role does prototyping play?

I regard prototyping as one of the most important parts of the design process for interactive systems.

They are simply too complex to be able to imagine all possible contingencies as static sketches, as was previously the case. The systems have to be felt and learned, much in the same way that product designers approach the materials for their works. Otherwise you only see the surface. Prototyping also quickly exposes problems and dead ends in the interaction, which can be immediately corrected and tested again. Simple usability tests can be carried out quickly and evaluated by the team or by volunteers. But prototyping also means independence for designers and creative coders, who no longer need to be dependent on and restricted by programmers. Designers have a more open-minded and experimental approach to new technologies and so can discover new possibilities.

Michael Zöllner is a professor of interaction design at the Hochschule Hof as well as the founder and partner of blink tank.

3.6

PROTOTYPING & TESTING

In the Discover and Define phases, as well as in the first stage of the Design phase, paper prototypes and roleplay can help to test interaction principles and processes and allow a better understanding of possible user behaviour. In the Design phase, they can also be used to test feasibility and usability. Before the design direction presentation, we test the critical design points in-house. With larger projects, about two weeks are scheduled after the DDP for usability and UX testing. One advantage of an agile project approach is that you don't have to create click-through prototypes for presentation purposes alone. This is another reason why you should try to persuade your collaborators to follow an agile process. Strictly speaking, prototypes can be part of any project phase, as they help you to understand the requirements, test interface concepts and check technical feasibility.

MOCK-UPS AND PAPER PROTOTYPES

Rough sketches and paper prototypes using doodles or wireframes are the simplest form of prototypes and can be introduced at a fairly early stage to get initial feedback from the client and focus group or to test feasibility. If possible, the prototype should reflect the proportions of the original.

A paper prototype of a mobile app made of Post-Its. Using an iPhone as a base means that the context of use can be simulated.

CLICK-THROUGH PROTOTYPES

Websites and software apps are initially implemented in the form of click-through prototypes, which can include varying degrees of detail. HTML click-throughs based on wireframes, for example, can be created using Axure, OmniGraffle and Visio, which allow wireframes to be exported as HTML. Also known as black/white prototypes, click-throughs are used for checking specific click paths and linear sequences, but not the details of the layout. More detailed click-throughs can be created if a layout design exists. If the platform you plan to use is not yet available, you can build the click-throughs in Flash or static HTML. If using an agile process, you can build prototypes using Ruby on Rails, for example, which allows dynamic content to be included at an early stage. Prototypes of this kind can be produced during any phase of the development process.

VIDEO PROTOTYPES

Films were being used to present design concepts as early as the 1930s at the Bauhaus. Video personas can be used to create vivid user journeys or user scenarios (P. 83) before the actual product even exists. We should make sure that the problem and starting position are clearly formulated and create a script or a storyboard (STORYBOARDS, P. 200) for the scenario. Videos are also useful for documenting free gestures to be used with interactive installations, rather than describing them elaborately using dance notation. Video technology is now relatively simple to use, and effective results can even be achieved using an iPhone and widely available software such as Apple iMovie or Microsoft Movie Maker.

SERVICE EXPERIENCE PROTOTYPING

Service experience prototyping is used to simulate a user experience in a service scenario, usually via roleplay (ROLEPLAY, P. 187). It allows the design team to test the predicted user experiences through the early interaction with products and services. This naturally applies to all other prototyping methods that are presented here. However, service experience prototyping refers in a particular way to the situation of service systems, e.g. the sequence of interactions at multiple touchpoints. Through roleplay, you can act out scenarios and find out which requirements exist at which touchpoints, or where problems could arise. A rough script that focuses on the central question should also be created. This script should be based on your personas and their user journeys. For interactive environments and installations it is useful to have physical prototypes or models ready to use. If not, you can use props. Service experiences can be tested outside; depending on the project, you could also use a public space to hold a flashmob event and monitor public reactions.

SET-UP / PROCESS ——— DISCOVER / DEFINE / **DESIGN** / DELIVER / DISTRIBUTE

PHYSICAL PROTOTYPING

Physical prototypes are models made of wood, cardboard, polystyrene, foam etc., designed to convey the look and feel of an interactive object or space. These models can then be used in roleplay exercises or for service experience prototyping. You need to be aware in advance of what you want the physical prototype to demonstrate. To replicate the feel of a piece of hardware, the actual material should be used. If you only want to show the size of a device, a cardboard model is sufficient. For space-based projects, architectural maquettes do the job (BMW MUSEUM, P. 288).

DO-IT-YOURSELF PROTOTYPING

To test interactive installations and environments, a technical prototype must first be built. Inexpensive microcontrollers, such as those made by Arduino, can be used to test, evaluate and connect sensors to software relatively easily. These are often pre-mounted on a so-called breadboard, to which sensors, motors, batteries and other electronic components can be attached.

A simple but quite powerful Java-based development environment called vvvv is also available, and is the development environment of choice for manipulating multimedia environments in real time. vvvv is an environment in which graphically represented elements (known as objects) can be connected to each other in real time via virtual cables. While the strength of vvvv is in its use of 3D real-time graphics, similar environments such as Max/MSP by Cycling74 and its open source counterpart Pure Data (Pd) are traditionally used for audio processing.

Hacks of existing hardware allow installation prototypes to be built quickly by taking advantage of existing, partly commercial, hardware and by using existing sensors and interfaces. To test gesture interactions without developing your own motion tracking system, it's particularly common to use something like Nintendo's Wiimote controller or Microsoft's Kinect (FREE GESTURES, P. 220).

USER ACCEPTANCE TESTING

Many successful products may never have existed if they had first been acceptance-tested with the target group. Unfortunately, however, this happens far too often today. Managers trust the judgment of the target group more than they do the design experts who have been hired to create an innovative product. This can go so far that the development of ideas is partly crowdsourced, i.e. delegated to the community. The results of leaving product innovation to users are demonstrated in the TV series *The Simpsons*. In the episode 'Oh Brother, Where Art Thou?' Homer Simpson learns of the existence of his half-brother Herb, who owns a car company. Herb regards Homer as the perfect average American and commissions his design team to create a car according to Homer's requirements. The car soon becomes a feature-overloaded monstrosity and the company goes bankrupt.

Just to be clear here, I am happy to involve users in the strategic design process, especially if their suggestions for improvement are based on their own experiences. But a user's judgment should never be regarded as representative, especially not when it comes to matters of taste. I will not therefore be discussing the kind of focus group tests for branding and design that agencies perform. Of course, it may be useful to consult the target group's opinion on specific aspects of the design or brand personality, but I think broader surveys are better suited to this than focus group tests, and the results of those surveys should

'If I had asked people what they wanted, they would have said "faster horses".'

HENRY FORD

always be treated with caution. In the following section I will limit discussions to usability testing.

USABILITY TESTING

Smaller tests can be carried out by the design team itself. In some cases it may make sense to do this in collaboration with the client, if for example the specific target group is more easily recruited by the client. Tests like this are useful to iron out uncertainties regarding the usability of the design, e.g. if you're introducing a new interaction paradigm that is non-standard.

Full usability tests are not usually carried out by the designer, but by specialized agencies that recruit subjects, draw up test cases and perform the tests. However, the designer should know enough about testing to compile the brief and interpret the results in a useful way. I've seen usability agencies perform very good analyses, but then submit completely misleading solutions. In a nutshell: if users can't find a button, the solution is not necessarily to make it bigger and paint it red. It may be better to choose a different screen layout, and thus shift the emphasis between different elements.

☰ USABILITY TESTING SEQUENCE

1 **ESTABLISH A FOCUS** at the start. Not everything needs to be queried in a usability test; questions should be limited to a few key points.

2 **PREPARE TEST CASES** and participant profiles, and define user tasks. The test cases should refer to specific user scenarios and personas.

3 **CHOOSE AN AGENCY**, brief them and book them. Which agency do you need? Do you need to test internationally? What methods does the agency use? Does the agency recruit participants, carry out the tests and follow through?

4 **COMPILE A BRIEF** when the agency has been selected, and decide on a shared definition of the test cases.

5 **PREPARE QUESTIONNAIRES FOR PARTICIPANTS**. Here you can collect socio-demographic information to match up with target group segments and personas, and record media preferences and existing levels of experience.

6 **BRIEF THE PARTICIPANTS** properly about their role and the situation; it may be prudent to split the test group. Five to seven test participants are sufficient for a pure usability test; if other aspects of

the user experience need to be studied, the number of participants should be doubled **(USER EXPERIENCE TESTING, P. 231)**.

7 **CONDUCT THE TEST**. In each session (about 45 minutes), participants are observed while interacting with the app and asked specific questions about their impressions. The design team should be present, and several countries can be represented if relevant **(PLAN THE ROLLOUT, P. 307)**. Participants should describe their thoughts out loud while engaged in a task.

8 **INTERVIEW THE PARTICIPANTS** about their experiences in depth. What were their overall impressions, what did they like, what was less impressive? Questions regarding brand-specific aspects can also be included **(USER EXPERIENCE TESTING, P. 231)**. The conversations can be recorded.

9 **PRESENT YOUR FINDINGS** to the client, in collaboration with the test agency. Misunderstandings and arguments can be avoided by analysing the findings together with the agency and discussing them before the presentation to ensure everyone is in agreement.

10 **DEBRIEF:** The experts come together, prioritize the issues and suggest solutions.

Usability and UX tests are conducted in the most relevant countries or regions, since the budget is usually not sufficient to do so in every market. However, it is important to choose a representative cross-section of cultures and levels of technology. If tests are only conducted in the home country or the most developed markets, it implies a disregard for all other markets and cultural differences. If possible, it is best to involve the design team in the tests to ensure the testing processes are comparable and to give immediate feedback on any cultural differences. The question of whether, and to what extent, brands should be regionally localized and adapted for different target cultures, however, often depends less on how close the target culture is to the brand's culture of origin than on the extent to which a company or brand has developed an independent corporate culture.

ⓘ Why five test users are enough for a usability test is described by Jakob Nielsen here:
⟶ bit.ly/14L4LB

USER EXPERIENCE TESTING

Conducted using qualitative methods, UX testing examines the entire experience that users have when interacting with a digital app. This builds up a comprehensive picture that takes into account the most important aspects of the user as well as the brand experience. The focus is not only on the effective and efficient use of a digital product or service, but also on factors such as emotions, joy of use and brand confidence.

TRY IT YOURSELF

When an existing product or service is being relaunched or optimized, experience has shown that designers should use the product or service themselves over the course of the project. A designer quickly establishes a proprietary attitude towards the brand and can build a list of requirements and ideas for improvement. If working prototypes have been created, these can also be tested. But don't lose your prototypes – like one Apple employee who'd been issued with a brand-new iPhone 4 did – unless you're aiming to cash in on the publicity.

FASHION GOES MOBILE

MARKUS ALLER
HUGO BOSS

&

JOACHIM BADER
CLANMO

Markus and Joachim, I would like to talk with you about the role of interactive and, in particular, mobile media for luxury brands. How important are online media and social media today at HUGO BOSS? And how has this changed in recent years?

Markus Aller: Their importance has grown enormously. This has to do, of course, with the arrival of e-commerce as a distribution channel. But web presence as a whole is crucial if we want to address the end user via mobile media. There are an infinite number of ways to reprocess the content that we generate in the company and make it mobile-friendly. And there's also the challenge of integrating retail. All of this has evolved tremendously in recent years.

Quite frankly, we used to think that we needed mobile to stay on trend, but didn't know much about content or concepts. In fact, the first thing we discovered was how to engage the user and

what we can actually use it for. The exciting thing is that now the company is willing to pursue mobile media in a professional way and not just as a peripheral project. It is a very, very important channel, and our monthly figures prove that, both in hits to the mobile website and downloads in the app store. The demand is there, which is why we're now creating appropriate content for mobile apps.

Joachim, you were an early adopter of mobile marketing. Today you're director of CLANMO. What has changed and what is your focus today?

Joachim Bader: Before 2008, mobile had nothing to do with what CLANMO now does: mobile brand experiences, mobile commerce and mobile social media. Back then, we were mainly campaign-driven. That could mean SMS, MMS, Bluetooth, sometimes games that you could download or even mobile websites. But it really was all about campaigns and less about what we do now. We create mobile hubs for our clients: the first point where the mobile user comes into contact with the brand. What's happening now is fascinating. Agency clients who started with mobile brand experiences now want mobile commerce.

Markus, you have various sub-brands, from BOSS Black to the premium brand BOSS Selection, to BOSS Orange, the younger label that also targets women. Are there BOSS brands that are better suited to mobile devices? To what extent does the brand architecture play a role?

Markus: It definitely plays a role. BOSS Black, for example, is the biggest line and the one that makes the most money. Therefore it's much more of a focus for the business than, say, BOSS Green, which accounts for just two percent of all revenue. The trend in mobile communications is towards HUGO, because HUGO is innovative and cool. That brand actually has the coolest content. HUGO and BOSS Black, followed by BOSS Orange, are currently the three lines that are best suited for mobile. A BOSS Green app would reach too few customers, even though there's some overlap; a Green customer may also be a Black customer, wearing suits for business and going golfing in his free time. Brand availability also varies country by country. In Japan, the use of mobile devices is much higher than traditional PCs or notebooks now. Most Japanese people use the mobile web to go online; home PCs are no longer popular there.

Joachim: The question we discussed at the very beginning was: Where is the mobile target

group located within HUGO BOSS as a whole? That's why we launched an iPhone app in 2009, because, back then, it was more of a lifestyle tool for early adopters who had quite a lot of money or disposable income. We jointly decided that this kind of platform was right for our brand positioning. Only later did we follow suit by launching a mobile portal for everyone. For most of the brands, we do it the other way around. For the BOSS brand, that was certainly the right way.

The platforms you currently use are primarily information-driven or campaign-driven. What other considerations are there?

Joachim: Of course, the collections are presented both on the iPhone app as well as the portal. There are also service features, such as a store finder, or the ability to create a Wish List of products you like. This goes beyond pure information. There are features that are unique to the iPhone, such as colour matching: you can take a picture of your shirt and can see what colour in the collection matches it – this only works with a cellphone. The goal for mobile should be to offer more than just a smaller version of the main site.

The point is to find the added value in mobile and make that the focus. Sometimes less is more, if you do it right.

On the other hand, don't forget that lots of people today who tap 'HUGO BOSS' into the search engine on their phones are expecting special offers. They no longer visit the website via a laptop or PC. For them, the cellphone has replaced the laptop. This is a new kind of user scenario, and means you can't just give them gimmicks if what they really want tosee is collections.

Markus: Knowing user needs is vital. Two years ago, we could still launch an iPhone app relatively easily without asking 'Does this really make sense?' For us, it was definitely useful because it pushed the market to embrace the mobile web. Without the iPhone, we would not be where we are now. There would also be no Galaxys or other competitors. Producing a tablet version of eMAG, our online magazine, certainly makes sense, because that's what it's there for. It the ideal platform for a combination of static and dynamic content, text, images and even music.

Does it make sense to sell fashion via mobile phones?

Markus: Absolutely. M-commerce will come. A good percentage of revenue share comes from store access via the mobile portal – surprisingly high even though the portal is not yet optimized.

Which products are sold in this way? How do you choose the range?

Markus: I wouldn't include as much detail in a mobile store as in a classic online store. We also

don't show the complete collection on the mobile site as we do on the main site; that's just too much. This allows us to set priorities, move away from product-driven campaigns and focus on m-commerce.

Joachim: I think the trend in the commerce sector is moving towards including everything. If we have a client who has 50,000 products, they'll all be on show. Of course, there will always be the 80: 20 rule: you make 80 percent of your sales with 20 percent of your products, but we don't yet know which ones these are. At HUGO BOSS we could also include everything, depending on the country; China has a different product portfolio to Germany, for example.

Markus: The main online store handles things in a similar way: America buys different products to Europe. But I think mobile campaigns should do it differently. You have a lot more options when you connect with social media.

What are collaborations like, both between the company and the agency, and between different agencies? What is the role of agencies at BOSS? Are they sounding boards or implementers?

Markus: We generally have a digital lead, an agency that we work with a lot on development and brainstorming. The agency lead typically comes from the online sector. And now, for the past two or three years, Joachim and his team have been our mobile lead. Things aren't always simple. At our last Agency Day there were almost thirty people. It was quite interesting to see everyone sitting at one table. But we don't use a large circle of agencies. I want to keep it deliberately small and define and assign clear responsibilities. I find this works very well.

Our agencies are not implementers, but their consulting services are very important. We're not experts and we need to get an overview of all digital channels. The agencies are the specialists.

There's give and take. We write briefs with clear goals or directions, but it's important that there's lively dialogue and an exchange of ideas between the mobile lead and the online lead.

This confirms one of the basic hypotheses behind this book: that the role of digital agencies has changed dramatically in the past few years. They've moved from being service providers, who were purely involved with implementation in that particular channel, towards becoming a sounding board for companies.

Markus: That is only because the companies and brands have now reached that point. I think agencies have had the ability to do this for quite

some time. I notice this with us. I've been here since 2000 and I've been through everything you can go through. In the past, the company's way of thinking was just not there yet. I could have briefed agencies from here to Timbuktu, but if they hadn't said 'We'll put our money where our mouth is and start shooting now,' nothing would have come of it. In the past, agencies got images from me and put them online, and then we added more content. But this integration and the changes within agencies that you mention could have happened much earlier. It depends on how open companies are.

Joachim: Digital agencies have become more important because of the growth of the medium. To me it's a matter of relevance. The more relevant something is, the more people expect of digital agencies, wanting them not only to adapt but to develop something new and original within the limits specified by the brand. It used to be expected that an interactive campaign would involve text messaging. Today a company has a basic framework, and wants the agency to supply the digital or mobile component of this framework – and that is a very big difference.

You create your traditional communication in house, in collaboration with out-of-house specialists such as photographers and stylists. What is the foundation of HUGO BOSS's marketing? Is it that the spirit of HUGO BOSS is strong here and retains that strength when it's passed on to agencies? And what does that mean in return for people who work on your team? What skills do they need to meet all these requirements?

234

235

Markus: In the end it comes down to motivation and believing in your own work. And taking advantage of the opportunity to approach each new project quite freely. You can feel that freedom on my team. Of course, there may be some restrictions on ideas if they're too complicated or too offensive. We don't need any super-specialists. I wasn't born an internet user, either; I used to do something else before this, and this is true of many others in this industry. You need openness to absorb new things and to be inspired. For example, when I leaf through magazines and newspapers, I see graphics and think 'That could be useful for our eMAG', or 'That image would be cool on an iPad'. I cut them out and pin them on the wall for the team. We all get commission because everyone has different interests and they all enrich each other.

Many people seem to feel that everything is getting increasingly analogue: tearing things out and pinning them on the wall....

Markus: I've always believed this. At one time, everyone said that the traditional way of doing things was dead because suddenly everything was digital. But I don't think so. Of course, some things die away, but that is justifiable because everything evolves. But lots of good things will remain relevant and leave their mark. *Wallpaper* and *Monocle*, for example, are print magazines that are here to stay.

Markus Aller is team leader of online media at HUGO BOSS. Joachim Bader is the managing director of CLANMO.

III

GOOD PRACTICE

—

Brand Communication on the Web

BYRK MÖBEL / HEINEKEN / JÄGERMEISTER /
EDDING WALL OF FAME /
BURBERRY / CONVERSE / THE GUARDIAN

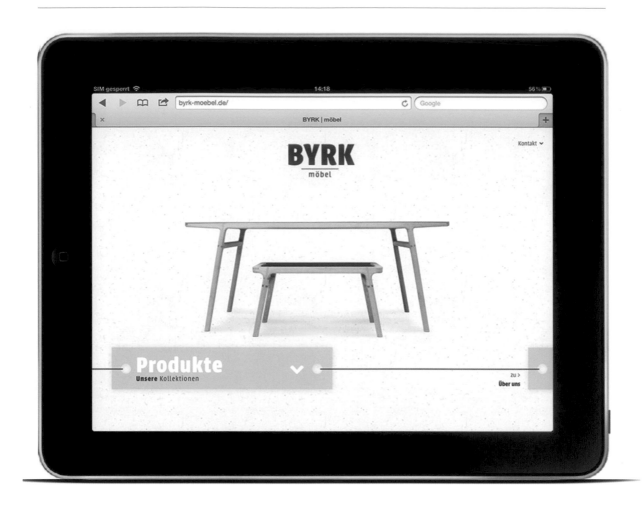

BYRK MÖBEL

THINK MOTO

Websites and mobile apps are more than just forms of advertising: they are often marketing, sales and service channels in one. It is therefore important to carefully consider context of use from the start. Who will use this app, when and why? Whether it is an e-business or a more traditional trade, it is important to identify the added value that the new medium can deliver.

For the German furniture brand BYRK Möbel, the website is not only a virtual showroom for customers but also serves as a corporate presentation platform at trade shows and with dealers. The site was therefore optimized for the iPad.

BYRK Möbel manufactures high-quality sustainable household furniture. Only organically produced materials are used in the firm's print communications and packaging, and their tactile quality is represented by the website's textured background.

www.byrk-moebel.de

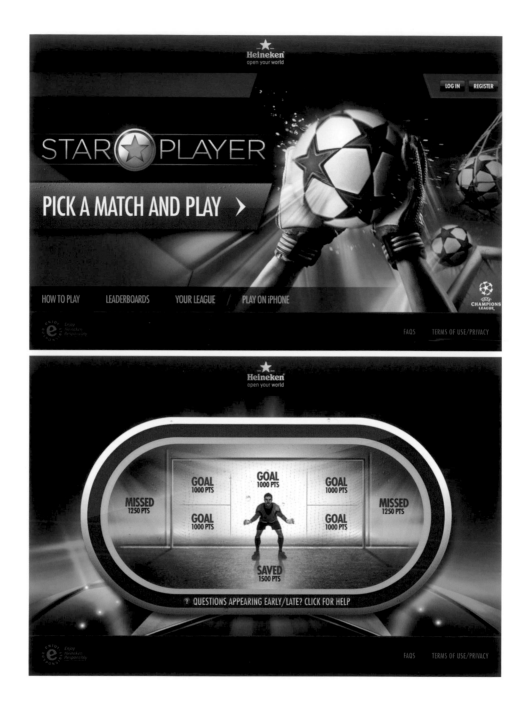

HEINEKEN

AKQA

Heineken has been an active sponsor of the UEFA Champions League since 2005. In 2010 initial measures were taken to go beyond mere brand awareness by developing a platform that actively involved users and created a tangible connection between Heineken beer, football and the UEFA Champions League. Based on the statistic that 72% of the audience watch the UEFA Champions League at home alone (source: UEFA), AKQA developed Heineken Star Player, a smartphone app that transformed watching a UEFA Champions League game on TV into a live social experience. During the game, questions are asked about the game in real time. If a penalty kick, free kick or corner kick is awarded, the user must predict where the ball will go. Users can team up with or compete against other players. The game is based on anticipation – a natural state while watching a match. The app is a great realization of the brand values of fun and passion and the business maxim 'consumer-inspired'.

JÄGERMEISTER

SYZYGY AND Hi-ReS!

The online presence of Jägermeister presents its products as heroes, alongside the well-known brand symbols: ice, glasses and the stag logo. The focus is the unmistakable bottle. The 3D website leads visitors into new areas that reflect the various facets of the brand. The technically complex website has a high degree of immersion – a site for the young party generation that wants to celebrate its favourite beverage.

www.jaegermeister.com

JÄGERMEISTER AT HOME

SYZYGY AND Hi-ReS!

In contrast to its main online presence, Jägermeister At Home attempts to reach an older, more restrained target group that prefers to celebrate at home rather than in a nightclub. The idea is that if the target audience won't come to Jägermeister, then Jägermeister will go to the target group. The goal of Jägermeister At Home was to find real stories told by real people. The strangest, funniest and most moving stories could end with a Jägermeister home visit. The winners got to throw a party at home with friends accompanied by lots of Jägermeister

on ice and a Jägermeister bartender. The event was shadowed by a Jägermeister camera crew and Jägermeister moderator and captured on film. The result was a series of very short films showing the target group relaxing at home, with their friends and Jägermeister, just the way they like it. The short films were presented to a wide audience on Jägermeister's YouTube channel and website, subtly spreading the campaign message.

www.jaegermeister.com

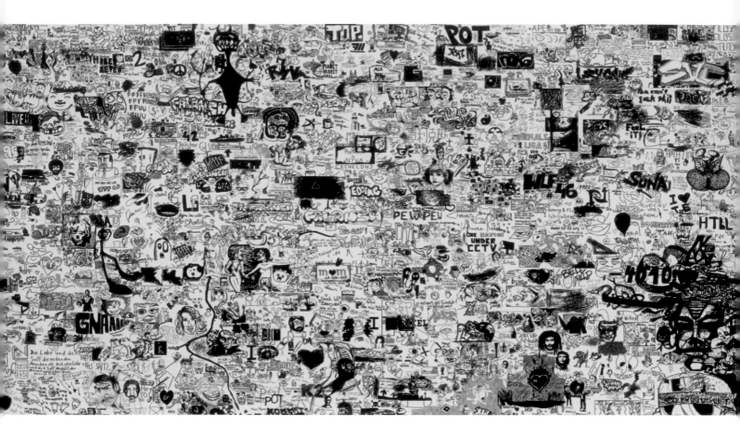

EDDING WALL OF FAME
KEMPERTRAUTMANN, DEMODERN

In January 2011, to celebrate the 50th anniversary of the pen manufacturer edding, the company launched a cross-media campaign. Part of this campaign was the edding Wall of Fame, an interactive online drawing board on which visitors could draw in real time using virtual edding pens, or choose to watch others draw. Over time, an enormous work of art was created, with millions of visitors worldwide taking part.

The edding Wall of Fame tries to recreate an analogue experience in feel, look and sound. The number of pens is limited; there are no erasers and no Undo function, just as with a real marker pen, and the typical sound made by a real edding is also emulated. In this way, the brand bridges the same gap its customers crossed a long time ago: working creatively in both analogue and digital media.

BURBERRY

Art of the Trench is a photosharing microsite for fans of Burberry trench coats. Burberry itself describes the site as a 'living document of the trench coat and the people who wear it'. The trench is a classic product by this iconic British brand and has a solid fan base, whose members were invited to share photos of themselves in a trench. Fashion blogger Scott Schuman (a.k.a. The Sartorialist) publicized the project to a broad spectrum of fashionistas. The Burberry team selected posts and put these on the microsite, which users could log onto via Facebook to comment on photos or 'like' and share them. In this way, Burberry managed to appeal to younger consumers, presenting itself in a media-appropriate manner without pandering to the new target group.

The viral marketing worked and, by 2010, a year after the launch of the page, Burberry had a 50% increase in profits. The Facebook page, which went online in July 2009, reached 3.8 million members in the first year. By September 2012, the total was 13 million.

CONVERSE
POWERFLASHER

Over its century of history, Converse has had its share of ups and downs, yet everyone knows the the star logo that makes 'Chucks' unmistakable. Converse's online presence logically places the star centrestage and succeeds in translating the typical Converse style into a relevant user experience.

The products are arranged in a star shape, and presented by a human avatar, who speaks to users and helps them with product selection. The fact that the scenes were filmed using a real actor makes them credible; the movements were subsequently digitally processed. The integration of news and campaigns is also suitably branded.

Saturday 2 May 2009

Britain's first swine flu cases are confirmed

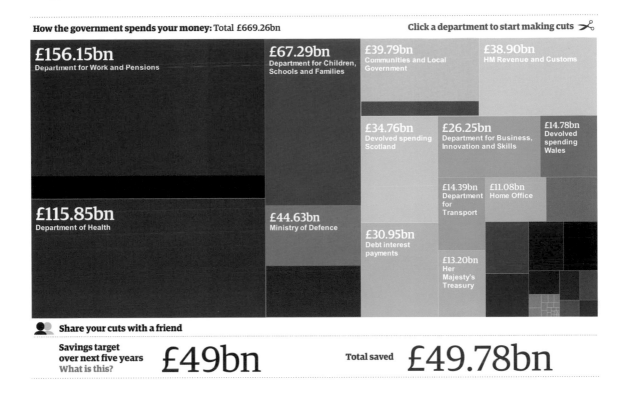

How the government spends your money: Total £669.26bn

Click a department to start making cuts ✂

£156.15bn
Department for Work and Pensions

£67.29bn
Department for Children,
Schools and Families

£39.79bn
Communities and Local
Government

£38.90bn
HM Revenue and Customs

£34.76bn
Devolved spending
Scotland

£26.25bn
Department for Business,
Innovation and Skills

£14.78bn
Devolved
spending
Wales

£14.39bn
Department
for
Transport

£11.08bn
Home Office

£115.85bn
Department of Health

£44.63bn
Ministry of Defence

£30.95bn
Debt interest
payments

£13.20bn
Her
Majesty's
Treasury

👥 Share your cuts with a friend

Savings target
over next five years
What is this?   £49bn

Total saved   £49.78bn

THE GUARDIAN

The Guardian is one of the UK's leading newspapers, known for its spacious, clear layout with large colour photographs and colourful information graphics. In 2006, for the first time, *The Guardian* published an article on its website before it had been published in print. In 2011, guardian.co.uk was the world's fifth most widely read newspaper website, not least because it continues to experiment with media-appropriate formats. In addition to collaborative journalism, in which readers contribute information and other material to articles, the interactive infographics are heavily responsible for extending *The Guardian*'s digital brand image.

Above: 'You Make the Cuts' visualizes UK government spending and lets users start applying the famous red pencil. The app has a double effect. As users click through the expenditures of different government departments and remove the items of their choice,

they get a sense of the importance of budgets. At the same time, users can share their suggested cuts and scrutinize decisions. This example demonstrates how a newspaper brand remains not only visually consistent, but also supports its claim of an open, transparent information culture.
→ bit.ly/8Z6yiH

Opposite: 'The Year in Review' is a series of interactive photo galleries, summarizing the main stories for each day in a given year. Additionally, shown in a photo spread, they offer a bird's eye perspective of that year's events. Users can bookmark stories, share these with friends, or participate in polls. The visual branding is consistent and fulfils one of the newspaper's central promises – to provide an overview of a complex world – by exploiting the potential of the digital medium.
→ bit.ly/6wpyOA

4

DELIVER

252
253

DOCUMENTS AND PRODUCTION

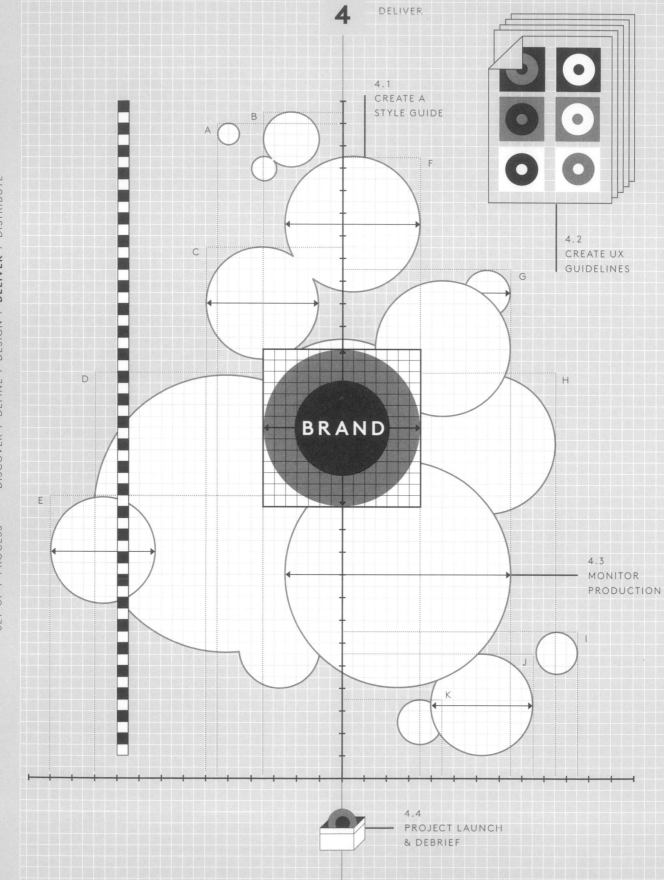

SET-UP / PROCESS —— DISCOVER / DEFINE / DESIGN / **DELIVER** / DISTRIBUTE

4.1
CREATE A
STYLE GUIDE

4.2
CREATE UX
GUIDELINES

A

B

C

D

E

F

G

H

I

J

K

BRAND

4.3
MONITOR
PRODUCTION

4.4
PROJECT LAUNCH
& DEBRIEF

The concept and design are complete. Now it's time to ensure that the design is properly implemented. To do this, we create style guides and UX guidelines and monitor the technical implementation.

In the Delivery phase, the design team documents the conceptual and creative decisions in a style guide and supplementary UX guidelines. However, during production, there may still be questions that the detailed design documentation (P. 177), the style guide and the UX guidelines cannot answer. We must therefore monitor implementation, support asset production and ensure quality. After the launch, a debrief takes place, in which what has been learned is documented and a case study is created.

4.1

CREATE A STYLE GUIDE

SET-UP / PROCESS —— DISCOVER / DEFINE / DESIGN / **DELIVER** / DISTRIBUTE

Style guides are key tools in brand management for businesses and provide a challenge for everybody who works with them. A style guide must convey easily and quickly how the brand image (P. 129) should be maintained at the brand touchpoints. The goal of a corporate style guide is to ensure that the brand visuals remain consistent and coherent across all channels. In other words, style guides control the brand experience. To this end, they must retain a degree of flexibility while including all relevant design rules. This particularly applies to digital media as these are subject to both technical restrictions and dynamic development.

Interactive corporate design is not merely an 'add-on' to traditional style guides. The influence of interactive media on the perception of brands is now so significant in many industries that features such as navigation, interaction paradigms, gestures, animation and sound should all be considered when designing a corporate identity. Unfortunately this happens far too rarely. A prerequisite for having interactive designers and traditional corporate designers work on a joint design strategy is finding a work process that brings together techniques from both realms. Ways of doing this are presented in the Define and Discover chapters.

The groundwork for the style guide has already been laid in the detailed design documentation (P. 177) because the DDD contains vital data about information architecture, user navigation and visual design. Much of this, however, refers specifically to the implementation of the project and documents the only relevant details. The style guide, however, must be more universal, in order to cover any future BIxD projects developed for the brand.

The design rules on which the style guide is based are defined and recorded during the Design phase. The structure of the style guide should be planned well in advance. However, it only makes sense to turn the style guide into a printable manual – usually in PDF format – or a web portal (BRAND MANAGEMENT PORTALS, P. 310) after the completion of the project, since rules may change before the end. At the end of the Design phase, I recommend creating a preliminary style guide, version 1.0, which, together with the DDD, can serve as a production template. After the launch and after an initial operating phase of several months, you should update to version 1.1. Following an international rollout (PLAN THE ROLLOUT, P. 307), there will be more additions that can be documented in version 1.2 in the form of a supplement for different markets.

✓ AN INTERACTIVE BRAND STYLE GUIDE SHOULD...

1　Ensure a consistent brand presence across all channels and markets, including country-specific considerations.

2　Ensure a unified customer experience that fits the target group and can also be applied to new products and services.

3　Demonstrate the creative scope for campaigns and advertising.

4　Raise the visual and formal quality of thexbrand identity as a whole.

5　Reduce the cost and complexity of the rollout and subsequent projects (PLAN THE ROLLOUT, P. 307).

6　Contain as few rules as possible, but as many as are needed to control the brand experience.

7　Be flexible in its application and demonstrate that interpretations may vary, ensuring that the style guide will remain relevant.

8　Explain the strategic basis behind the rules: this will help when passing on the design rules to others (BRAND FILTERS, P. 137).

9　Be always available and regularly updated.

10　Provide style sheets, templates, code snippets and UX guidelines in addition to style rules (P. 270).

STYLE GUIDE
TARGET GROUPS

A style guide should always be consulted when something new is developed for the brand – whether it is a new app, an ad campaign or an additional service. A style guide for interactive media is aimed at the editors and the internal design and development team, as well as agencies and external service providers. Depending on the type of project, these are:

ON THE CLIENT SIDE:

- web manager and online editors
- internal web developer and system programmers
- internal creation and content development (marketing, campaign planning)
- brand management
- corporate communications
- product management
- customer services

ON THE AGENCY/SERVICE PROVIDER SIDE:

- designers in creative agencies, design agencies and advertising agencies
- media planners in media agencies
- programmers and technical service providers

Business and distribution partners can also be target groups for style guides if they include advertising materials on their online platforms or in their brochures. These cases have to be considered early on and rules for co-branding taken into account.

THE FEATURES OF
DIGITAL MEDIA

Corporate designers may be used to creating style guides for print media, but digital media have their own special features that should be considered when an interactive style guide is being created.

1   DIGITAL MEDIA ARE DYNAMIC

Digital media are constantly evolving. Technical standards have short life cycles. New developments like the iPad become very big, very quickly, and this is also true of apps. Google, blogs, Twitter and Facebook look like they are here to stay. The photosharing app Instagram was sold for $1 billion to Facebook just a year and a half after its launch. On the other hand, Second Life and Myspace are yesterday's news.

On average, a leading website changes its look about every eighteen months. This dynamic should be built in when creating a BIxD style guide. Insisting on predefined rules may seem logical but, in cases of doubt, only leads to a brand looking outdated quickly. Another important point is that the specific context of use of an interactive touchpoint must be considered. Websites or mobile apps are used in a particular context, and the same applies to an even greater extent to interactive installations in public spaces. The user may be in a hurry and not expecting a wide range of interactions, so brand elements must be presented clearly and concisely.

2   DIGITAL MEDIA ARE MULTIMEDIA

Digital apps include motion – from simple interactive animations to video clips – and sound, which enhance the intensity of the experience. The use of animation, video or sound needs to be regulated in the same way as the logo, font and colours. However, these aspects should not be viewed in isolation for the website or app, but considered under existing guidelines for traditional media such as TV, radio ads or events.

3   DIGITAL MEDIA ARE NETWORKED

Connectivity is a central feature of digital media. Software and hardware are interlinked and allow the seamless transmission of information (and experiences) between different platforms, so that the same data can be accessed anywhere in different everyday situations. The challenge for designers is to prepare the data to suit multiple devices. For screen-based media that is nothing new: e-books, movies or multimedia notes can be synced between devices via the cloud, e.g. you can continue to watch a video on your tablet at the same point where you stopped watching it on your desktop PC. Objects and

everyday devices are also increasingly networked. The challenge for brand guidelines primarily involves defining behavioural and operating models to fit the brand.

4   DIGITAL MEDIA ARE FLEXIBLE

Today there is a variety of different display formats, from smartphones, tablets and notebooks to workstations with 30-inch screens. These have different screen resolutions and width-to-height ratios. In addition, users, especially in browser-based apps, can change the size of the window itself. Websites, apps and desktop software must work visually at different sizes. The leading brand management elements must be recognizable in all formats and reproduced in a brand-appropriate way.

5   DIGITAL MEDIA ARE SHARED

Digital media are communication media, like the BBSs of the early 1990s, the text-based virtual worlds of MUSHes (multi-user shared habitats), graphic virtual worlds such as Second Life a few years ago, or social media platforms such as blogs, Facebook, Pinterest or Flickr. Digital media create social spaces of communication and collaboration, for playing and sharing. The social potential has contributed to the success of the internet and purely digital business models such as eBay or Amazon initially built heavily on the community aspect: eBay was more than an auction platform; it was a community of people who shared special interests and hobbies and could discuss these

SET-UP / PROCESS ———— DISCOVER / DEFINE / DESIGN / **DELIVER** / DISTRIBUTE

worldwide via the platform. The same is true for Amazon: it's not just about buying books; it's about being a reader, creating wish lists, sharing purchases and writing reviews.

Traditional companies made early attempts to exploit this potential, but even today, their dealings with social media can be fraught with uncertainties and misunderstandings. These often stem from the fact that Facebook and Twitter are treated in the same way as conventional marketing channels without taking the company business model or brand strategy into account. First of all, you must determine which digital touchpoints are appropriate for a brand (TOUCHPOINTS, P. 116). The specific product category should also be considered (INTERVIEW, P. 152). Aimless me-too enthusiasm is counter-productive.

The BIxD process presented in this book can help to answer these questions. How does the brand want people to participate? Are openness, closeness, and intimacy relevant to the product category? Does the brand fit the target group and the business model? And how can a traditional, closely controlled brand be transformed into a more open and relaxed brand? The issues that interactive branding guidelines have to cover – whether these are style guides or UX guidelines (P. 270) – are complex.

HOW MANY STYLE GUIDES DOES A BRAND NEED?

It may be useful or even necessary to lay down a separate set of rules for each of a brand's digital channels. A solid foundation could include rules for the following:

- style guide for the company portal, the corporate website or online shop
- UX guidelines (P. 270)
- style guide for microsites
- style guide for app software for customers and within the company
- templates and guidelines for email marketing
- templates and guidelines for videos and/or podcasts
- templates for interactive presentations in PowerPoint
- behaviour guidelines for social media

In addition, you will also need guidelines for overarching concepts, such as tone of voice and user guidance, which must remain consistent across countries and across markets; the mechanisms and steps for customizing a site; the integration and use of social media; the building and management of a brand community – and more.

The result is a complex set of interconnected documents, which are difficult to create and, because they are so closely linked, even more difficult to maintain. It is therefore a good idea to begin with a comprehensive web style guide that goes further than the two to three sample layouts shown in the corporate design manual, which many companies still use a basis for all their digital output. In a basic web style guide of this kind, special emphasis should be placed on clearly identifying the key branded elements and on emphasizing flexibility and modularity.

STYLE SHEETS AND STYLE GUIDE POSTERS

To maintain an overview of the visual language, interface elements and modules, designers can collect all the elements together in a single document (e.g. Photoshop, InDesign or Fireworks) during the Design phase. This file should contain the correct settings for typography, shadows, gradients, and element sizes and can be used directly by the developer. It can also be printed out during production and used by editors in the creation of content, which is why, at think moto, we like to call it a 'style guide poster'. During the Design phase, this kind of 'master' file is invaluable for reference, especially when multiple designers are working on the same project.

BENEFITS OF ONLINE STYLE GUIDES

Style guides, like other sets of rules, should be reviewed regularly and revised if needed. This is especially true for web style guides. The need for corporate change and the introduction of new company-wide policies can quickly result in organizational and logistical problems within large multinationals. Problems may arise with an app, for example, because obsolete versions are still in circulation.

A possible solution to these problems is an online style guide that displays the rules in an interactive form. In addition, websites can be used to provide implementation examples, prototypes or templates and style sheets for downloading. Large companies usually have a brand portal that can be used for this task (BRAND MANAGEMENT PORTALS, P. 310). But remember that an online style guide or a brand portal is a brand touchpoint and therefore should follow the rules of the style guide itself. We should lead by example if we expect employees and service providers to apply the same rules later.

An online style guide or brand management portal with examples and templates for work, code downloads, a forum or Wiki and a contact for brand management can significantly reduce costs, save time and improve quality, as well as creating the opportunity for gathering and discussing ideas. Nonetheless, online style guides may also have disadvantages. For companies with stringent security requirements or a more conservative corporate culture and therefore a more cautious attitude to the internal use of digital media, a print version may be more appropriate. In addition, printed documents can be browsed, annotated, hung on the wall and so on. It is therefore advisable to produce a handout to accompany the launch of an online style guide (SWISSCOM, P. 338).

✔ THE BENEFITS OF ONLINE STYLE GUIDES

▸ **UP TO DATE:** The current version is always available; this avoids errors created by outdated information and questions that have already been answered.

▸ **MODULAR:** Simple links can be created between different sets of rules.

▸ **COST-EFFECTIVE TO CREATE AND DISTRIBUTE:** A website is easier to update than an InDesign document exported as a PDF, and is more cost-effective than providing a printed document.

▸ **INTERACTIVE:** Details can be more clearly conveyed in interactive form than on paper. Dimensions can appear with the click of a mouse, guided tours can explain complex processes (STORYTELLING, PRODUCT PROMOS AND GUIDED TOURS, P. 306), and on-demand glossaries or interactive question-and-answer sessions can aid customer choice.

▸ **EXPANDABLE:** It is easy to add new rules to an online style guide, for example, if country- or app-specific exceptions are introduced during an international rollout.

BRAND BOOKS

The launch of a new brand identity should be accompanied by a brand book or brochure about the product launch. If the majority of the company's employees are not familiar with the project, they should be informed about the strategy that lies behind it. Some stakeholders, however, need more detailed guidelines to conduct their work. It is impractical to include both in a single document.

A style guide must provide a clear set of rules and should be as unpretentious as possible. However, a brand book can and should evoke emotion, convey the spirit of the new look and invite the reader into the world of the brand.

CONSTRUCTING A WEB STYLE GUIDE

A style guide ensures that a brand identity is consistently and effectively maintained across all media. The goal is to achieve a positive brand image and increase the recognizability of a brand, product or company. The style guide documents the design rules based on predefined visual categories (P. 209).

Take, for example, the online portal of an international company. The style guide will look something like this.

SAMPLE CONTENT FOR A WEB STYLE GUIDE

1   INTRODUCTION

The introduction includes a contents page, a glossary and a document history, which makes it clear where and when changes have been made. Specific target group information should also be included, as should instructions explaining which sections of the style guide are relevant for which target group.

2   STRATEGIC BACKGROUND

A style guide should not repeat the project strategy in detail, but should stick to the central issues: the goal of the project, a summary of the basic brand strategy, the navigation path and the brand filters. A summary of the design direction presentation (P. 176) will help to explain why design decisions have been made. Optionally, other sub-concepts such as customized web content or the use of social media may be added.

3   VISUAL DESIGN FOUNDATIONS

Similar to a style guide for traditional media, this section presents the basic visual design rules, including header and logo use on websites and on mobile devices, typography, colour, treatment of static and moving images, icons, forms, tables, charts, infographics, grids and sound design. These visual categories are defined during the Design phase (P. 209).

4   NAVIGATION SYSTEM

A website's navigation system must take multiple devices into account. Every level of navigation should be presented. The sitemap and the web landscape are appended in a simplified version of the style guide or presented in 'Structure and Page Types' (section 6). Alternative navigation paths are demonstrated, such as filters for specific product features or specific ways to visualize cross-links between relevant content. Navigation methods, such as drop-down menus or animated roll-overs, can be described in both text and images. Even better, a prototype could be made that takes the UX guidelines (P. 270) into account.

5   LAYOUT ELEMENTS (MODULES AND INTERACTION ELEMENTS)

Layout elements such as modules, teasers and buttons help to create structure and emphasize content and features. They establish a visual language, which, in turn, can be divided into different functional categories (P. 209). The use and positioning of layout elements should be described, along with their colour, size, dimensions, etc.

6   STRUCTURE AND PAGE TYPES

Style consistency must not only be addressed at page level. Information architecture – the structure of different page types across multiple sites or apps – is crucial for online brand recognition and needs to be addressed, including localized adaptations where applicable (PLAN THE ROLLOUT, P. 307). A simplified representation of the templates, the layout grid and the sitemap will give a better understanding of the structural principles. Sitemaps and wireframes are complex documents and should not be included in the style guide.

7 TEMPLATES

Templates typically consist of multiple containers and modules, which, in turn, are made up of elements (such as headers, text blocks and images). Modular design allows websites to maintain a unified look while remaining flexible in their organization. The individual templates are documented in wireframes for development. The style guide usually only shows final layouts, but you can choose to extract descriptions from the wireframe if they are relevant. Premade templates and style sheets can be made available for download through a brand management portal (P. 310).

8 TECHNICAL REQUIREMENTS

A style guide always includes the technical requirements for an app. In the case of websites, this usually means the browser versions and screen resolutions for which they have been optimized. For software and apps, it means the operating system. A brief summary of the technological architecture can be included if it is relevant for maintaining and operating the app.

9 DESIGN MANAGEMENT AND CONTACT INFORMATION

The internal handling of the brand, the structures and processes of design management (P. 309) and continuous product development (UX LEAN AND BIxD, P. 319) are described in this section. This includes the allocation of responsibilities within the company or project team and contact information in the case of questions.

10 APPENDICES

Additional documents can be added to the back of a style guide to form a sort of reference library. These may include the style guide poster with style sheets (P. 261), the original requirements, a link to an online version of the style guide or to the brand management portal (P. 310) and other relevant documents, such as the detailed design documentation (P. 177) or the UX guidelines (P. 270).

MULTISCREEN STRATEGIES

CHRISTOPHE STOLL &
JOHANNES SCHARDT

PRECIOUS

You are a 'design studio for strategic design and visual languages'. What distinguishes your approach to design?

Christophe: We are designers who ask lots of questions and practice constructive criticism. We want to understand what we're doing and why something is being done, and what the business processes are that lead to certain decisions. We need to understand what we do. We need to understand the material, the scope and the context.

Johannes: Let's take the example of Native Instruments: They have a research and development department that works on product design and – at an early stage in the development process – thinks about which features and functions should exist. But we do more than simply paint in the details; we initiate an iterative development process that also includes

discussions – sometimes heated ones – with their own in-house designers. The separation of development and visual design doesn't work.

What role does the brand play in projects like this? For example, to what extent does Native Instruments as a brand – and by that I don't just mean the logo – play a role?

Christophe: Actually, there is a wide gap between what we as a brand feel is important, and what is traditionally regarded as a brand – the logo, the website, the marketing, the packaging, the classic attributes. For us, a brand is something else: logo, fonts and colours are important, but we like to look beyond the graphic facade and look for brand-building potential there. There's often only one rule: put the logo on it. That's okay, but it is not enough. Instead we prefer to think: what is the core concept and which visual language fits it best? What is the style that characterizes the software?

And what are the recurring patterns? How can you reuse them in different software products? What constitutes the brand? How do specific interactions work? How do you choose a filter? These elements are much more important for us.

A challenge for brands is to create a consistent experience and not to ignore the fact that different platforms have different interaction patterns. You call this a multiscreen strategy. How do you go about creating one?

Christophe: The basic dilemma is that we're fascinated by gadgets and the technologies that go with them. It is also fun for us to try out the latest stuff, because you have to do it when it's your job. But on the other hand, you can easily get too focused on the technology and risk losing sight of the user. What good is that to the user?

What does it mean to have different screens and different formats and to be constantly connected and have a screen with you at all times? We're fascinated by this idea.

That is why – from a very early stage – we've always considered everything from the user's point of view as well.

Is there something that's a bottom line for you? When you're designing for multiple screens, is there anything that should always be considered?

Christophe: We call it an ecosystem of screens. It's an appropriate metaphor.

We no longer design for individual products, but rather for services or systems, and the systems can have multiple touchpoints.

We focus primarily on devices, although we've also created devices that go beyond standard consumer-driven products, such as embedded touchscreens. But the intriguing question is: how can everything be connected? The challenge here is not just thinking about the products, but also about the relationships between products and the relationships between products and users; it means thinking in networks. How do these things affect each other? What happens if I switch from one device to another? We design the relationships just as actively as we design the individual UIs.

Can you illustrate this using Native Instruments as an example?

Johannes: You can't squeeze an entire music production studio or another piece of complex desktop software onto a small device. Instead, we asked: when might a user want to incorporate a mobile device as part of their workflow? And then it is natural to think in terms of sketches. Imagine you're out and about, have an idea and want to jot down a beat or record a melody. This is the direction that we've pushed things in. Visually, the desktop UI and mobile UI are closely compliant with one another.

In addition to user scenarios and questions regarding the functions and the features of the mobile version, the interesting question is: how can the visual language of the Native Instruments brand be transferred to a realm that has its own patterns? So there's the challenge: how can we apply what we have built for Native Instruments to the iPhone world, without ending up with a generic iPhone app that looks too much like it was made by Apple? Even a technical feature like the high-resolution retina screen is a challenge because it creates a different aesthetic.

While we're doing this interview, your client who set up shop here two weeks ago is right next door. What is your collaboration with clients like?

Johannes: We're still in the very early stages of the process and we're working very closely with the client's ideas. For us, this is actually an ideal scenario, or at least one that we like very much. We've worked with some start-ups in similar situations. You can't just pick up a brief and work on it independently of the development process, and then present results later.

For a fixed phase of a project you become part of a small and motivated team and work in very close contact with all the major decision-makers.

Then at some point you might leave the team, and pass the work on to a more established and mature in-house team and take part only at specific points.

Christophe: Many start-ups also get designers involved from the start. They have developers who understand the platform and then in-house designers from an early stage. This does not mean that they don't ever work with people like us. But they have in-house designers who speak the language of designers: they can work together well and flexibly with small studios that can do one thing particularly well because they understand it. It is no longer the case that a marketing manager needs someone who 'can meet him at eye level' or talk to him using the same vocabulary because he doesn't understand what the designers are doing.

What added value can a designer give a start-up, beyond designing products and corporate identities?

Christophe: It depends. When a start-up is technically driven, then you're employed as a designer and bring your own design thinking.

You can ask questions like: 'Have you ever thought about this another way? And have you considered what that means from a user perspective? Or what happens when you think and work more visually?' So it can really be a question of basic orientation. We are now working with a company that isn't a start-up, but is a new project by a former start-up.

Since we only work on development, we've got a complete development department. It's all about being advocates for the user.

We have to keep considering the user's point of view and reinforcing the idea that design is more than pasting together existing modules to make an interface that works.

268
—
269

Christophe Stoll and Johannes Schardt, Precious, Hamburg.

4.2

CREATE UX GUIDELINES

While a style guide mainly describes the visual identity of an interactive product and is usually aimed primarily at marketing and editorial staff, UX guidelines focus on the UX and interaction design, and so are aimed more at designers and developers who build or develop the product. The dividing line between style guide and UX guidelines is blurred because in the best cases, the style guide and the UX guidelines are identical. This is not always possible, however: e.g. if the branding department requires a traditional style guide in PDF format, or if the design team are solely responsible for the UX strategy and the creation of a comprehensive style guide is not part of the project. In addition, classic style guide manuals cannot cover complex issues such as describing interaction paradigms for interaction designers and developers, or for complex multi-brand frameworks, as in the case study for Sagem Wireless (P. 273). Last but not least, the decision on whether UX guidelines are needed in addition to a style guide depends on the corporate culture and the specific project. If the project involves providing an open platform to deliver third-party content or apps – e.g. the user interface of a mobile device – UX guidelines may not be appropriate.

▸ document the behaviour of
an interactive app, not just its
visual identity

▸ provide design frameworks for
visual and UX design

▸ provide interaction patterns in
pattern libraries

▸ describe complex brand frameworks
or multiscreen strategies that
cannot be illustrated within a
classic style guide structure

⟶ SEE NOKIA N9 UX GUIDELINES, P. 342

INTERACTION GUIDELINES

Interaction guidelines include rules that control
the behaviour of the interactive product, e.g.
animations, rollover states, navigation system.
Interaction guidelines can be added to the style
guide in the form of a handbook. However, it may
be a better idea to create Flash demos or short films
that represent specific aspects of the interaction in
moving images. For example, an interactive movie
was created by the agency Tribal DDB in London to
convey the dynamics and timing of web animations
in a playful way, while the interaction guidelines
were provided as a PDF for downloading.

UX DESIGN FRAMEWORKS

A user experience design framework replaces
the classic visual style guide, supplementary
documents and interaction guidelines with an
online platform that provides the visual design
guidelines in a way that is interactive and always
up to date, alongside code libraries, icons and
templates for downloading as well as examples
and demos. These frameworks are particularly
suitable for platform providers, such as operating
system vendors or providers of online virtual
environments. They serve multiple target groups
and aim to mobilize as many developers and
designers as the platform needs, while printed
style guides are usually not intended for the
public (NOKIA N9 UX GUIDELINES, P. 342).

PATTERN LIBRARIES

Companies that provide operating systems or other technological platforms for software or apps often offer pattern libraries. This will ensure that the applications not only look similar, but also provide a uniform user experience. Apple's brand-shaping interaction patterns for the iPhone and iPad are not only well documented but also patented. Via the App Store's submission process, which every app for iPhone and iPad must go through, Apple can ensure that all providers adhere to them. Apple's success is due not least to the fact that consistent attention is paid to compliance with OS X and iOS interaction patterns. On the other hand, Apple itself can easily update and modify its central control patterns, such as scroll direction, for the release of a new operating system version. It does this by implementing an overarching paradigm, such as multitouch control, consistently across all Apple devices.

Libraries of interaction design patterns are also useful for traditional software firms or companies that offer a more extensive digital product line. For example, educational publishers such as Cornelsen want all their software solutions to offer consistent control paradigms that allow the user to quickly switch between products and also help to build brand loyalty. This uniformity gives the brand's interactive products a feeling of familiarity.

MANY BRANDS, ONE EXPERIENCE

Hardware manufacturers and suppliers of operating systems and software platforms are faced with the challenge of providing not only a platform for third-party apps, but also offering these to brands that wish to apply their own branding to the hardware or system. This leads to the creation of co-branding solutions, which, in the best cases, combine a brand and user experience, and embody the brand values of both companies.

These are not white-label solutions, where the hardware manufacturer or OS provider remains invisible, but branded frameworks that allow other branded services to be offered. This creates partnerships, and it is important that the brands are well matched. Design agency Fjord developed this kind of multi-brand experience framework with the French mobile phone company Sagem Wireless, based on the Android mobile operating system. The brand toolkit for Sagem consisted of components for four different levels on which the interface could be customized (see opposite).

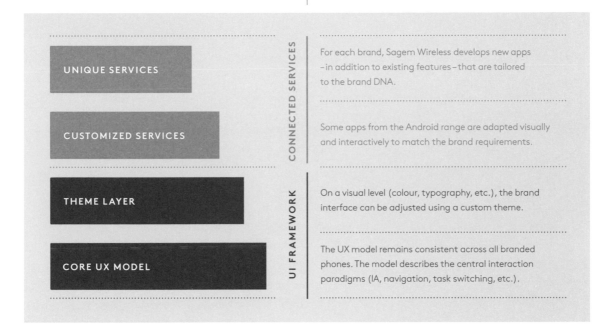

For each brand, Sagem Wireless develops new apps – in addition to existing features – that are tailored to the brand DNA.

Some apps from the Android range are adapted visually and interactively to match the brand requirements.

On a visual level (colour, typography, etc.), the brand interface can be adjusted using a custom theme.

The UX model remains consistent across all branded phones. The model describes the central interaction paradigms (IA, navigation, task switching, etc.).

CONCLUSION

Style guides and UX guidelines should always have an instructional remit. They are not paintboxes from which you can randomly select different colours – even if some less design-savvy stakeholders want to use them that way. Instead, they are intended to convey and illustrate the design foundations of a brand, showing how the brand feels in different contexts. If a style guide is to achieve this, it must be flexible. Nothing hurts the brand more than when it is run bureaucratically and the brand manager's mission is to push for stricter compliance rules.

MANY BRANDS, ONE EXPERIENCE

The Sagem Wireless branding toolkit includes four levels on which the Android operating system can be customized to meet co-branding requirements: the core UX model, the theming layer, the customized services already offered by Android and its own unique services (agency: Fjord).

4.3

MONITOR PRODUCTION

As thoroughly as we designers document our work, experience shows that we can always do more. I have often been shocked by the final outcome of a project if we do not stay actively involved during the technical implementation. The reasons for this may be political: the in-house IT department takes control, not the brand or marketing department, and the technical service providers are not willing to cooperate because they wanted to be involved in the design. More often, however, it is due to a lack of understanding or eye for detail on both the client and service side, or to time constraints. In order to meet a deadline, for example, entire task sets may have been put aside before the launch, and postponed to a later stage. Whatever the reasons may be, it's frustrating for everyone involved when a half-baked solution goes online.

If the service providers argue that the front-end functionality is unworkable or too complicated to implement, you should look for a design team – either an agency or freelancers – who can take over the development of the HTML or Flash templates, which the team can later expand on. The in-house IT or tech providers may simply lack the necessary competence, perhaps because they specialize in back-end programming, but sometimes they merely lack of a sense of adventure and the will to try something new. Putting the design team in control of front-end development has many advantages and benefits a great deal from an agile project approach that begins in the Design phase.

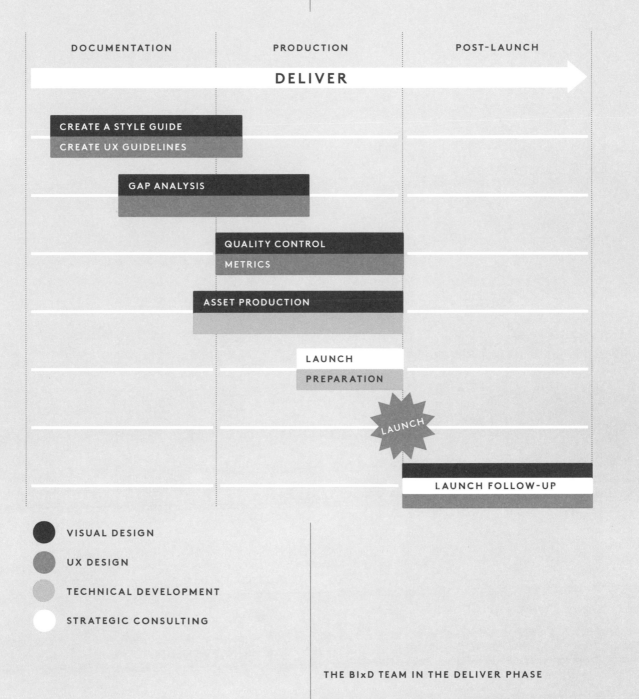

DOCUMENTATION | PRODUCTION | POST-LAUNCH

DELIVER

CREATE A STYLE GUIDE
CREATE UX GUIDELINES

GAP ANALYSIS

QUALITY CONTROL
METRICS

ASSET PRODUCTION

LAUNCH
PREPARATION

LAUNCH

LAUNCH FOLLOW-UP

- VISUAL DESIGN
- UX DESIGN
- TECHNICAL DEVELOPMENT
- STRATEGIC CONSULTING

THE BIxD TEAM IN THE DELIVER PHASE

During the Deliver phase, the design team can make itself doubly useful by helping to monitor the production and carrying out quality control metrics. But they should also have plenty of other tasks to occupy them, both before and after delivery.

SET-UP / PROCESS ——— DISCOVER / DEFINE / DESIGN / **DELIVER** / DISTRIBUTE

Even when it is not possible to be extensively involved, getting the design team to take part in the Deliver phase is as important as involving developers during the Design phase. As a quality control metric, this involvement should be planned in advance, as it always saves time and money in the end.

GAP ANALYSIS AND MODULE LIST

The module list includes all the module types used in the templates and shows the programmer at a glance which modules should be used where. This list is usually created in the Design phase by a UX designer while developing the modules with wireframes (DESIGN THE USER EXPERIENCE, P. 191).

The module list becomes the basis for the gap analysis: a comparison of the various documents from the DDD stage (P. 177) – wireframes, process flows, sitemap, layouts, etc. – with the aim of identifying ambiguities, inconsistencies or missing information. The gap analysis is a quality control metric.

QUALITY CONTROL ————

Companies that regularly develop digital products often have their own quality control department, which is responsible for planning and executing tests and quality controls. The design team can nonetheless play an important role here, because while it's possible to check that the UX and visual design guidelines have been followed at the end, this fact is not always immediately apparent. The design team should therefore plan to test the apps from the beginning, even though the client seldom demands this. In addition, you should schedule a first update of the style guide immediately after implementation (CREATE A STYLE GUIDE, P. 256), because errors that arise in the first implementation of the design will also reoccur later. Where appropriate, new rules should also be added to the style guide. The development team becomes the first test group for the style guide and UX guidelines.

ADDITIONAL QUALITY CONTROL METRICS
COULD INCLUDE:

- Performing another brand check during the production phase. Have the design goal and UX goal been met? Does everything fit the brand filters (e.g. navigation, performance, animations)? Have all technical requirements been met?

- Monitoring asset production, especially with challenging and brand-defining elements; this includes the support and training of editors.

- Collecting frequently asked questions and their responses, and adding them to the UX guidelines or the brand management portal.

- Reviewing the development stages and recording these in an independent issue tracker. It is important to use previously agreed-on language. A glossary helps everyone to stick to the same terminology.

- Becoming a beta tester. Use your own product! Follow up testing and tracking.

- Supplementing guidelines when you notice gaps or see where misunderstandings arise; provide input for the editorial guidelines.

PRODUCING AND MAINTAINING CONTENT

It is a good exercise for a designer to have maintained the content of a web portal or an online store at least one or twice, because it allows you to become aware of everday issues in the life of the editor. It is helpful, of course, if the designer does not have to start learning about the system at that point, but has become familiar with it at an early stage. It also makes sense for the design team to populate the system with data. In this case, all relevant content and assets are created by the designer. These can be used later by the editors or administrators as templates.

The client does not always appreciate having to pay for additional asset production, and too often regards it as a responsibility of the design team. Kim Goodwin therefore advises allocating 15 to 25% of the time budgeted for the detailed design stage to asset production.

4.4

PROJECT
LAUNCH
& DEBRIEF

The entire project team has been working hard on the launch of a new project, the moment when a website goes live or an interactive installation is activated. There is a certain amount of anticipation connected with this moment and this should be acknowledged by the project manager or team leader. Installations or interactive architecture can be unveiled like art exhibits.

The launch of a website should always be followed by at least a thank-you email to the team, even if the work of the client's team is only just beginning. There is still some way to go for your own design team as well.

PLAN THE LAUNCH

Before the launch there is usually a lot of hustle and bustle and – not infrequently – a certain degree of tension within the team. Planning the launch is therefore often forgotten. Yet the deadline is equally important for the team, the client and the outside world and should be planned accordingly. Websites are not usually fully launched until a few users have accessed the site and there is still some time for testing and fine tuning. It may also take a while for mobile apps to go on sale at the app store.

Both the client's and the agency's PR departments should become involved in the launch planning at an early stage. Ideally, they should have already determined who is communicating what. Unnecessary tensions can arise if the agency overshadows the client and dominates the media and the search engine results in the first few weeks after the launch.

PROJECT DEBRIEF

An in-house project debrief is a way of collecting solutions and suggestions for potential use in future projects. Technological, conceptual or design patterns can be identified and used again later. There's always something worth carrying forward for next time.

The in-house debrief should be held soon after the project's completion. All the team members should take part and jointly evaluate the process and its outcome. All comments and lessons learned are recorded by the project manager using a standardized form and are approved by the entire team. Try to be brief and focus on the key points.

If everything went well, the debrief is often forgotten along with the client and any other external collaborators. But for long-term client relationships, it is important to review what can be learned from projects and to use this knowledge during future collaborations. In addition to reviewing the project's schedule, budget and scope, the issue of communication between the client and the design team should also be addressed if need be.

QUALITY CONTROL REVIEW

CRITERIA	DETAILS	PRAISE / CRITICISM	LESSONS	WHO	NOTES
1 PROFESSIONAL QUALITY					
BRAND FIT	Does the result fit the brand filters?	→	→	→	→
USER EXPERIENCE	What is the user experience like?	→	→	→	→
BUSINESS	Were the business goals achieved? Are we on strategy?	→	→	→	→
2 PROCESS QUALITY (WORKFLOW & PROJECT MANAGEMENT)					
BRIEF / REQUIREMENTS	How accurate was the brief? Were the requirements modified in terms of the starting position and goal?	→	→	→	→
SOURCE MATERIAL	Was the material supplied sufficient? Was it delivered on time?	→	→	→	→
DOCUMENTATION	Did the documentation meet the requirements? What was the quality of the presentations?	→	→	→	→
RESOURCE PLANNING	Was the team well prepared (e.g. on schedule and professional)?	→	→	→	→
TEAMWORK	What was cooperation like within the design team?	→	→	→	→
EXTERNAL COMMUNICATION	What was the quality of communication with the client and external service providers?	→	→	→	→
PROJECT ORGANIZATION	Was the project properly prepared and were all stakeholders sufficiently involved?	→	→	→	→
TIME AND BUDGET	Was the project completed on time and on budget?	→	→	→	→

EVALUATION SCALE

1   exceeded expectations
2   expectations were met
3   okay/mediocre
4   expectations were not met
5   missed the target/negative impact

QUALITY CONTROL REVIEW

Using a form such as this, scores for individual aspects can be assigned and the project evaluated. These can be used to assess the process and the technical outcome, as well as the performance of the agency and the client.

CREATE A CASE STUDY

Shortly after a project has been successfully completed, the work should be documented in the form of a case study, which the team can use later in presentations or as inspiration. The case study is based on the original brief and describes the initial situation and background of the project as well as the goals and solutions, the latter of which can be accompanied by quotes from the client. Facts and figures that prove the success of the project can be added later, along with any awards received. The case study should reflect what made this project notable for the client and the agency. Video case studies are particularly useful when documenting interactive and multimedia aspects of a digital brand experience, or the making of a BIxD project. They are also useful as award submissions because they provide the judges with a quick first impression of the project.

✔ **THINGS TO DO AFTER THE LAUNCH:**

▸ Debrief as a team and with the client (P. 279).

▸ Back up all the data from the project.

▸ Clean up material (unwanted material is returned to the client or shredded).

▸ Store future inspiration: if any aspects of the project could potentially be reused on other projects, add them to a team Wiki or idea library.

▸ Go through notes and update roadmap.

▸ Document what has been learned. If the project was representative, it can be used as a template.

▸ Record hours and compile invoices.

▸ Create and prepare demos and user presentations for the press and in-house stakeholders.

▸ Create a case study (incl. demo and showreel, etc.)

▸ Coordinate PR and social media before the launch and maintain it afterwards.

▸ Celebrate your success together.

INTERACTIVE BRAND COMMUNICATION FOR BENETTON

ALFIO POZZONI

FABRICA

Tell me, what exactly is Fabrica?

Fabrica is a communications research centre founded by Luciano Benetton in 1994 with the aim of combining culture and industry and offering young people from around the world an opportunity for creative growth and multicultural exchange. Fabrica is based in Treviso, in a 17th-century villa that has been restored by Japanese architect Tadao Ando. We invite young artists and designers to develop multidisciplinary projects in the fields of design, visual communications, photography, digital interaction, video, music and publishing, under the guidance of experts.

What is the role of Fabrica within the Benetton brand? How do you work with other departments at Benetton?

Fabrica's primary role is to promote the brand, in line with Luciano Benetton's belief that

'communication should never be commissioned from outside the company but conceived within its heart'. This currently means researching integrated communication channels and finding new ways for the company to talk to people. We work with those who give voice to the brand.

Interactive media have become an essential part of brand communication. In 2010 you created IT'S:MY:TIME, the first global online casting session for Benetton. What were your experiences from a brand perspective? How did it relate to Benetton's brand DNA?

IT'S:MY:TIME was a huge success; more than 65,000 participants created their own profile on the website, crossposted it to other social media, uploaded hundreds of photos and video clips, and added millions of comments and votes. It was the first all-digital model casting session with a global reach.

Every Benetton campaign has resulted from a huge amount of social research.

IT'S:MY:TIME was a continuation of the product catalogues Benetton used to shoot in the streets of Beijing, Tokyo and Gaza, with ordinary people as their stars. With IT'S:MY:TIME, we wanted people to come to us. We didn't want to launch a new social network but to aggregate personal content through young people's favourite channels: Facebook and Twitter for messaging and posting pictures and YouTube for videos. The network brought together these different styles of self-expression, and offered a space where users could be imaginative, sharing their tastes, ideas, praise and criticism. Via this vast virtual arena, Benetton took a fresh and exclusive social sampling of the inspirations and aspirations of young people and their outlook on the future.

Another installation, Exquisite Clock, was selected to be part of the Victoria and Albert Museum's exhibition 'Decode: Digital Design Sensations'.

The 'Decode' exhibition was a major survey of the best contemporary digital art and design from around the world. Launched in London at the V&A in 2009, it travelled to Beijing (CAFA Art Museum) in 2010 and Moscow (Garage Centre for Contemporary Culture) in 2011. Exquisite Clock is a clock made of numbers taken from everyday life – seen, captured and uploaded by people from all over the world. Based on an online database,

the clock exists as a web 2.0 website, an iPhone app and as a series of site-specific installations. The V&A Exquisite Clock was a hanging sculpture made up of deconstructed computers, screens and cables that visitors could add to and interact with.

While these projects seem to be pieces of art, others have a clear communication objective in mind. The Colors of Movement installation was created for Benetton store windows and is installed in several cities. Who comes up with the ideas for these branded interactions?

Actually, Colors of Movement is one of the many interactive apps we are using in a project called Benetton Live Windows (P. 294). This project is focused on customer experience and driven by the need for the brand to be more alive and visible on the street. It involves flagship stores on high streets, places where brands are engaged in a low-intensity war for consumers' attention. We're working at the intersection of design, marketing, urban life, consumer behaviour and technology. We aim to engage people on the street and turn them into customers. That's why we chose to develop a concept – huge HD screens that cover the whole store window – to create an enhanced relationship between the brand and people.

Colors of Movement is based on the magic of simplicity. It's you, on screen, in colour: a relationship that reflects the very heart of the brand. The user's image is split up into three RGB colours, each streamed with a delay. It's an invitation to move that needs no explanation:

you just play. People are entertained by this magic mirror effect and love to capture it on their phones and share it with their friends and followers.

The experience of seeing yourself on a huge scale in a shop window on a crowded street isn't just fun – it enhances the customer experience and turns it into a social event.

What other interactive apps are you developing?

We currently have two different approaches. The first one allows users to interact with their own image in the store window. This is the basis behind Colors of Movement, Ripple and Time Loop. The user's image is captured by an ordinary webcam behind the glass and put on screen by the app. The outcome is fun, playful, surprising. It is a trigger for body actions – we're not into touch apps that don't demand anything more than pushing a button.

The second approach uses more sophisticated hardware, such as 3D sensors. In this case, the user's body actions trigger video effects. In Run For Fun, users can run opposite a life-size model on screen. The user's pace makes the model run faster or slower. The experience is concluded by a score showing the calories burned, to make

the experience more meaningful and rewarding. Another app that sits between these two approaches is Face in the Hole. Users can put their own face inside a fashion photo, in place of the model's face. After posing in a photo booth, they see the final image on a large screen. People love to laugh at themselves – a big guy was keen to choose a beautiful female body to put his face on and a bald man wanted to see himself with dreadlocks on his head. Wherever the app was running, we saw a magnetic effect that attracted dozens of people who spontaneously queued to try the experience. The audience itself was part of the show, and everybody was welcome to watch everybody else.

Who works at Fabrica? How do designers work with other disciplines like developers or brand experts? Is there a Fabrica-specific process?

We have a multidisciplinary team that brings together many skills: videomaking and editing, animation, photography, graphics, copywriting, sound design, interactive technologies. We produce a huge quantity of content that can be presented in multiple formats. We don't have a one-size-fits-all approach: each store has its own specific design. We want technology to be as transparent as possible, so users barely notice it. Of course, technology is the core of the project but our main goal is to develop a suitable language for feeding that channel and allowing a deeper experience for users.

Alfio Pozzoni is Special Projects Director at Fabrica, Treviso.

IV

GOOD PRACTICE

——

Brand Communication in Public Spaces

AUDI CITY / BMW MUSEUM / LEGO CODES /
IBM SMARTER PLANET BILLBOARDS / BENETTON LIVE WINDOWS /
4010 TELEKOM SHOP / LEGO DIGITAL BOX

AUDI CITY

In summer 2012 Audi opened the first AUDI CITY in London near Piccadilly Circus. There, in a compact space, Audi set up a showroom of the future. Efficient use of space enables Audi to display its entire model range in a way that fits the brand and its tagline 'Vorsprung durch Technik' (forwards through technology). Audi also has the youngest customers in the premium car segment.

In AUDI CITY visitors can select and assemble their vehicles virtually. The car can be configured on touch terminals via gesture control, so that client managers and potential customers can jointly work on the design. A life-size image of the dream car is then back-projected on the wall. AUDI CITY also offers analogue samples of paint, fabric and wood finishes. The car can be ordered on site or viewed again at home in the myAudi section of the company website.

GOOD PRACTICE —— BRAND COMMUNICATION IN PUBLIC SPACES

BMW MUSEUM

ART + COM

The BMW Museum is not simply a presentation of the car manufacturer's history. It is also the perfect touchpoint for branded interactions, creating digital brand experiences at the intersection of architecture, exhibition design and new media. Large-scale choreographed sound and light projections remove spatial limitations and allow the architecture to come alive, highlighting the 125 exhibits. Interactive installations and so-called 'auxiliary' displays serve as mediators of information and content.

Opposite: This kinetic sculpture stands at the starting point of the three-stage journey through the BMW design process. ART + COM created an artwork that symbolizes a metaphor for the flow of ideas and metaphorically translates the virtual design process into three-dimensional space. The installation consists of 714 metal balls that hang on thin steel cables in an area measuring 6 m² (64 sq. ft). Individually controlled by a computer via micro motors, the balls move as if they were directed solely by the power of thought, creating a cycle of free abstractions and typical BMW vehicle shapes, lasting for several minutes. Beginning as chaotic 'thoughts', the choreography progresses through a sequence of associative ideas and geometric forms until representations of BMW cars emerge. The concept for this complex kinetic sculpture was first tested for feasibility by ART + COM using a simple prototype (INTERVIEW, P. 312).

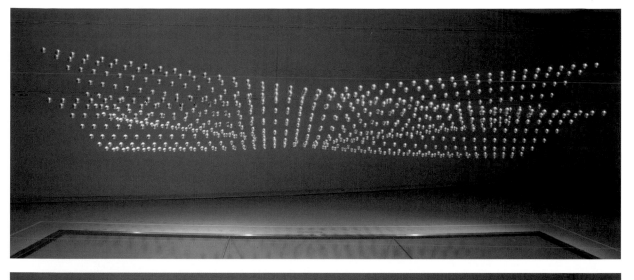

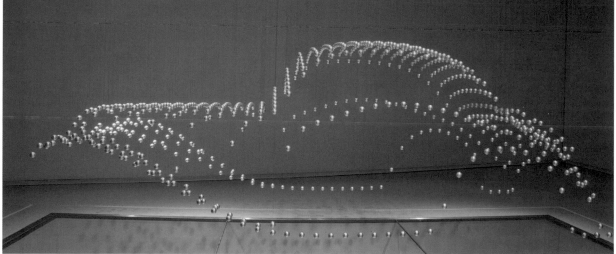

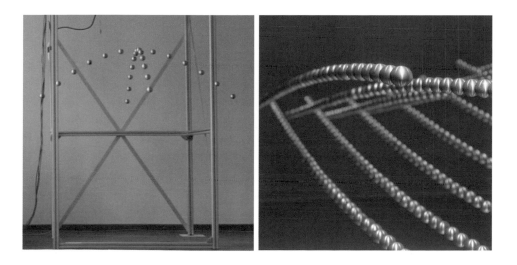

LEGO CODES

LUKAS LINDEMANN ROSINSKI

The requirements for this project were two-fold. The business requirement was to promote the sale of LEGO on the website of the German online store myToys. From a brand perspective, however, LEGO had to be the focus. The LEGO brand is synonymous with imagination, creativity and joy, but LEGO also represents learning and what happens when we experiment, improvise and explore. A single brand-consistent app should – depending on its focus – convey all of these values.

myToys.de is an online store with the tagline 'everything for children', selling 17,000 products from well-known children's brands. The agency's task was to advertise LEGO, a lead product on myToys. The aim was to develop an innovative campaign for LEGO products that stimulated people's instinct to play and inspired them to delve into the imaginative world of LEGO.

The project had to maintain an interesting balancing act: advertising LEGO in a brand-consistent way, but doing so on behalf of another brand (myToys.de). The concept itself is based entirely on the product: posters built out of LEGO, showing QR codes that can be read using a mobile phone. When the QR code is scanned, the phone displays one of the many things you can build using the LEGO bricks from which the code was built, and displays a web link allowing you to order the relevant LEGO set directly from myToys. The myToys logo appears on the posters in small type, but only comes into play in the second step, when the QR code is scanned. The toy retailer's innovative presentation highlights their claim of fast service.

IBM SMARTER PLANET BILLBOARDS

OGILVY & MATHER

This colour-sensitive billboard for IBM's Smarter Planet campaign provides a graphic demonstration of the company's desire to develop user-tailored technology and service solutions. The colour of the Smarter Planet logo on the billboard changes to match the colour of the observer's clothing – an allusion to the psychological effect of colours when making purchasing decisions.

IBM advertises its 'smarter supply chain' in locations frequented by business decision-makers, and allows the user to become part of the brand interface.

GOOD PRACTICE —— BRAND COMMUNICATION IN PUBLIC SPACES

BENETTON LIVE WINDOWS
FABRICA

Benetton Live Windows is an on-going series of interactive apps developed for the windows of Benetton flagship stores around the world. With Live Windows, Benetton has created a tool for communication in an urban context that allows the brand to interact with passers-by, even before they reach the store. The goal of Fabrica's concept was to create more dialogue with the flagship stores.

The basic design initially remained true to the look of the company's classic print ads. Close-ups of young people from all over the world are shown on enormous and seamlessly connected LCD monitors that fill the whole of the store's windows. Later, interactive apps were added and developed into a kind of video membrane through which the brand can engage in a dialogue with the public and allow people to communicate with one other.

Playlists are tailored for each store and real-time central control is possible via the network. The flagship stores in Milan, Munich, Moscow, Shanghai, Barcelona, Istanbul, Paris and London are currently connected. The apps will be further developed and supported across the network.

4010 TELEKOM SHOP
MUTABOR

4010 is Deutsche Telekom's concept store, located in Berlin's Mitte district. The name is derived from the colour profile of Telekom's magenta branding: RAL4010. The aim of the 200-m² store is to present Telekom products to urban youth at eye level. The result is a platform for dialogue, which interweaves the ideas of community and shopping and offers a place to linger and explore. The concept is more gallery than shop, more an experience than a point of sale, and yet everything comes together. A special feature is the transformability of the store. Within a very short time, all products and their stands can be removed, making the space available for showcases, readings and workshops. New services and products

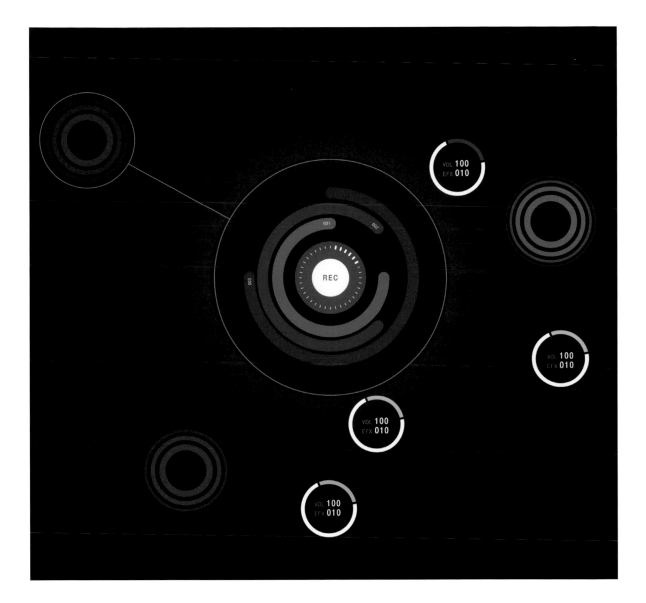

are presented in close association with Telekom's youth marketing, such as Electronic Beats, an offering that sharpens the brand image of Telekom through the target group itself. Part of the media presentation is an interactive touchscreen app that allows users to intuitively compose ringtones using a graphic interface and to send these ringtones to

their own phones free of charge. To do this, the phone simply has to be placed on the table. In collaboration with the Berlin-based DJ and producer Ian Pooley, a toolkit of electronic sound files was created that allows endless combinations and modifications. Track by track, the user can create a personalized ringtone on virtual turntables.

LEGO DIGITAL BOX

LEGO DIGITAL/OLAV GJERLUFSEN AND METAIO

In-store purchasing decisions are driven by the product experience that potential buyers have at the point of sale. This is especially true for the toy industry. Ideally, customers want to be able to handle the product. For complex – and expensive – LEGO products, sales help is needed that explains the product in a simple but compelling way. A product that is made up entirely of individual parts should be made tangible in the truest sense of the word – and, ideally, without drastic changes to the store or the product and its packaging.

Based on AR software by metaio, LEGO has developed a point-of-sale app called Digital Box. A system of kiosks uses markerless tracking technology to recognize the different LEGO packs and to overlay these with 3D animations that show the finished assembled product in detail. Customers hold a LEGO box in front of a camera and see the real-time rendered 3D data displayed on the product box on the adjacent screen.

5

DIS
STRIBUTE

BIxD
ROLLOUT
AND
UPDATES

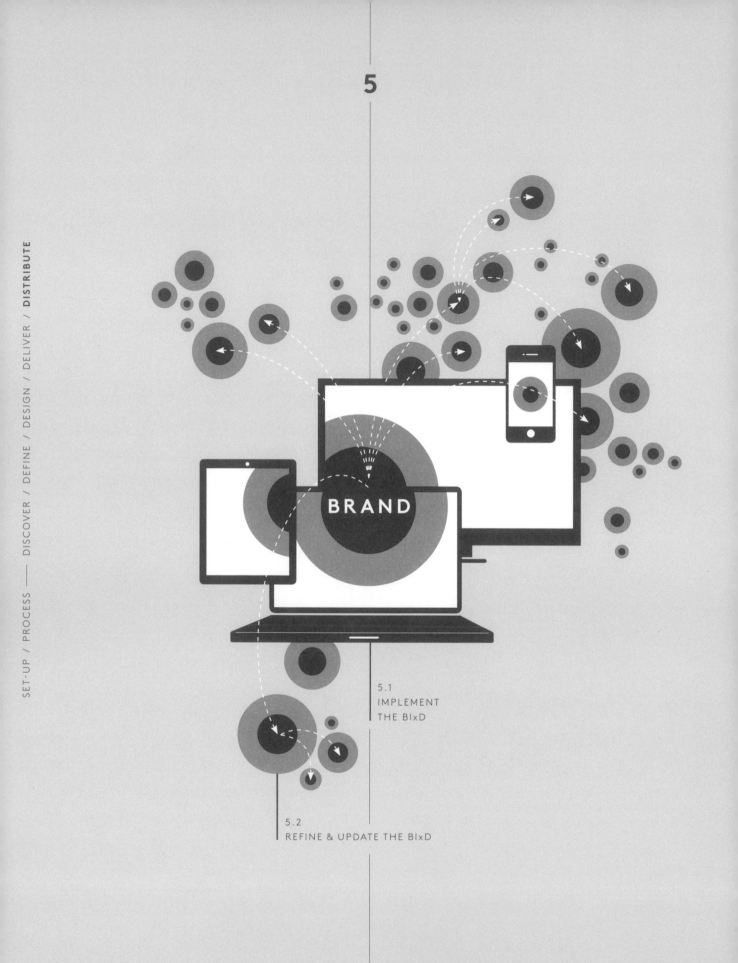

BRAND

5.1
IMPLEMENT
THE BIxD

5.2
REFINE & UPDATE THE BIxD

When the launch happens, the most important stage is over. Or is it? Not quite. The lifespan of a new digital brand, product or service is only just beginning.

Whether branded interactions grow and thrive after the launch depends on how they are nurtured and developed. The final phase of the BIxD process involves essential post-project tasks and documentation. These range from explaining the project both in and outside the company, employee training and supporting the rollout, potential implementation in new markets or on new platforms, to performance assessment, evaluation and further development of the project.

5.1

IMPLEMENT THE BIxD

SET-UP / PROCESS ——— DISCOVER / DEFINE / DESIGN / DELIVER / **DISTRIBUTE**

'A user experience design for a technology is, at its core, a set of suggestions for human behaviour. Because the only thing that can be guaranteed is that people will not behave according to plan, it becomes the designer's responsibility to design for flexibility.'

MIKE KUNIAVSKY, *Smart Things*

After the launch, we find out how a brand, product or service is received and regarded by users. For us, it's exciting to see how users interact with the app and what will happen when it is developed further. A 'living' brand or product begins to change almost immediately, as users find new ways to use it, and editors shape its content and appearance. The brand is set in motion, and it's important for the design team to watch these developments and incorporate what they learn in their future work. For international projects, the rollout in different markets also needs preparation. How should you convey the project to other countries, cultures and corporate divisions? Ideally, these should have been included as a focus group and stakeholders at an earlier stage, but this is often not the case.

And what about new employees who are hired after the launch or when an editorial team is being built up slowly? Although you can try to anticipate all eventualities, the first few months after a launch are often pretty hectic.

COMMUNICATING THE BIxD

A new interactive corporate design, the relaunch of a corporate or sales website or a digital service always means a change for people inside and outside the company. People can be afraid of change, reacting with scepticism when something familiar alters or when something new interrupts an everyday routine. New ideas often have to battle against prejudice, and if something does not run smoothly from the beginning, it will have an even harder time of it later on. It is therefore vital to communicate the BIxD properly.

However, BIxD is not a democratic process, which is why only a core team and, if necessary, a focus group (P. 56) should be involved in its early development. Later, however, it must be understood and accepted by employees, service providers, agencies and dealers. It's important to take any fears about the new product seriously and to deal with employees with empathy, while trying to remain neutral. Getting entangled in office politics may mean you lose credibility and support and suddenly find yourself on the wrong side if there's a change of leadership. In contrast, if you've made your design decisions based closely on the requirements and have justified them during the Design phase, you should have an easier time reacting objectively to comments, avoiding arguments over matters of taste and defusing subjective criticism.

Workshops on dealing with interactive products and employee training are a good opportunity to bring together people from different departments and to encourage them to talk to each other and exchange work practices. Many things are easier when people simply communicate.

TRAINING STAFF

The training of employees and service providers who will work with the system should not only cover technical details. The application of style guide rules must also be explained. An awareness of compliance with guidelines should be established – but room for leeway must also be demonstrated. Often the problem is not that people are too lax with the style guide but that they are too rigid. The result is that agencies have no room for innovation and further development, leading to new projects looking completely outdated after a year or two.

SET-UP / PROCESS ——— DISCOVER / DEFINE / DESIGN / DELIVER / **DISTRIBUTE**

Training courses are a great opportunity to meet the staff. You should take their questions and concerns seriously and show interest in their fields. This way, in addition to the training, you can also learn about in-house processes and get some interesting insights. Many tasks that seem obvious to designers may be strange or unusual to the client's employees. This is where you can offer assistance and make their jobs easier.

Courses are also valuable as a sales tool. Just because the project has already been launched does not mean that we no longer need to sell it. Agencies who know this will make sure that the training is on brand in both its planning and execution.

> ### ✔ THE BASIC FRAMEWORK FOR A TRAINING COURSE

▸ the goal of the training
▸ the subject of the training
▸ the number of participants
▸ the length of the session
▸ who is doing the training?
▸ who is being trained?
▸ what IT skills do the participants need?
▸ any equipment that is needed

'Stories illustrate points better than simply stating the points themselves because, if the story is good enough, you usually don't have to state your point at all; the hearer thinks about what you have said and figures out the point independently.'
ROGER SCHANK

STORYTELLING, PRODUCT PROMOS AND GUIDED TOURS

A story allows us to communicate complex technical relationships in an engaging way. Stories touch the emotions of the reader or listener, and so are easier to remember than purely factual information. Storytelling should therefore be used not only during planning and design, but also during the implementation of branded interactions. Depending on the objective, the user or even the product can become the protagonist of the story. A good story includes a conflict: a central problem that the protagonist resolves over the course of the story. The short version of a story about a BIxD project should be encapsulated in a few sentences, so that it can be told to a co-worker or supervisor during an elevator ride.

In the Design chapter (P. 227), I discussed a video prototyping method that allows user scenarios and interactive situations to be documented using screen- and space-based media. These video prototypes are easy to develop into product promos or guided tours, which can be shown for marketing purposes at presentations or on YouTube. They are particularly useful for innovative products and services that introduce new operating concepts that require explanation. For the interactive learning platform LernCoachies.de by the German educational publisher Cornelsen, we developed a guided tour that introduces first-time student users to the underlying concept and the basic interface elements in a fun and brand-focused way. The tour is also used as a marketing tool on tradeshow stands and on product presentations on YouTube and Facebook.

ℹ An elevator pitch is a 30-second summary of a product or service whose goal is to convey an idea or a concept in the shortest possible time. An elevator pitch is often formulated by start-up entrepreneurs to get potential investors interested in their idea.

PLAN THE ROLLOUT

A rollout plan describes which features are implemented where and when, in which market segments of which country or which section of a system. The new design is rolled out across all digital touchpoints of a brand. Looking at the metrics catalogue (P. 148) can refresh your memory about which metrics and features have been earmarked for the rollout and which additional steps have been planned. The timing for the rollout is specified in a roadmap. Special or exclusive features for specific countries may be postponed until later, depending on priorities. Often a stripped-down basic version for smaller markets and a more elaborate or customizable version for larger markets will be required.

A rollout is planned and budgeted as a separate project, so the design team should know from the beginning where the finance is coming from. Usually only a portion of the cost is borne by global brand management, with each country paying for their own share of the rollout, which means that they also want and should have a say in things. The rollout begins with a stakeholder analysis across all markets, if this was not conducted in the Discover phase. It is best to involve partner countries in the Discover and Define phases as a focus group (P. 56), otherwise surprises may arise later.

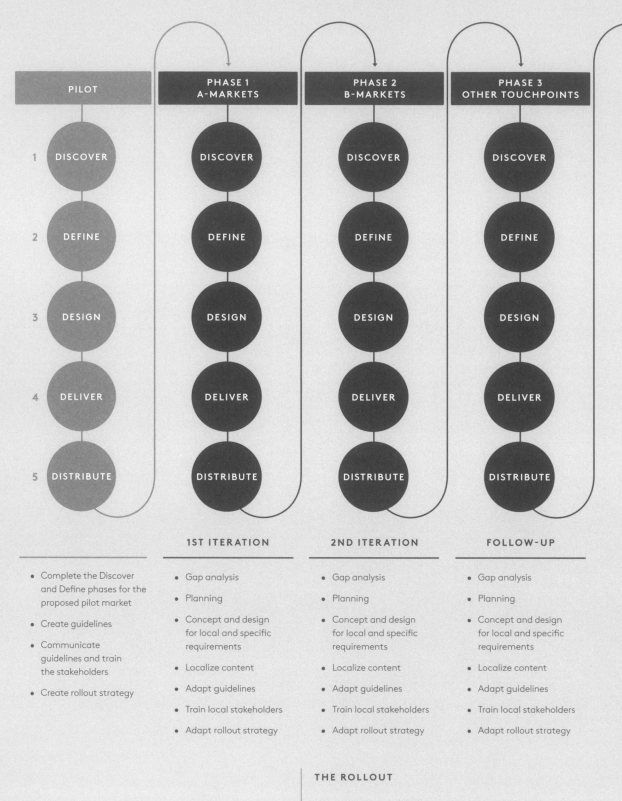

PILOT	PHASE 1 A-MARKETS	PHASE 2 B-MARKETS	PHASE 3 OTHER TOUCHPOINTS

1   DISCOVER   DISCOVER   DISCOVER   DISCOVER

2   DEFINE   DEFINE   DEFINE   DEFINE

3   DESIGN   DESIGN   DESIGN   DESIGN

4   DELIVER   DELIVER   DELIVER   DELIVER

5   DISTRIBUTE   DISTRIBUTE   DISTRIBUTE   DISTRIBUTE

	1ST ITERATION	2ND ITERATION	FOLLOW-UP

- Complete the Discover and Define phases for the proposed pilot market
- Create guidelines
- Communicate guidelines and train the stakeholders
- Create rollout strategy

1ST ITERATION
- Gap analysis
- Planning
- Concept and design for local and specific requirements
- Localize content
- Adapt guidelines
- Train local stakeholders
- Adapt rollout strategy

2ND ITERATION
- Gap analysis
- Planning
- Concept and design for local and specific requirements
- Localize content
- Adapt guidelines
- Train local stakeholders
- Adapt rollout strategy

FOLLOW-UP
- Gap analysis
- Planning
- Concept and design for local and specific requirements
- Localize content
- Adapt guidelines
- Train local stakeholders
- Adapt rollout strategy

THE ROLLOUT

International rollouts for branded interaction projects include a number of phases. After each of them, the style guide and the UX guidelines should be adjusted and updated.

It's possible that stakeholders may suddenly emerge who were not previously involved. In this case, you will need to take time to integrate these stakeholders and explain the project history. The rollout plan is compiled by the project manager together with the design team, editors and development team. The planned steps should be coordinated with the marketing plans for each country. Major dates and events in national markets must be taken into account as well as the activities of competitors and trade show dates. Localized translations of text should be centrally commissioned by the service provider; each country is responsible for quality control or assigns the job of proofreading to an in-house editor.

An international rollout happens in stages. First, countries are divided into groups, then it is decided which country will be rolled out when. You could start with a small pilot project to see if supplements to the original style guide are necessary. Sometimes there are markets that are more independent from the parent company, with locally established business and brand strategies. Enough time must be allowed for these to be properly accommodated by the style guide, templates and guidelines. Cultural differences must be taken into account not only in the design itself, but also when presenting and discussing the design (COMMUNICATING THE BIxD, P. 305). In some cultures, for example, employees may never openly express opinions that differ from those of their superiors. You should be aware of such customs in advance and, where necessary, seek the advice of a crosscultural consultant.

DESIGN MANAGEMENT

Design involves responsibility. As interactive designers, we change the way thousands of people deal with a product or service, how they feel, what the brand means to them. It's not always easy for us to handle this responsibility.

Design management is used to strategically coordinate all design projects within a company and organize them in a sustainable way. Designers can only influence this process when they are integrated into the company. However, after a project is complete, agencies are usually out of the picture. Freelance designers or teams, meanwhile, have the advantage of being able to work closely with the client. In any event, it is worthwhile to discuss the potential of continuing collaboration with the client. Some companies will realize the advantages of this – ultimately both parties can benefit from an ongoing exchange, especially in periods when there is less to do. In recent years, even companies whose core business is not directly involved with interactive media have begun to recognize that digital brand management is a top management issue. The responsibility for developing digital apps lies with a company's own in-house IT department, which tends to be less concerned about issues that affect the brand. It's still rare to have a UX team working on a corporate website, yet the situation is slowly changing. Designers are increasingly seen as brand consultants and involved in ongoing exchange and dialogue; they must therefore be included in the budget planning.

If an interactive design team creates a corporate design, it is important to monitor the project at least part of the way to the launch, in order to test that the design guidelines will work during the implementation phase. The problem with many guidelines is that they're often made up on the spot by corporate design and branding agencies. This means that they're not tried and tested and may be a poor fit for the limitations and potential of interactive media, and yet they are intended to serve the technical service providers as an implementation guide. Misunderstandings between traditional corporate designers and IT developers are rife and can often be seen in the results. An interactive style guide must therefore be developed based on a functioning project.

For major international companies with multiple regional marketing and microsites implemented by different service providers, you should develop at least one prototype. This can then serve a design archetype, from which other designs can be developed. The less we are involved as designers in the implementation process, the clearer and more precise the communications and project documentation must be (CREATE UX GUIDELINES, P. 270). Brand management portals not only help by providing style guides and UX guidelines, but also communication and quality assurance.

BRAND MANAGEMENT PORTALS

Brand management portals are web-based systems that contain style guides and assets as well as tools for corporate identity management, which are made available to in-house and external collaborators. They ensure that departments such as public relations, marketing, sales, product management and customer services, as well as external service providers and agencies worldwide, always have access to the most up-to-date materials. Access permissions and workflows ensure that everyone can access the information relevant to their role. These portals can also be used for campaign planning and may offer web-to-print services, allowing customized letterheads and other printed materials to be ordered.

LAUNCH

year 1 – 1st to 3rd quarter	year 2 – 1st and 2nd quarter	year 2 – 3rd and 4th quarter	year 3
RECOGNITION	**ESTABLISHMENT**	**DIFFERENTIATION**	**REINFORCEMENT**
awareness understanding	presence sympathy	acceptance appreciation	loyalty authority

PHASE 1: BEFORE THE LAUNCH
Basic website and booking software,
online marketing, newsletter sign-ups,
SEO + SEM, web specials for the launch

PHASE 2: LAUNCH
Site optimization: News section, newsletter,
pre- and post-flight email, text messaging service.
Online PR: blog and social media, interactive
out-of-home metrics.

PHASE 3: MARKET ENTRY
Customization: Development of
customized accounts, including customer
history, expansion of service offerings,
mobile apps.

PHASE 4: MARKET STABILIZATION
Introduction of a loyalty programme,
ongoing development of product and
service offerings.

LAUNCH PHASES

Four-step rollout plan for the launch of a new airline and
the accompanying digital metrics. Each phase climbs to
a new level of the brand experience pyramid **(P. 141)**.

INTERACTION IN PUBLIC SPACES

JOACHIM SAUTER
ART + COM

Mr Sauter, you once defined four physical formats for digital media: screen apps, interactive objects and installations, interactive spaces, and interactive architecture. I would first like to talk about screen apps. To what extent can these be used for branded projects in public spaces?

In our experience, the focus for brands is on installations. It is the most efficient branded format because it is where we can appeal to people the most intensely.

But overall it's clear that interactive installations, spaces and architecture are all extremely topical, which was not always the case. The internet has been with us now for around twenty years or more; we move in virtual spaces and sit isolated at home in front of our computers or mobile devices, while we communicate, search for information or look for entertainment. People want to go back out into physical spaces and deal with each other in a physical context. And this is true both in the cultural sphere and in the worlds of brands. The key difference from the pre-digital era is that people are computer-savvy now; they have been using them for ten or fifteen years or even longer. They know what the benefits of the medium are – interaction, collaboration, networking – and want to see these in physical spaces. If you're a brand designer but you have no idea about these things, you won't be able to speak to people in the brand space.

At ART + COM we focus on these three formats, which usually work together. There's a smooth transition between an installation that occupies less space, an installation that occupies more space, and one that actually *is* the architecture. Most of the works include a combination of formats, where we use both installations and an immersive space.

A good example of this is the BMW Museum, where you have a central space – the space in the middle of the museum – which is equipped as a fully immersive room, but is very restrained and reflects the brand atmospherically rather than literally.

That room serves multiple functions, in terms of both the brand and the architecture. It's reactive. Even when the museum is relatively empty, an identification with the space takes place, because visitors become part of the room and part of its expression.

In contrast to similar museums, this central space in the BMW museum is relatively small. But if you design a space that's defined by its media, you can enlarge it. Through the use of three-dimensional and motion graphics, the perception of it grows larger. In addition, visitors return to this central space again and again and see it differently each time. We therefore create a mental map that we use to expand the perceived space. The brand values can be conveyed there in a non-cinematic way. In the case of BMW, this means dynamics, challenge and precision. These are ideas that can be captured in dynamic digital imagery. I think it's brave and commendable of BMW to say 'We won't display any products here, old or new.

In retrospect, this choice has been justified. The space has become a place where you can sense the brand without analysing it.

There's a work in the BMW Museum that brings the brand to life in a special way: the kinetic sculpture at the start of the museum tour. It is not an interactive work, but, as an installation, it has become part of the outward brand communication. Many people are familiar with it from the ad campaign for the 5 Series.

The kinetic sculpture stands in the first room of the museum. Here the task was to present the design process and its importance for the BMW brand. A classic way to do this is to present designers on monitors as talking heads or tape drawings. We said to ourselves: this entry space is a business card that must convey the brand values in a challenging way. 'Challenge' is indeed one of the most important brand values at BMW.

We wanted a surface floating in space, which reflected the design process metaphorically over time.

We experimented with nets and fabric suspended on strings. Then we had the idea of the spheres. We visualized this, and at BMW they immediately said: 'Are you insane? You can't tell the story of car design with metal balls.'

But we made a prototype and the client soon realized that these were much more than ball bearings. They relay the brand values, the precision and the interdependence of everything on everything else.

How large does a prototype for a project like that need to be, for you to tell whether or not it will work?

For BMW, we used 25 balls instead of 700, which provided a very effective structure. We combined the 25 balls, which were blue, with a virtual model. Both were run in parallel, so we got a pretty good idea. We didn't do the final calculations ourselves.

I find it interesting that an installation like that could suddenly become the lead concept for the entire brand.

That was the goal: to see how far we could go, how much of an impact we could have on the brand.

If someone from the company had said during the museum's planning phase that the museum would later influence the brand's message, no one would have believed it.

But the installation later became the basis for the launch campaign for the new 5 Series sedan.

You worked on the BMW Museum with Atelier Brückner, who were responsible for the architecture, and with Ruedi Baur, who was in charge of graphic design. What was the collaboration like? Were there a few people who led the project? Were there joint brainstorming sessions with everyone involved?

We at ART + COM, as a media agency, were initially hired to design the museum, because BMW said: 'This is a technical museum, and we want it to be strongly characterized by media.'

Then we hired Atelier Brückner for the interior design. From the beginning we worked very closely together, and with BMW too. It helped that we were the first ones hired.

I've seen it often enough: the building has been built, the interior is finished, the layout is finished, and now we install a few media stations.

In this case, it was a more inclusive process from the beginning. And the process was very dynamic. We had great discussions and learned a lot from each other. We also brought Ruedi Baur on board early on, as well as idee und klang, who did the audio, and Marc Tamschick, the motion graphic artist who designed the 'visual symphony' on the upper levels. It was an integrated team in which no one took the lead. We were all on an equal footing.

What is the nature of the agency process at ART + COM?

We don't see ourselves as an agency but as an office, because we've always tried to focus on the design and development aspect. In terms of our history and our attitude and our processes, we've developed entirely independent structures. There's no single process, but several structural phases.

Most projects are done without a pitch. Instead we begin with a question.

Then there's a proposal for a kick-off workshop, for which we are paid. The workshop also includes a rebrief, in which we try to understand what the actual job is behind the commission. Then, after a phase lasting two to four weeks, we deliver a brochure or give a presentation in which we describe our initial ideas, often including visuals. Then there can be phases lasting from six months to three years. Usually there is a second design phase with a refined concept, in which it's still possible to back out. Otherwise, the project is carried out.

So the team is interdisciplinary from the beginning; there are always both developers and designers around.

Precisely. The future for us is moving away from active displays, such as screens, touch tables and projections. We do a lot of passive displays, for example, just kinetic objects. It is only possible to develop these things by working with programmers and mechatronics. Particularly for more complex tasks, such as creating the table that tells the story of BMW, we call in content developers.

How do you define content developers? Or concept developers?

We all develop concepts.

That's why there are designers, engineers and content developers with us. They handle content and prepare it for the design phase.

Which design disciplines are included?

Back in the days when there were no media designers, we had all disciplines on board. Now there are digital media designers. Most start here when they are young and stay here a long time. They are graduates of my class (Digital Design at the Universität der Künste, Berlin), media designers from the Royal College of Art or interaction designers. These are people who understand the disciplines of computational design, physical computing, etc.

Many of the ideas come from an understanding of technology. Designers today should be able to program. You should at least have some knowledge of the Processing programming language and be able to program a little hardware.

I could not imagine hiring anyone today who does not know the basics of Processing and who couldn't discuss sensors. That would be difficult.

What can be done to prevent an interactive public work, especially interactive facades and

architecture, from looking outdated quickly? This is particularly important for a brand like BMW, as its major attribute is its progressiveness.

It's simple: you make things that don't age and show no technology. In the BMW Museum you can't see the technology. The LEDs behind the facade are concealed. People don't know how it is done.

The focus is on the outer surfaces, which are dynamic. How it's done doesn't matter. After twenty years, the ball installation will still – knock on wood – be fascinating, because it doesn't come across as technical. As another example, telling the story of something across the surface of a table and making it interactive is not something that will date. This is a basic principle.

What can easily become obsolete – although this is true of other media as well – is the visuals. These are often characterized by the latest technologies. It was the case with bitmap fonts on the web, then with the Flash aesthetic, which crossed over to TV, and now it's happening with Processing.

Yes. In a few years people will say that they want new installations for these facades. A poster looks old after ten years, too, but you can switch it for another. It is important that technology is not in the foreground. You should never base something on technology but always on the content and the experience instead. Then things are permanent and durable.

Joachim Sauter is the founder and creative director of ART + COM and a professor of New Media at the Universität der Künste, Berlin.

REFINE &
UPDATE
THE BIxD

*'From little buck slips
to big buildings, the
design challenges of
a large organization
are neverending.'*

PAUL RAND

The communication of BIxD, the implementation
of interactive branding and the further
development of BIxD projects are closely
interwoven. A working project creates
requirements and requirements lead to metrics
and new projects. These must be communicated
and implemented throughout a company. To
ensure the quality of branded interactions
and their brand fit over the long term, quality
control metrics that go beyond project-based
quality assurance (P. 276) must be executed
regularly. Around twice a year, the design team
should examine the consistency of the product

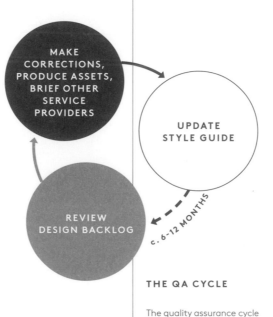

MAKE CORRECTIONS, PRODUCE ASSETS, BRIEF OTHER SERVICE PROVIDERS

UPDATE STYLE GUIDE

REVIEW DESIGN BACKLOG

c. 6-12 MONTHS

THE QA CYCLE

The quality assurance cycle
following a BIxD launch.

at all digital touchpoints, produce new assets if necessary and adjust the style guide. Better yet, the design team should be permanently involved in the project and available right after the launch to perform quality assurance services and answer any questions.

As previously emphasized, branded interactions are living things that are constantly being transformed by the actions of users and stakeholders. An active development process does not leave these changes to chance, and therefore involves:

- regular project reviews that compare actual costs with the planned budget and the quality of results
- documenting what you've learned and compiling case studies
- helping to prepare and perform tests and evaluating test results (The design team should always be aware of the results of these tests!)
- regular comparison of the strategy and the brand filter
- adjusting the product architecture
- helping to measure and track efficiency
- regular competitor analysis (evaluating what works for others and what does not)
- monitoring social media
- observing trends: the need for action may come from market trends, society, culture, technology or politics

However, active development requires corporate and project structures that allow needs to be perceived, evaluated, prioritized and implemented in an ongoing way. This means that the interaction between the company and agencies involved – especially between product management, the design team and the technical service providers – must be appropriately organized. The integration of lean UX workflows into existing processes provides a structure for this cooperation, as we will see in the following chapter.

LEAN UX AND BIxD

In the past, UX design has been extremely focused on deliverables. The intended results and documentation were defined at the start of the project and then developed over its course. This method still makes sense for some tasks, such as recurring project types (WORKFLOW MODELS, P. 42). But when developing an innovative product or service, we must react quickly if we want to shorten the time to market, or respond quickly to new discoveries or changing conditions. We are performing open heart surgery, in a matter of speaking, and feasibility does not rely on evaluation or a specific choice of platform.

Once a design is decided upon, it should be evaluated and then flows into the agile process. The development team must define what additional input is needed. If a BIxD style guide and UX guidelines already exist, it doesn't matter if every pixel isn't in the right place or every function isn't described in huge detail.

Lean UX is a conceptual extension of terms such as lean management and lean production. Both describe processes for continuous product improvement. This continuous improvement process (CIP) or *kaizen* (Japanese for 'change for the better') was the key to the economic success of Japan's car industry after the Second World War. Since then, the concept of lean management has been transferred to many areas of corporate life. Lean UX refers to a process for the continuous development of the user experience over a sequence of fast iterations – consisting of UX design, visual prototyping and UX testing– and is therefore the technical equivalent of an agile work process.

A prerequisite for lean UX is the implementation of continuous workflow management. In my experience, the key element of a lean UX process should be a regular workshop, preferably monthly, based around Scrum terminology; at think moto we call this the monthly backlog meeting. A workshop of this type helps with UX implementation, technology and product management. The product ownership – another Scrum term that refers to responsibility for the products being created – is shared by the product manager on the client side, the UX lead and the tech managers.

In the monthly backlog meeting, the product ownership team discusses and prioritizes new requirements that have been introduced by the stakeholders, who are invited to the meeting if any further information is needed on a given topic. The requirements are formulated as user stories (P. 90) and documented in the form of so-called backlog items as soon as all the necessary information is available. In addition, the level of completion of backlog items from previous meetings is discussed – these may be UX, visual design or software results. However, the monthly backlog meeting is a purely organizational meeting, and specific requirements are not to be discussed. We write the backlog items by hand on pre-prepared cards; how the UX and development team use them later is their own decision. We used this model when developing the interactive learning platform LernCoachies.de. Our technology partner manages the backlog items in JIRA, while we add the items as to-dos in Trello. It is important that the same backlog item IDs are used, to enable smooth communication.

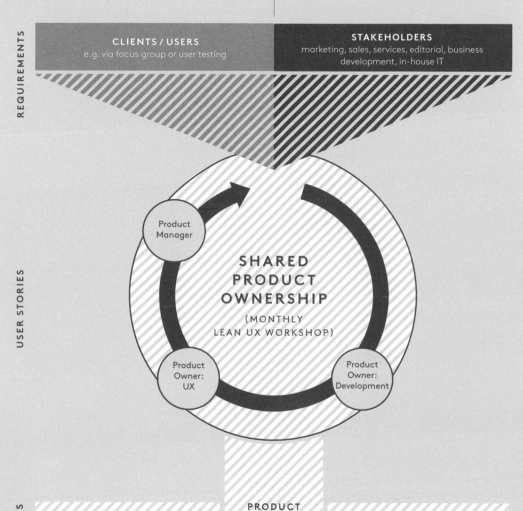

REQUIREMENTS

CLIENTS / USERS
e.g. via focus group or user testing

STAKEHOLDERS
marketing, sales, services, editorial, business
development, in-house IT

USER STORIES

Product
Manager

**SHARED
PRODUCT
OWNERSHIP**
(MONTHLY
LEAN UX WORKSHOP)

Product
Owner:
UX

Product
Owner:
Development

BACKLOG ITEMS

**PRODUCT
BACKLOG**

EXPERIENCE DESIGNER
UX Designer / Visual Designer

SCRUM TEAM (DEVELOPMENT)
Front-end Developer / Back-end Developer

320
—
321

LEAN UX MODEL

Lean UX in practice: In a monthly workshop, the product owners
representing UX, development and business compile a product
backlog for the Scrum and design teams.

SET-UP / PROCESS ──── DISCOVER / DEFINE / DESIGN / DELIVER / **DISTRIBUTE**

BACKLOG ITEM TEMPLATE

STAKEHOLDER	→		VALUE FOR STAKEHOLDER (1–3)	→
BACKLOG ITEM TYPE	→		BUSINESS VALUE**	→
PRIORITY	→		USER BENEFIT**	→
APPROVED	→		BRAND BENEFIT**	→

SHORT DESCRIPTION / USER STORY	→
BACKGROUND / MOTIVATION	→
DATA / MATERIAL NEEDED	→
CONFLICTS AND INTERDEPENDENT TASKS	→

*   calculated based on the business benefit,
        user benefit, brand benefit, and cost x 2
        (SEE P. 148).

**   1 = must have
        2 = nice to have
        3 = postpone until next phase

BACKLOG ITEM TEMPLATE

Requirements are formulated as user stories during
the backlog meeting. A backlog item template helps
to document the different aspects of a backlog item.

If designers and programmers work together in a lean UX process, everyone – regardless of their discipline – can contribute ideas, without drawing boundaries between the disciplines. Comments from team members are welcome; as designers, we should always be open to suggestions from the development team. The product owner from the design team ensures that brand and UX topics remain under the control of the BIxD teams. Because both the design and the development team, as well as stakeholders, regularly make proposals and comments during the iteration process, the projects reflects the work of all of these groups. This creates loyalty and trust within the team and strengthens it against criticism from outside. In this way, lean UX can build greater commitment between team members.

ⓘ In agile product development, the product backlog is a list that includes everything the product being developed should contain. The requirements listed in the product backlog are known as backlog items. They are described from a user perspective and processed in-house by the Scrum team. The BIxD team is usually not part of the Scrum (development) team, but should work closely with them.

A good source for more information about lean UX:
⟶ bit.ly/1hErzdj

TEST, MEASURE, OPTIMIZE

The success of a project can only be measured if targets – success metrics or key performance indicators (KPIs) – have already been defined. These must be objectively measurable: 'more stylish' is not measurable, but the number of hits a website receives is. The design team should not be kept out of this step completely, even if metrics is a dry subject; in fact, designers should insist on being involved in testing and on being shown the results.

Web analytics, tracking and analysing user behaviour are already a top priority in many companies. These are used to find out where users come from, what they do and for how long, how frequently they come back, and so on. Designers should not be over-influenced by these findings and should continue to trust their own intuition rather than beginning the design process with fixed figures in their head. But there are still a lot of questions that can be answered with conventional website tracking:

- How do individual user segments behave (P. 74)?
- How do users evolve over time? What is the nature of the customer life cycle (P. 120)?
- Do users change segments after a while, e.g. from beginner to professional?
- Are specific functions or design ideas being accepted?

- How long does it take for the user to accept changes?
- What kind of call to action works best?
- Where are the entry and exit points?
- How often do users return to specific segments?
- How can the segments be better differentiated?

These results are documented and made available to everyone involved, perhaps by posting them on a Wiki or the brand portal. In order to assess a BIxD project, various tests (P. 226) and web analytics must be combined.

THE SUCCESS OF BIxD IS MEASURED AS FOLLOWS:

- How useful is the site (in terms of expectations)?
- How well are the user's specific objectives and tasks fulfilled?
- How quickly are a user's emotional needs and brand expectations fulfilled?
- How much confidence does the user have in the site?
- How much confidence does the user have in the brand and the product?
- How useful is the product or service (in terms of expectations)?

OBSERVE DEVELOPMENTS

Those who are temporarily absorbed in the depths of a BIxD project can soon forget to keep an eye on outside developments. Tunnel vision can be dangerous for designers. You can quickly take on a corporate view of organizational structures, processes and the product portfolio and become fixated on visual design requirements. UX and visual designers who supervise a brand, product or service in the long term from a customer perspective should constantly monitor their competitors and changes in the market. Long-term trends can also be assessed and incorporated into further developments. We use these to create future-state scenarios anticipating social and technological changes that may affect people's behaviour and create a need for new products, services and interactive environments. Techniques such as 'A day in the life' (P. 87) can be used to develop these scenarios.

ADJUST THE PRODUCT OR SERVICE MODEL

Companies often function as planned economies. Products are generally planned over a five-year period. Objectives and touchstones are defined at the beginning and alternatives suggested if certain criteria are not fulfilled. Circumstances and requirements can change very quickly however, especially in interactive media; you must learn over the course of a project and recognize if new criteria have become more relevant than those originally defined. Business models change as markets change. Digital brands, products and services have the advantage of being able to respond quickly to changes, as long as a company-wide design and brand management exists, overseeing developments, testing and optimizing regularly, and documenting what has been learned. Products and services must be constantly monitored to determine whether they fulfil their objective or whether the goal has changed. If necessary, new products and services must be developed and the brand strategy adjusted.

FUTURE COOPERATION

Successful and sustainable corporate partnership and cooperation requires a degree of pragmatism and a 'can do' attitude. Companies, especially those that already understand the importance of design to their business, usually want an agency or a design team to proactively take the lead. This is, after all, what they are paying for. If you're content simply to wait for the next brief to come along, won't start work unless everything you need has already been provided, and are willing to give design advice but not to do any of the design yourself, you cannot expect to be taken seriously as a consultant.

On the other hand, when closely cooperating with a company in a consultancy role, you soon learn that corporate structures cannot be changed overnight, even in smaller firms. Those seeking long-term change must seek partnerships, actively contribute and make repeated efforts to convince

the company to follow their ideas. This is best done by thoroughly documenting your small successes in order to build trust and credibility. Sometimes it helps to suggest tests or to conduct these on your own, if you're convinced you can find a solution. Don't let yourself be too easily satisfied. Every design team should know whether their work has lasting quality.

If you can live up to your own claims, follow the BIxD process step by step, ensure your designs have a strong strategic foundation in the brand, the business and the user, develop ideas creatively and test them using brand filters, you can deliver great designs. I hope this book will prepare the way.

DESIGNING A MOBILE OPERATING SYSTEM

PETER SKILLMAN

NOKIA

You were working as UX lead for Palm OS before you were hired by Nokia to work on the MeeGo UX design. What exactly was your role in the project?

I've been involved in design throughout my whole career, spanning hardware architecture to integration of technology, industrial design and user experience. Over the past four years I've been focusing on UX issues for mobile operating systems. When I arrived at Nokia, I focused on the Nokia N9 and MeeGo (the operating system of Nokia N9), and that project is one of the things in my career that I'm the most proud of. It was the work of a passionate team.

I came from the Stanford product design culture of David Kelley Design and IDEO, where I worked for seven years. After IDEO, I joined Palm and spent eleven years involved in design, technology, mechanical engineering and the creation of new ideas that triggered a wave of start-ups. Then

I worked on interface design and user experience for several years, including initial work on the Palm WebOS UX.

So what was most interesting about working on the MeeGo UX design?

It started with an understanding that the foundation of any mobile experience is how you start up apps, switch between apps, and handle notifications.

The key to success is finding a clear and simple approach to handling these core fundamentals.

You can switch between the three home screens of the Nokia N9 with a swipe. You start apps through the launcher, switch apps through the multitasking screen, and handle notifications in the events view. The epiphany for us was the integration of swipe, an entirely new paradigm. This means you can use gesture interaction and be fully present in the moment. It also allowed us to eliminate keys and make the device simpler to use. What you remove is as important as what you put in.

Let's go a little further into the UX approach. What were the concepts from the very beginning?

The concept for the Nokia N9 was the creation of a better way to use a mobile phone: a larger screen, swiping, effortless core user journeys and multiple home screens, but with an entirely different approach from that of our competitors.

The concepts really started with how we try to solve basic customer needs. For example, the idea of the 'effortless journey' is about minimizing the number of clicks. This goes back to Larry Constantine's principles of user interface design.

The six principles include: how to achieve a minimum number of clicks, how to achieve convenient handling, how to design feedback modes so errors can be easily corrected, how to achieve consistency and familiarity, etc. We asked ourselves: 'How do we build a better phone?' And it started with this idea that you can replace keys with swiping, so there's no need to reach for buttons. The way you place your hands and swipe from side to side or from top to bottom is very natural. It's easy and effortless, like sliding a piece of paper off a tabletop.

Switching between apps with a flick feels natural and allows you to design a product that is almost all screen.

From a visual point of view, it's about reducing visual noise, keeping things as simple as possible, allowing personalization in smart dynamic ways, using familiar language that's approachable and friendly, with a clear colour logic, beautiful graphics and richly emotive movements that bring a smile to people's faces. It's not just about utility; it's about crafting a product that creates delight, something you want to use because it feels good.

How are these UX and visual design principles taken from Nokia's past and incorporated into the Nokia brand of today?

Nokia has created some great products and, in the past, hardware was the dominant theme. What we're doing with the Nokia N9 is a fundamental change where the experience becomes the brand. You can tell a story about how the product makes a difference in your life, and make it in a simple, direct, delightful and visually rich way. This is what the Nokia N9 is about, and it is influencing the rest of the brand and is the foundation of what we're doing moving forward.

The Nokia N9 is driving cultural change at Nokia. Let's start with the font. When I arrived we wanted to change the font, because the old font is not a good UI font. It comes from a category of fonts known as Grotesque, ironically. We created a new font called Nokia Pure: it has a tall x-height and big, open letters and belongs to a category of fonts called Humanist. So we went from Grotesque to Humanist and basically the UI font Nokia Pure became the brand font.

So the brand is evolving and simplifying in a very human way from the UI to a complete shift in product making, including a massive change in industrial design language and several other aspects, such as service interaction.

The UI is becoming the brand. The experience is becoming the brand.

I want to ask: have there been any explicit requirements from a branding perspective in terms of 'this is what Nokia stands for' and 'this is how we translate it into an operating system, into an experience'?

Well, I think what you are seeing right now is a major transition at Nokia from a brand perspective, and I think this transition will take several years, given the scale and the size of Nokia. There are many small examples that seem minor but become game-changing when viewed in aggregate. Take the icons: we are shifting the metaphors towards authenticity by including realistic reflections. This isn't just a fake glossy coating on each icon. Instead, you only get reflections on objects such as a camera lens icon, which reflects light like a real camera lens would. But if you have a calendar, there's no highlight creating a glossy reflection, because calendars on paper are matt. So we're very explicit with these metaphors.

We're now driving that across Symbian, we'll push that into Series 40 phones and we'll push the font across all of the product lines. We are explicitly driving consistency and familiarity, where every operating system is almost an abstraction of what we have begun to do with Nokia N9, and that transition will take some time.

I really like what you did with the Nokia N9 and I think this is great work in UX terms and also in terms of creating a brand experience. But how does this relate to the strategic change within Nokia to go with Windows Phone?

Let's start with some very simple elements. If you overlay Nokia Pure and the Windows Phone font Segoe, there is not a font in the world that is more similar than Segoe is. And that was pure luck. It's all down to the fact that the Windows Phone design team at Microsoft shares almost all of the same design values as we do: bold typography, lively movement, making people's lives easier. If you look at the Windows Phone design principles, they apply in an almost eerie way to exactly what we did on Nokia N9 and the evolution of these ideas may find their way into future Nokia Lumia products.

It is critical that we have the ability to build a credible high-end smartphone ecosystem and this is the only way that we can do it – with Windows Phone as our main operating system.

It's not going to exist at the low end, and there are some really incredible things we can do taking principles from Nokia N9 to more accessible phones and applying them there. I can't say any more than that, but there are going to be some really interesting things that Nokia does in more affordable products that will define the brand as it evolves.

Nevertheless, the decision to go with Windows Phone was made after you started this job at Nokia. So your intention was to create a new interface, a new experience, as you said, to create a better phone for Nokia, and this experience would have been connected solely and uniquely with the Nokia brand. Now you're sharing this brand experience with Windows Phone and with other hardware providers. How is that for you as a designer? What takeaway is there for Nokia that exists beyond the operating system for the Nokia N9?

After working on the design of the Nokia N9, I'm now focusing on the UX design of our more accessible phones. We seek to build a rich user experience at the low end, where we ship approximately a million phones a day. The bulk of our current sales are in the mobile phone business. When you look at what we can do with these lower-cost phones, there's such an enormous potential to change the impression of what Nokia is: today it is about reliability and durability. These are the values that people apply to the brand and are based on the perception of the company as it was and not as it will be. Design has a big role influencing change at Nokia. The Nokia Lumia family combined with a richer experience at the low end will completely change people's impression of the existing brand identity. But as I said, it'll probably take a few years before all of these changes take place. You'll start to see some of these elements – the icons, the fonts and swipe – and over time, these will become design leitmotifs for a company that's transitioning towards a different kind of experience.

As a major platform provider for Windows Phone, will you have an impact on the further development of Windows Phone?

Absolutely. We should never disassociate the user experience, the industrial design, the developer ecosystem, and services and apps. They all exist together as one, and we contribute to and influence the user experience. We have complete authorship of the industrial design and the hardware, and we're also putting significant effort into building the ecosystem and specific apps.

Looking at the product marketing website and the guidelines website, it seems like Nokia has managed to create a consistent product identity in marketing as well as for the product itself. It seems like authorship exists. How can authorship and design be created, and what are the conditions needed in a company like Nokia and on a design team, to come up with a strong and unique UX and branding approach?

The design team as a whole, and I really mean the entire team, spent a lot of time with in-house groups and agencies communicating what their values were. We were allowed to break some rules,

because it was a product intended for exploration and learning. We were actually freed from some of the more entrenched beliefs about how Nokia does things. This freedom allowed some really good work to come out and I think swipe.nokia.com is a good example, as are the user experience guidelines. This work came from the design team. swipe.nokia.com was created entirely by marketing but heavily influenced by the product experience. It's kind of a delightful expression of 'hey, let's take a risk'.

Great design can only evolve when you don't have excessive constraints on what you can and can't do.

You were talking about the user-centred design approach that you've chosen. You come from an IDEO background, so what you've actually started to do is change Nokia, from my perspective, from a very product-driven organization to a user-centred organization. Would you agree with that?

It wasn't driven by me alone. There is a core group of people, including some people in product marketing, in brand and across the board who signed up to this ideology. And a shared belief that Nokia must change to stay relevant. Most importantly Marko Ahtisaari, Head of Nokia Design, created the conditions for success and heavily participated in every element of the Nokia N9 design work. He's really pushing our agenda.

How do you make sure that these guidelines – and I'm not talking only about the UX guidelines for Nokia N9, but about this completely new approach that you were just talking about – are distributed throughout the company? What steps are being taken now and how can you steer this communication process within the company?

I think the best advertisement for that system of values is a successful product, a product that people are proud of. And this is one of the best devices this company has created. People are paying attention. Successful product experiences become the best carrier of that mission, because they are emulated and people look to those examples and those patterns to create a consistent identity to push forward.

We have an intense passion for detail – to constantly refine and repeat the message that details matter at every level. It's really only through the end-to-end experience that you can develop a true brand identity and all of those touchpoints matter. The user experience is just one tiny component. Besides design, there are several other factors that define business success: marketing, sales, distribution, channels, software, QA, etc. All these elements are part of what makes asuccessful business, but design in the modern age is one of those core foundations, and without it, the structure can crumble.

Peter Skillman, Vice President UX Design, Nokia

V

GOOD PRACTICE

—

Brand Management

DZ BANK WEB STYLE GUIDES / LINDE INTERACTIVE BRAND ARCHITECTURE /
T-MOBILE WEB USER EXPERIENCE / SWISSCOM / BBC GEL / NOKIA N9 UX GUIDELINES
VOLKSWAGEN UK INTERACTIVE GUIDELINES / LEO BURNETT SOCIALSHOP

DZ BANK WEB STYLE GUIDES

It is not yet the norm for style guides for interactive media to be taken into consideration at the beginning of the corporate design process. It is therefore all the more important later, when the print media guidelines are adapted for web use, that the specific features of the medium are observed and the guidelines emphasized. For the header of the DZ BANK website, for example, a variant of the logo set in a plain orange rectangle was used; on the company's printed material, the logo is set in multiple colours that would have looked too fussy on the web. On the site's subpages, the use of orange is reduced even further, with the logo appearing against photographic page headers that look light and sophisticated.

www.dzbank.de

GESTALTUNGSSYSTEMATIK. HEADER.

Für den Benutzer ist der Header im Kopfbereich der erste, prominenteste und vor allem prägendste Berührungspunkt mit der Marke „DZ BANK". Der Header bildet die Bühne, auf der zum einen die wichtigsten markenbildenden Elemente und Anwendungen verortet sind und zum anderen die globalen Einstiegspunkte und die Haupt- und Metanavigation.

Der Header existiert in zwei Zuständen.

Startseite:
Die Startseite stellt für den Benutzer das zentrale Eingangs-tor dar, auf der er von der DZ BANK willkommen geheißen wird. In diesem Kontext übernimmt der Header die Funktion der Bühne, auf der die emotionale Inszenierung der Marke durch interaktive Anwendungen, Imagefilme oder prominenten Schlüsselbilder stattfindet. Zusätzlich werden dem Benutzer Direkteinstiege und die globalen Einstiegspunkte zu den Zielgruppenportalen angeboten, über die er seine Interessen/Ziele identifizieren kann.

Zielgruppenportale:
Auf den jeweiligen Portalseiten wird der Header farblich kodiert und mit den markenbildenden Elementen wie Logo und Vernetzungsgrafik belegt. Darüber hinaus ist im Header-Bereich die globale Navigation und die Hauptnavi-gation verortet.

VERWEIS

» Detailinformation zum Header finden sie im Kapitel „GESTAL-TETE EINHEITEN"

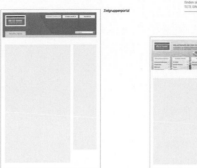

Zielgruppenportal

Startseite

DESIGN-TEMPLATES. ÜBERBLICK.

STARTSEITE – DE

PORTALEINSTIEGSSEITE   PRIVATKUNDEN

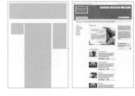

STARTSEITE – COM

ÜBERSICHTSSEITE – 2-SPALTIG   PRIVATKUNDEN PRODUKTE

BASISELEMENTE. TYPOGRAFIE. FRUTIGER VS. ARIAL.

Für die DZ BANK Website werden die Schriften Frutiger LT und Arial verwendet. Die Frutiger LT 45 Light für die Hervorhebung von Fixationspunkten und die Arial für pflegeintensive Inhalte sowie für systemgenerierte Aus zeichnungen, Texte und Interaktionselemente.

Die Frutiger LT ist die neue Hausschrift der DZ BANK. Die 1976 entwickelte Frutiger gehört zu den zehn erfolgreichs-ten Schriften in Deutschland. In 2000 wurde die Frutiger technisch überarbeitet und in Frutiger LT umbenannt. Die Frutiger LT ist keine Systemschrift und muss für die Verwendung auf der Website als Grafik generiert werden.

Die Verwendung der Frutiger LT für die Fixationspunkte (Punkte, die bei webbasierten Informationsangeboten durch die sprunghaften Augenbewegungen vornehmlich erfasst werden) dient neben der Hervorhebungsfunktion also auch der markenbildenden Funktion.

BRAND MANAGEMENT

GOOD PRACTICE

LINDE INTERACTIVE BRAND ARCHITECTURE

The Linde Group is a global group of companies with many branded affiliates and over 160 web presences that can be accessed via a central homepage, Linde.com. The site provides visitors with an overview and a quick introduction to the company's complex brand architecture.

The left side leads to the Linde Group's corporate website, while the right side links to its international business website Linde-Worldwide.com, where the user may select one of the company's three divisions or one of the individual countries on the large map.

www.linde.com

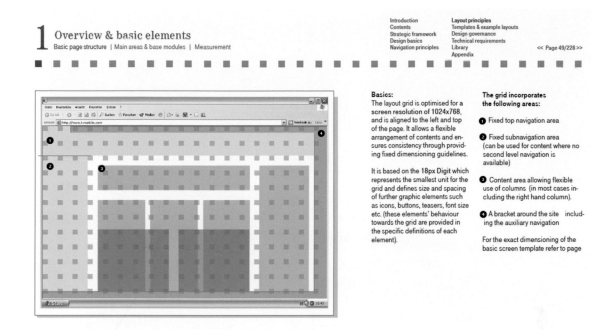

Introduction
Contents
Strategic framework
Design basics
Navigation principles

Layout principles
Templates & example layouts
Design governance
Technical requirements
Library
Appendix

<< Page 49/228 >>

1 Overview & basic elements
Basic page structure | Main areas & base modules | Measurement

Basics:
The layout grid is optimised for a screen resolution of 1024x768, and is aligned to the left and top of the page. It allows a flexible arrangement of contents and ensures consistency through providing fixed dimensioning guidelines.

It is based on the 18px Digit which represents the smallest unit for the grid and defines size and spacing of further graphic elements such as icons, buttons, teasers, font size etc. (these elements' behaviour towards the grid are provided in the specific definitions of each element).

The grid incorporates the following areas:

❶ Fixed top navigation area

❷ Fixed subnavigation area (can be used for content where no second level navigation is available)

❸ Content area allowing flexible use of columns (in most cases including the right hand column).

❹ A bracket around the site including the auxiliary navigation

For the exact dimensioning of the basic screen template refer to page

4 Template description
A-1 | A-2 | B-1 | B-2 | C-1 | C-2 | C-3 | C-4 | C-5 | C-6 | C-7 | C-8 | C-9 | C-10 | D-1

A-1 HOME

Sketch:

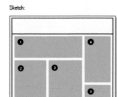

Example design:

C-1 Phones List

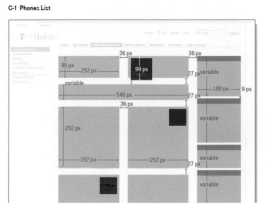

T-MOBILE WEB
USER EXPERIENCE

The layout grid for T-Mobile's international presence is based on a shared brand element: the square blocks or 'digits' of the logo, which symbolize digital data transfer and which frequently appear in the company's advertising. With ease, precision, originality and elegance, T-Mobile introduced a brand review matrix, which includes a brand filter and is an important part of the style guide.

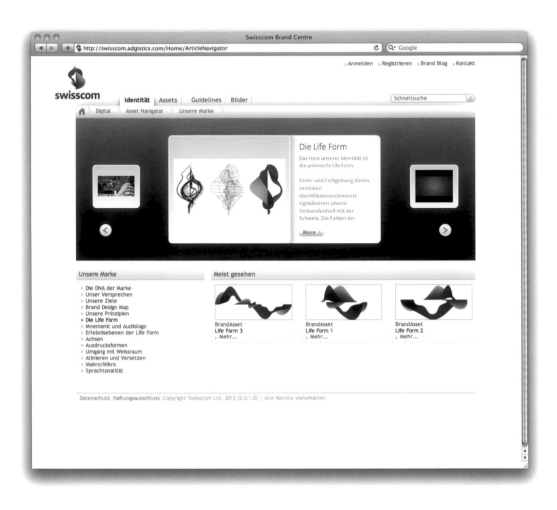

SWISSCOM

The Swisscom Brand Center is an open brand portal
that presents all aspects of Swisscom's corporate
design online; it also explains the brand identity and
graphic guidelines and offers assets for download.
The Flash navigation allows users to zoom in on
different features on the overview pages, creating
a playful way to access the content that reflects
the dynamic brand identity (GOOD PRACTICE, P. 161).
The accompanying blog ensures that the portal
appears lively and approachable.

swisscom.adgistics.com

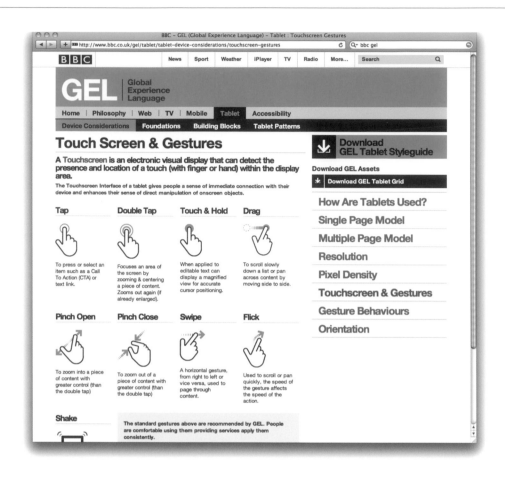

BBC GEL

The BBC is the UK's largest broadcaster and is considered a pioneer in embracing new technologies. In addition to its radio and TV stations, the BBC offers a wide range of web services, and its TV and radio shows are accessible online via BBC iPlayer, which is available for various devices. The website is continually being developed and expanded by the UX and BBC design team to improve the user experience.

In 2010, the GEL (Global Experience Language) guidelines were jointly developed with Neville Brody's Research Studios, and are documented in an online portal that is open to all designers involved in online development: 'The design philosophy underpins everything we do as a user experience and design

team. It informs the way our services look, the way they behave and the way we operate as a team. ' GEL initially focused on the BBC's own homepages, but was subsequently supplemented by guidelines for mobile, tablets and iPlayer, and includes a range of accessibility guidelines.

The portal provides design principles, guidelines and grids. Because it is publically funded by licence fees, the BBC also places value on making the work of the UX and design teams transparent to the public via a blog: a good example of the mediation of BIxD to a broad stakeholder group.

www.bbc.co.uk/gel

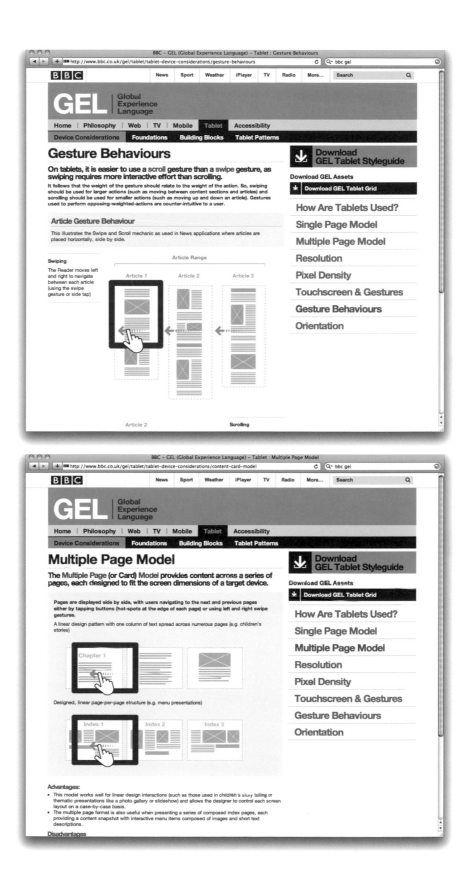

GOOD PRACTICE —— BRAND MANAGEMENT

NOKIA N9 UX GUIDELINES

On its sleek yet functional website, Nokia provides guidelines, demos, templates and samples for the design of apps for the Nokia N9. The basic design principles are presented in the 'Getting Started' section (INTERVIEW, P. 326). The Core UI Framework explains the key functions of the smartphone, while the Pattern Library allows app developers to ensure a consistent N9 user experience. The Core UI Toolkit contains all the interface elements as vector

graphics for direct use in apps and is available for download. The design of the UX guidelines site itself is low-key, so that the app examples and explanatory infographics are foregrounded.

Opposite, below: The navigation's colour coding uses shades from the N9 colour palette.

www.developer.nokia.com/swipe/ux/

BUTTONS 05.11.10

480x854

Core button sizes & distribution

Normal

Normal | Normal

Normal | Normal | Normal

Normal
Normal
Normal

Normal

Normal | Normal

Normal | Normal | Normal

Normal | Normal | Normal | Normal

Core button sizes & distribution

Normal

Normal | Normal

Normal | Normal | Normal

Normal
Normal
Normal

Normal

Normal | Normal

Normal | Normal | Normal

Normal | Normal | Normal | Normal

Normal button states

Normal

Pressed

Disabled

Selected

Selected Disabled

Core button states

Normal

Pressed

Selected

Negative button states

Negative

Pressed

Disabled

Accent colour button states

Accent Colour

Pressed

Disabled

Negative button states

Negative

Pressed

Disabled

Accent colour button states

Accent Colour

Pressed

Disabled

Split button sizes & distribution

Normal | Normal

Normal | Normal | Normal

Normal
Normal

Normal
Normal

Normal
Normal
Normal
Normal

Normal | Normal

Normal | Normal | Normal

Normal | Normal | Normal | Normal

Split button sizes & distribution

Normal | Normal

Normal | Normal | Normal

Normal
Normal

Normal
Normal
Normal

Normal
Normal
Normal
Normal

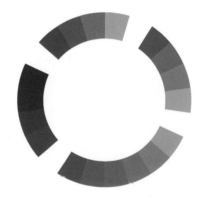

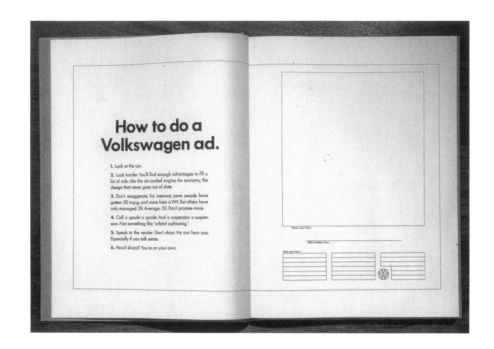

GOOD PRACTICE —— BRAND MANAGEMENT

VOLKSWAGEN UK INTERACTIVE GUIDELINES
TRIBAL DDB

'How to do a Volkswagen ad': these guidelines from a 1960s Volkswagen print ad by the agency DDB summed everything up in six brief and witty points. The online presence of Volkswagen UK resolutely follows this tradition: no exaggerations, no huge videos, no buzzwords. On its very sleek homepage, Volkswagen UK first asks what the user wants: a new car, a used car or a company car. If you choose 'I want a new Volkswagen', you can select a model then move to the Configure page – another special feature – where you can then view the car in more detail.

To ensure that the site remains consistent, even when external service providers are involved, Tribal DDB created a set of online interactive guidelines. Under the headings 'Look,' 'Touch' and 'Listen', the graphics, animations and sound samples can be experienced interactively.

www.volkswagen.co.uk

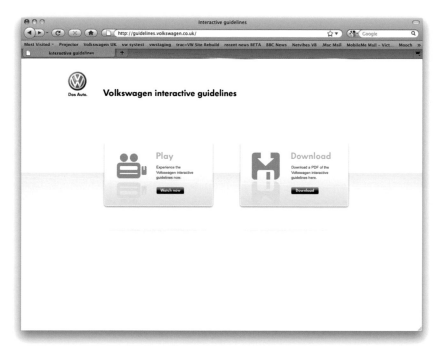

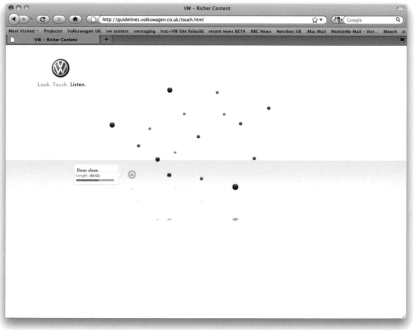

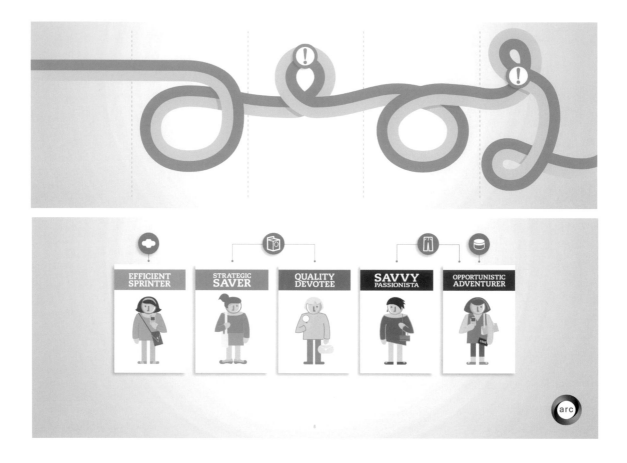

LEO BURNETT SOCIALSHOP

Leo Burnett's experience design framework 'SocialShop' is not just an example of brand management; it also demonstrates how brand management must embrace interaction. SocialShop describes the purchasing behaviour of six different buyer types based on shopping journeys for different product categories (RISK/REWARD™, P. 64). SocialShop is an extension of the broader quantitative study PeopleShop, which surveyed 8,000 shoppers, examined more than 40 online and offline touchpoints and created user journeys for more than 20 product categories.

Opposite, above: The shopping journey of an Opportunistic Adventurer – an impulse buyer looking for bargains – when buying a pair of designer jeans.

Opposite, below: The behaviour of a Savvy Passionista for whom the product and the experience associated with the acquisition is more important than the price. In both of these cases, the purchase takes place in a store, but online media nonetheless play a crucial role in the decision-making process.

© Leo Burnett

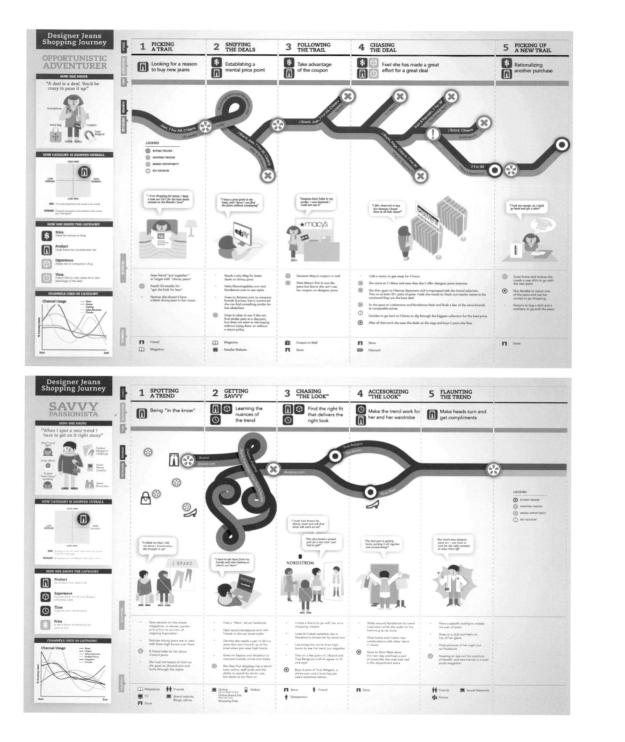